DATE DUE

DEMCO 38-296

American Political History

American Political History

Essays on the State of the Discipline

edited by

John F. Marszalek and Wilson D. Miscamble, C.S.C.

with essays by

Michael Les Benedict
Carl N. Degler
Jane Sherron De Hart
Robert V. Remini, and
R. Hal Williams

University of Notre Dame Press
Notre Dame and London

Library of Congress Cataloging-in-Publication-Data

American political history: essays on the state of the discipline /
    John F. Marszalek and Wilson D. Miscamble, editors.
        p.   cm.
    Includes bibliographical references.
    ISBN 0-268-00651-2 (alk. paper).—ISBN 0-268-00652-0 (pbk. 4: alk. paper)
    1. United States—Politics and government—Historiography.
    2. United States—Politics and government.   I. Miscamble, Wilson D.,
    1953–   . II. Marszalek, John F., 1939–   .
    E183.A547   1997
    973—dc20   96-28969
                                                                         CIP

To
Vincent P. De Santis
Historian, Teacher, and Friend

Table of Contents

Acknowledgements

The symposium in which versions of the major papers in this volume were first delivered was supported by a generous grant from the Paul M. and Barbara Henkels Endowment, College of Arts and Letters, University of Notre Dame. The editors are grateful to Associate Dean Jennifer Warlick for her assistance in facilitating this grant. The conference was also supported by a generous donation from Mrs. Alice Rogers of St. Paul, Minnesota.

In the preparation of this volume the editors received assistance from Peggy Bonner, Rita Christopher, and Jeanne Marszalek at Mississippi State and from Jackie Wyatt, Jane Wroblewski, and Laura G. Holland at Notre Dame. The editors are also grateful to Jim Langford and his staff, especially Rebecca De Boer, at the University of Notre Dame Press for their work on the production of this volume.

Most of all, the editors are grateful to Vincent De Santis for his friendship and scholarly example and assistance over many years. It is a pleasure to dedicate this volume to him.

Introduction

John F. Marszalek

On October 13 and 14, 1995, more than one hundred historians from around the nation gathered at the University of Notre Dame to participate in a conference entitled "American Political History—The State of the Discipline." The inspiration for this symposium was the desire of its co-conveners to honor Vincent P. De Santis, a major historian of the American past. A graduate of Johns Hopkins University, where he studied under C. Vann Woodward, De Santis joined the Notre Dame History Department in 1949, assumed emeritus status in 1982, and has continued teaching part-time ever since.

The co-conveners believed that the best way to honor Professor De Santis was to invite distinguished historians to participate in a symposium discussing the present state of political history, the field to which De Santis made his own important contributions. Each of the five speakers made an extended formal presentation on a specific aspect of political history and then engaged the audience in a wide-ranging discussion. In addition, the symposium included a formal banquet honoring De Santis. Among those doing the honors were De Santis's major professor, C. Vann Woodward; his graduate school colleague, Suzanne Carson Lowitt; Notre Dame president Edward Malloy, C.S.C.; and longtime colleague and friend, Robert Gunderson.[1]

The success of the symposium and the timeliness of the topic provided impetus for the publication of this anthology, which contains the papers presented by the five speakers as well as an essay on the scholarly career of Vincent De Santis. Political history is undergoing substantial change, some would say attack, so an anthology addressing its present state is particularly important. That it should honor Vincent De Santis is similarly significant, for his career, displaying integrity, dedication, and insight, spans half a century of service and scholarship.

In the last several decades, American political history has found itself in an unaccustomed position. Long the mainstay of historical writing in the United States, it has been seriously challenged by the "New Social History" with its emphasis on the study of the past from the bottom up, analyses of the experience of the masses of people rather than that of governing elites. According to William E. Leuchtenburg in his April, 1986 presidential address to the Organization of American Historians, by the middle of the 1980s "the status of the political historian had sunk. . . . Political historians were all right in their way, but you might not want to bring one home to meet the family."[2]

Yet, said Leuchtenburg, he was willing to predict that political history would be "the historian's next frontier."[3] Lawrence W. Levine, a later president of the Organization of American Historians, went even further in the spring of 1993. He denied that the historical profession had ever "abandoned politics and other 'significant' subjects in favor of parochial, politically correct areas," citing a recent American Historical Association's collection of historiographical essays to support his contention.[4] The editor, Eric Foner, stated in the introduction that despite the growing importance of social history, the essays in the collection did "not lend credence to recent complaints that historians are no longer concerned with politics, economics, the Constitution, and intellectual history." They still are, Foner insisted, but "politics now means much more than the activities of party leaders."[5]

Considering this and other lively discussions in the profession over the present and future of political history, it would have been easy for the five essayists in this anthology to slip into an attack or a defense of the discipline. Such a reactionary approach might have been valuable, but instead, the thrust of the essays is more proactive. The essayists, all historians of the first rank, discuss where the discipline stands at the end of the twentieth century, what insights it is still producing, what methodology it is utilizing to provide these insights, and what yet needs to be done. In so doing, the essayists show clearly how vibrant the field remains yet how different is its approach from that of the past, with its emphasis on campaigns, elections, and terms of office.

The five major essays which make up this anthology deal with different aspects of political history. The first two provide broad overviews; the next two present in-depth analyses of specific periods of the American political past; and the last explores a major genre of the discipline, biography. The essays are all broad and wide-ranging, insightful, and thought-provoking.

Carl Degler, Margaret Byrne Professor Emeritus of History at Stanford University and past president of the major professional historical organizations, is the author of the book's first essay. Degler, brilliantly sweeping across the entire history of the United States and making comparisons to Europe's major democracies, throws light on the present state of American politics, i. e., the conservative attack on the federal government. He argues persuasively that Americans have tried to restrict the power of the federal government throughout most of the nation's history. Unlike European democratic parliamentary government, the American system makes it difficult for the national government to govern effectively. But that is the way Americans have preferred it; they have consistently believed that their individual liberties are being protected in the gridlock produced by the system of checks and balances. As Degler phrases it, "politics in America is really much more than votes or issues or elections. It is rather a sign or a manifestation of a people's conception of themselves." This historical reality, Degler concludes, will continue, with smaller American electoral participation, greater governmental deadlock, and lower social well-being than that possessed by other democratic nations. "Our once fortunate history," he concludes, "has now become the burden of American politics."

Jane Sherron De Hart, Professor of History at the University of California, Santa Barbara, and a noted historian of twentieth century United States women's history, is the author of the second essay. De Hart demonstrates how the methodology and insights of gender provide new perspective on American political history. In this essay she discusses political culture, state formation, policy, citizenship, and nationalism. To highlight only one of her areas of analysis, De Hart points out that citizenship in the early American Republic was defined in white masculine terms. "Women served the state by serving their husbands and, by extension, their households," she notes. Thus, arguments against women voting included the belief that "a husband's ballot sufficed for both." In fact, De Hart argues, gender, sexuality, ethnicity, and race have all played crucial roles "in the construction and production of national identity," but none have been or are "natural entities." Rather, they are all "social constructions" traceable to time and place and ideology. In short, according to De Hart, American citizenship has never borne "a mark of fixed status." Instead, it has been and is "a practice," subject to ever constant influence and change.

Having considered political history through the widest lens, the anthology next considers two specific periods of the American past: Reconstruction and the Gilded Age.

Michael Les Benedict, Professor of History at Ohio State University and a leading scholar of Reconstruction, utilizes statistical methodology to analyze the complicated politics of the Reconstruction years. A few previous histories have attempted such an approach; this essay, more directly than others, ties public policy to the political system and grass-roots voting behavior and demonstrates "the way public opinion was translated into public policy." Benedict, providing an in-depth look at politics in both the South and the North, argues that Reconstruction politics was much more than a white racist reaction to black participation in the political system. Because elections were so frequent, contemporary politicians in both the North and the South were especially vigilant observers of election returns because of their value in predicting public opinion and the winning issue for the election that was always just around the corner.

In the South, white Republicans espoused an issue that would bring whites under their banner, "the promise of prosperity," trying at the same time to play down black interests, which they correctly saw as a Democratic issue driving whites away from the Republican fold. When the natural refusal of blacks to remain in the background helped create further intra-party strife, southern white conservatives (Democrats) overwhelmed the splintered Republicans.

In the North, Republicans tied "equal civil and political rights for African Americans with the triumph of loyalty and Unionism in the war" and produced a winning political issue. But then, under Democratic and factional Republican pressure, they changed the political formula. Instead of tying the Civil War issue to freedmen's rights, they attached the war to Democratic treason. In so doing, they broke the bond between the Union and black citizenship and thereby eliminated a key protection for the freed people. "Thus it was not increased racism that led to the erosion of northern support for Reconstruction," Benedict concludes, "it was the erosion of support for Reconstruction that led to increased racism."

R. Hal Williams, Professor of History at Southern Methodist University and an important scholar of the late nineteenth century, discusses the political history of the period whose politics and politicians were once the subject of universal ridicule. In more recent times, historians have come to admire in Gilded Age politics some of the very things that historians had earlier attacked, i.e., an electorate emotionally devoted to its political parties and one that enthusiastically voted in huge numbers in the rapidly repeating cycle of closely contested elections.

In addition to studying the impact of elections, Williams says, recent historians of the Gilded Age have also utilized new methodologies of research, explored issues of community and gender, analyzed words and style, and incorporated the insights of social history. The result is the discovery of much new information, including the fact that states and localities played more important roles in these years than previously understood, and actually began the reform of American life for which the Progressive Era of the early twentieth century is justly famous. At the same time, though politics was intrinsically masculine, women played an important political role, seen most clearly in the politically significant activities of the temperance movement and the women's clubs. In summary, the Gilded Age was a hotbed of politics, and historians are using a variety of methodologies to unearth exciting data about it.

The final major essay in this anthology is the product of prolific biographer Robert V. Remini, Emeritus Professor of History at the University of Illinois at Chicago and visiting Professor of American Studies at the University of Notre Dame. Remini says that "for American political biography, it is the best of times, it is the worst of times." He makes it clear, however, that he is not pleased with the present state of historical writing. While the public thirsts for good biography, the bigger the book the better, Remini says, too many historians are engaged in writing about "the 'holy trinity' of modern historical research": class, race, and gender. The result, he insists, is that no one but a few other historians reads these works, and, as a result, the historical profession is increasingly becoming marginalized. "We seem hellbent on killing our profession," Remini concludes.

Should all historians write only what the public wants and in that way regain its popularity? No, Remini believes, "We must be free to pursue what we believe will lead to a better understanding and appreciation of the past; and in that pursuit every historian must choose the methodology that is personally congenial and most appropriate to the subject." Historians must respect each other's research, however, and recognize that if they want the public to look to them for their knowledge of history, they must not totally ignore public wants and needs.

What, then, do the five essayists tell us of the state of political history in the late 1990s? They believe it is in a state of transition from the traditional approach of earlier years to the more complex mixture of today. In previous generations, the writing about American politics was normally white, male, and elitist. Today it takes into account people of all colors and social class: men, women, and children. In fact, the relationship among the varied groups that comprise the United States is now as much a matter of study in American politics as were the nation's presidents in earlier studies. Race relations and gender are now essential aspects of any political study, their exclusion indicating to the reader an obvious omission in the explanation of any historical period under study.

Political history in the 1990s is therefore a complicated study. Political historians, influenced by social history, are telling a much wider and deeper story than they ever dreamed of, even a few short years ago. They now routinely ask questions and utilize approaches that their predecessors seldom considered. In the hands of master historians, political history is alive and well, and hardly old-fashioned or unsophisticated. In its myriad forms, it still has a great deal to tell us about the American past, as the essays in this anthology and the extensive notes accompanying them clearly demonstrate.

Notes

1. A video tape of the October 13, 1995 banquet program is available through the Center for Continuing Education, University of Notre Dame.

2. William E. Leuchtenburg, "The Pertinence of Political History: Reflections on the Significance of the State in America," *Journal of American History* 73 (December 1986): 587.

3. Ibid, 589.

4. Lawrence W. Levine, "Clio, Canons, and Culture," *Journal of American History* 80 (December 1993): 864.

5. Eric Foner, ed., introduction to *The New American History* (Philadelphia, 1990), xi–x; cited in Leuchtenberg, "Pertinence of Political History."

1

History Counts: The Burden of American Politics

Carl N. Degler

Although I like to think of myself as a social historian, my deepest and longest connection with history has been politics. My earliest political memory is my betting a nickel with a contemporary on the election of 1928, a bet which I lost. During my college days my friends called me "New Deal Degler." Those of you who know your twentieth-century politics know that behind both of those personal political events stood social issues of import. To me, in short, political history is important because it reflects and epitomizes the great social and economic issues of any modern society, but especially that of the United States.

Historically, no people has been as politically aware as Americans, and thus when we observe the politics of America today, we can only wonder, if not weep. Despite the so-called revolution of 1994, the latest polls tell us that Americans are no more happy about their politics than they were in 1992. In August, 1995, a CBS / New York Times poll reported that only 26 percent of the American people thought Congress or the president was doing a good job; 79 percent—the highest figure in several decades—said "the Government was pretty much run by a few big interests looking out for themselves."[1]

Yet as a political people, Americans have much to appreciate and even to be proud of. American political parties are the oldest in the world, having begun in the 1790s. The constitution on which those parties and our political life depend is similarly the oldest written constitution. No other country opened up its suffrage so early, so freely, and so broadly as that of the United States. By 1860 universal white male suffrage prevailed except in a handful of states, and by 1870 black males were also able to vote. In some states even aliens were permitted to vote if they intended to become citizens. In Britain a comparable suffrage was not achieved until 1884.

Nothing is more applauded about the American political system than the way it moved from being merely a loose collection of thirteen weak states on the Atlantic rim of North America to the most powerful and prosperous polity in the world. Then came 1994, and the great Republican revolt against Big Government. Should it be designated as a "revolution," as some Republicans have claimed? If you mean by revolution a decided shift in beliefs and values, then I do not think 1994 constitutes a "revolution." To me a revolution implies not only a change or a departure from the past, but more importantly, an opening to a new way of doing things. My contention is that 1994 is not a revolution simply because it is not a movement in a different or fresh direction. Instead, 1994 should be seen as nothing more than a resumption of a very old outlook, one that the American people put together at the beginning of their experience as a free people. Put another way, the story of the growth of American federal power is not to be perceived as a stately evolution running from the Civil War to the Populists to the Progressives and the achievements of the New Deal, Fair Deal, the Great Society, and the Nixon years, as we usually view it. Rather, that growth of federal authority—that Leviathan, as one opponent has recently called it—is actually an aberration, a response, as economists say, to exogenous or outside forces rather than endogenous or internal developments. What I am talking about here are not politicians and parties but the character, the historical nature, if you will, of the American people. For it is they who have created and sustained the politics of this country from the beginning right down to the present.

To fill out that assertion, let us begin by looking at the way in which Americans organized themselves after their revolution against the centralizing power of the British king and parliament. The essence of the Constitution they created in 1787 was to restrict the power of the new federal government by separating the three branches of government and providing the well-known checks and balances to make sure there would be no concentration of power. Indeed, as my old professor at Columbia, Henry Steele Commager, used to remind us: the separation was so strict that without the invention of political parties during the Washington Administration there would have been no way for the executive and legislature to get together to coordinate the business of government. Yet even today we recognize that, despite the presence of parties, frustration and deadlock are still built into the peculiarly American division of powers. For years American political scientists and lay people have argued for something like a European parliamentary system, enabling the executive and the legislature to work together by having the majority in the legislature determine the executive. But the American people have never paid much heed to those cries of distress. Placed in broader terms, Americans feared the concentration of governmental power after the Revolution and they fear it still.

Or consider the Bill of Rights, which opponents of the new Constitution almost immediately insisted upon. It, too, reflects that same fear of power, especially the power of the federal government over the individual. As recently as January, 1995, Senator Robert Dole promised the Senate "that we will dust off the 10th Amendment and restore it to its rightful place in the Constitution,"[2] that is, to leave any power not delegated to the federal government to the states or the people. Or, consider the Senate itself, which, like the Bill of Rights, was a device to control federal power by providing each state with equal representation. No major industrial democracy except the United States permits its upper house to have equal power with its popular body. Britain's House of Commons put serious limits on the once equal House of Lords as early as 1911. And though the Bundesrat—the upper house of the German *Parlament*—can limit aspects of legislation enacted by the Bundestag, it has neither the equal power nor the prestige of the United States Senate. The Senates in France and in Italy are also only limiting or delaying bodies.

The original purpose of the Senate, of course, was to protect the power of the states against possible dominance by the newly constituted federal Union. And that emphasis upon local interests has persisted through both houses of Congress. Constituents still look to their representatives or senators to respond to individual or local interests; members of both houses work hard to have dams, roads, and bridges constructed in their constituencies. The result is government by local interests, which is what the late Speaker, Tip O'Neill, meant when he frequently remarked that "all politics is local."

In parliamentary forms of government, representatives have no comparably direct connections with their immediate constituents. Party connections control the legislatures since the parties determine the executive authority. In Germany, for example, only half of the votes in a Bundestag election are cast for a particular candidate; the other half are given to party lists of candidates, not individuals. In Britain there is no requirement, as there is in the United States, for a member of Parliament to live in his district. In the United States, in short, members of Congress, because of independent support from constituents or outsiders, easily escape from party control or from presidential appeals in behalf of national policy.

And just because the Constitution provided for checks and balances, the progress of legislation in the United States is uniquely slowed down, if not stymied. What parliamentary government—and all other major industrial powers are parliamentary in structure—has to struggle each year to enact the federal budget because the president presents it but the Congress determines what it will contain? And since over the last fifty years over half of the presidents have had Congresses of different parties, delay and frustration have been frequent. Under the parliamentary system of the European democracies, executive and legislature are united through party majorities. Governments can fall under such a system, of course, but deadlock does not ensue as it can and does under our presidential system.

One of the several ironies of the American political system is that Congress was clearly intended by the Founders to be the center of governmental power. As the theory of the old Whig party asserted—and President Grover Cleveland at the end of the nineteenth century repeated—the president is supposed to carry out the wishes of the people's representatives, not to lead or dominate the country. Yet, almost from the outset of the new federal system, the president has been at the center of popular politics. From the days of Andrew Jackson to the present, aspiring party leaders and organizations have first looked to find a presidential candidate around whom a party could be formed. That is why talk of a third party in the 1996 presidential election concentrates on possibilities like Ross Perot or Colin Powell.

The president figures so prominently in the system because he—or she—is really two persons: a party leader of government and a symbol of the nation's sense of identity. Because of that special significance and popular attention, presidential campaigns have become unconscionably lengthy, costly, and ultimately boring as well as uniquely American. No European election depends upon such a mindless consumption of time and money with an emphasis upon personality rather than policy. European parliamentary governments, of course, escape the conflicts and confusions of roles by separating them. The national symbol can be a monarch as in Britain or Spain, or a president as in Germany and Italy. Policy and party conflicts are the province of the leaders of the parliaments, and neither the election of presidents nor of prime ministers is a lengthy or costly procedure as the presidential elections in the United States have been for a century or more.

For many of you, these observations on the differences and disadvantages of the separation of powers in the United States are surely familiar. The larger question is, why has that sense of limited government persisted? It is true that parliamentary government is a relatively recent development, just as European parties are younger than ours. Americans had no chance to try the European system, since they invented their government so much earlier.

That still leaves the question: why has that earliest of free governments not been changed or updated? I think we have to look to the nature of the American people if we are to understand the longevity of our political system. This is what I meant at the outset when I said that politics in America is really much more than votes or issues or elections. It is rather a sign or a manifestation of a people's conception of themselves. Who then are Americans and how has their conception of themselves shaped the political system in which we still act?

The core of the American outlook is the individual or what modern political philosophy would call liberalism. But that is not the liberalism scorned by Newt Gingrich or Ronald Reagan; instead, it is the liberalism of Edmund Burke and John Locke, that is, a liberalism intended to free the individual from the ancient and confining regulations and traditions of government, church, and class in Europe. The freedom that Americans enjoyed and sought to preserve in their local communities was a freedom that many European liberals in the last half of the nineteenth century were still hoping and struggling to achieve.

Put in more practical terms, individual freedom meant freedom of economic enterprise, of seizing opportunities for individual success. This aspect of freedom was most obvious by the early years of the nineteenth century, a time that historian Charles Sellers calls the era of the "market revolution."[3] We used to call it the Age of Jackson. Arthur Schlesinger, Jr. contended that Andrew Jackson's destruction of the

Second Bank of the United States was a sign of anti-business policies. We now know it was an attack on monopoly, by which Jacksonians meant those privileges government bestowed on a few, such as the Bank, to the disadvantage of the many. And that was, of course, quite in line with Jacksonian Chief Justice Roger Taney's overthrow of John Marshall's principle of the sanctity of contract. Taney's aim was to open up competition among business enterprises in order to expand the economic development of the nation. Behind Taney's purpose stood Tocqueville's general observation that "in no other country in the world is the love of property keener or more alert than in the United States and nowhere else does the majority display less inclination toward doctrines which in any way threaten the way property is owned."[4] Politically, the idea was summarized at the masthead of the Jacksonian era's Washington *Globe*: "The World is Governed too much."[5]

It is true that government tried to shape the American economy, especially in the first half of the nineteenth century when individual enterprise was not yet prepared to satisfy large-scale economic needs. Thus the state of New York built the Erie Canal, a project that inspired several other states to support canal building. And later, even the federal government did its bit by subsidizing the private construction of railroads, especially those intended to link the Mississippi Valley to the Pacific coast. Significantly, however, the federal government only aided private enterprise, it never attempted to run railroads itself, as several European countries did in the nineteenth century. The federal government also opened up millions of acres of land at very low cost to farmers, cattle ranchers, and mining companies in order to expand economic opportunities for individuals. That same freedom of enterprise easily permitted some white Americans to enslave black Americans in an effort to achieve individual success. Millions of impoverished Europeans risked lives, forsook families, and broke traditions to seize the opportunities that American freedom promised. Over and over again, an important meaning of freedom was that winning or losing was up to the individual.

Political parties then and since have only occasionally challenged the goal of economic freedom for individuals. The parties certainly contested issues and policies in the 1790s and after, but their fundamental values were not at issue. The parties never challenged the liberal assumptions on which Americans had come to agree: popular participation in government by a defined electorate of white men who had some property or stake in the social order, a belief in revolution against unjust government, the rejection of aristocracy, the absence of any connection between church and government while accepting the importance of organized religion, and freedom for individual enterprise. These were values that in Europe were still sources of conflict rather than of consensus. As Tocqueville told us, protection of property was a given in America. Indeed, one of the principal defenses of slavery in the early nineteenth century was the great loss of labor and property that emancipation would entail. Lincoln himself recognized that concern when in 1862 he recommended that Congress consider setting up a fund to compensate the slaveholders, and thus avoid what he rightly anticipated as a much greater cost of continued civil war.

By the 1840s American parties were already well established, though only two at any one time seemed to last very long. Political historian Joel Silbey has called those years before 1860 the golden age of parties: they were open, and voters were informed and interested. Between 1840 and 1860, about 77 percent of the electorate voted.[6] One measure of the relevance and importance of parties at those times was that the creation of the new Republican party in the mid-1850s laid the fuse that soon led to the explosion of civil war in 1861.

The importance of the early parties was measured in a less dramatic but concrete way when historian Eric McKitrick compared the presence of political parties in the North with the absence of parties in the Confederacy. Although one might have thought that absence of parties would bring about unity of purpose, just the opposite occurred in the Confederate states. Since the newly created government lacked any party structure, Confederate President Jefferson Davis had only his own personality and policies to win supporters for his administration and its aims. President Lincoln, on the other hand, could turn to his Republican governors, legislators, and party functionaries who would rally behind his policies simply because of party, despite what they might have thought about him personally.[7] That example sharply reveals the absolute necessity of strong popular parties and party loyalty in a presidential system of government.

Despite the conflicts between parties before 1860, it becomes clear that even in the face of civil war, Americans were amazingly united on the character of their political system. It was the existence of slavery, not the American system, that split the country. One needs only to compare the Constitution of the Confederacy with that the United States to recognize the agreement in political values. The Confederate Constitution did not even justify secession, though the right to secede had been a bone of contention between North and South for years. The main constitutional innovations of the Confederates were minimal: the establishment of a six-year term for president and a line-item veto! The agreement in political outlook between North and South was also apparent in the way many Confederates justified secession. They described themselves in their conflict with the North as descendants of the revolutionary Americans who had fought against the tyranny of George III.

It is true that emancipation marked the greatest use of governmental power in the course of the nineteenth century; it resulted in a loss of Southern wealth amounting to perhaps two billion dollars when the federal budget in 1861 was only about $66 million. During a decade of reconstructing the former Confederacy, the federal government also imposed new authority over the defeated Confederates, but, it must be admitted, without much conviction. The well-known American conception that government should be local soon came into play. As early as 1872, a large segment of the Republican party joined with Democrats to end Reconstruction, largely because it denied self-government to the southern states.

Significantly, two major Congressional efforts to employ national power in behalf of former slaves failed to be enacted: the Blair bill in the 1880s for funding the education of blacks in the South, and the Lodge bill of 1890 to protect black voting in the southern states. Instead, the national government concerned itself in behalf of business by maintaining the protective tariff and by freeing private enterprise from monopolistic power with, respectively, the passage of the Interstate Commerce Act and the Sherman Anti-Trust Act of 1890. But when Congress in 1887 enacted a $10,000 appropriation for seed grain in behalf of destitute farmers in Texas, President Cleveland's veto nicely defined the limits on federal authority. Congress should learn the lesson, Cleveland sternly reminded the legislators, that "though the people support the Government, the Government should not support the people."[8]

During the post-Civil War years, the Democratic and Republican parties flourished. As Morton Keller tells us, "the high stakes of patronage and power that went with public office gave American politics a quality all its own. Its scale and articulation required hundreds of thousands of functionaries, more 'than all other political machinery in the rest of the civilized world,' said Henry J. Ford in 1898 in his book *The Rise and Growth of American Politics.*"[9] Issues, of course, were another matter. They were not what today we would call crucial or threatening, largely because the American people did not expect the federal government to deal with big questions. At the same time, the high level of voter participation in elections certainly reflected the people's enthusiasm for politics. Between 80 and 85 percent of the eligible citizens generally cast their ballots. With such high percentages, it is clear that Americans of all classes were voting, including the workers in cities and factories in the burgeoning industrial economy of late-nineteenth-century America.

But you will say that was the nineteenth century. Did that not all change after 1900 when the Progressive movement took over under the aegis of Republican Theodore Roosevelt and Democrat Woodrow Wilson? Yes, it is true that not since the Civil War had the federal government injected itself, particularly in controlling railroads, drugs, food, and banking, so deeply into the economic life of Americans. Two events in the 1890s helped to shape that upsurge of national authority. One was the rise of a third party—the People's or Populist party, which in 1892 demanded that the federal government help farmers suffering from a long-term fall in farm prices. The other was the depression of 1893, the first national economic collapse since the United States had become a major industrial society. The political impact of the depression of 1893 was unprecedented. Indeed, the defeat of the Democratic Congress in the elections of 1894 exceeded by far the transfer of seats in the 1994 election, exactly one hundred years later. Just as the Civil War had spawned a temporary increase in governmental power during the Reconstruction of the South, so the waning of the impact of the Depression of 1893 among Progressives became evident during the 1920s. Farmers once again found themselves in trouble, labor unions declined sharply in membership, and millions of citizens failed to vote, but large and small businesses flourished. The decline in voter participation had begun even during the Progressive years. By the 1920s voter participation had fallen to 60 percent.

What does the decline in voter participation tell us about American politics? Well, for one thing it changes the historic meaning of democracy in America. After all, the widening of the suffrage over the course of the nineteenth and early twentieth centuries had assumed that people wanted to participate, and that the political system required participation. When voters fail to turn out they are denying, or at least doubting, the validity of a democratic election. It is surely relevant that some countries, like Australia and the Czech Republic, require citizens to vote by law. After all, can one justify an election when a popular decision is made by less than half of the people, as happens in the United States today?

The major significance of the poor participation in American elections since the early twentieth century is that in all of the western democracies the people vote in high proportions, often reaching 85 to 90 percent. Today in the United States, a landslide like that of Ronald Reagan over Jimmy Carter in 1980 was achieved by only 28 percent of the eligible voters: (Almost half of the electorate did not vote at all!). That can be contrasted with Giscard d'Estaing's 40 percent in the French Presidential election of 1981 when he *lost* to Francois Mitterand![10] Why do twentieth-century Americans fail to vote, especially when contrasted with the votings in comparably advanced societies in Europe?

Part of the answer, political scientist Walter Dean Burnham has suggested, is that it stems from the old-fashioned nature of our parties. For one thing, American parties began in a far different milieu from today. The individual and the family were largely responsible for day-to-day life; government neither helped nor interfered very much. By the end of the nineteenth century, a majority of Americans had ceased to be independent farmers, artisans, and shopkeepers; instead they were now workers employed by others in factories and cities. According to Burnham, the old, established parties no longer spoke to these employed Americans, who began to drift away from apparently irrelevant political organizations. Burnham concludes that the absence of a strong socialist movement and party prevented many Americans from breaking out of the two parties, which had been created in the course of a nascent market society.

In Europe, socialism had long been an alternative party seeking to meet the problems spawned by industrial-urban society. This was especially evident in Germany, the only challenger, aside from the United States, to Britain's long-held industrial domination. In 1912, when the recently created Socialist party in the United States under Eugene V. Debs achieved one of its largest popular votes ever, only a single

Socialist won a seat in Congress. That same year the Socialists in Germany captured 110 seats, the largest number of any party in the Reichstag. Labor unions provided a substantial part of the German socialists' electoral success, but organized labor in the United States was only a tiny proportion of the industrial work force. Today—and even after Margaret Thatcher's assault upon unions—40 percent of British workers and a third of German workers are organized as compared with 17 percent in the United States.[11] But then labor unions, like socialism, depend for their support not upon individualistic workers but upon those who need and want cooperative solidarity with fellow workers, that is, they subordinate some of their individuality. That sense of cooperative support has long been largely foreign to the individualistic values inherent in the American political and economic system. The socialist alternative that was widespread in Europe is not available in the United States because of long-held individualistic values, just as the presence of a built-in conflict between president and Congress reminds us of the endurance of the American fear of concentration of power. In short, Americans still live in the political house they built two hundred years ago.

But did Americans not finally make fundamental changes in their traditional values during the Great Depression of the 1930s? Wasn't the New Deal, after all, a massive transformation in the use of federal power? Certainly, a number of policies, from Social Security, TVA, the National Labor Relations Board, Minimum Wages and Maximum Hours, to legislation to support farmers and provide work for the unemployed, are concrete measures of that transformation. But the source of that transformation—the Great Depression—was not a fundamental change in values among Americans; rather, it was the impact of unusual circumstances, circumstances that so frightened Americans as to acquiesce—temporarily—in what they had long doubted: the ability of free Americans to trust any Congress or president that concentrates power.

Has the American distrust of federal authority finally been assuaged? Will the Republican Contract with America be just an episode in American politics rather than a new transformation—as worried conservative economist Robert Higgs fears in his book *Crisis and Leviathan*?[12] I do not think Higgs needs to worry. Certainly, the Great Depression and the Second World War exerted an immense impact on the way the federal government exercised authority. Yet in actuality, when we perceive the New Deal as a manifestation of enhanced federal power, we are largely doing so in comparison with what went before: the hands-off federal government during the 1920s, which culminated in the volunteerism of Herbert Hoover. Projected against the long history of American politics, the impact of the New Deal shrinks to an aberration, rather than a fundamental shift in values and practices.

Compared with Europe, for example, America was and is still a weakly organized central government. Social security began in America only in the 1930s, largely driven by populist figures like Huey Long and Francis Townsend, not Franklin Roosevelt. It was Otto von Bismarck, after all, who first instituted old-age pensions and health insurance in Germany in the late nineteenth century. The British labor leader Herbert Morrison, visiting the United States in 1936, was puzzled by the vociferous public debate then going on over the Wagner Housing bill because, in Morrison's mind, its goals were far less ambitious than the British housing act of 1890.[13] And at no time during the New Deal, with the possible exception of TVA, did the United States nationalize any industry, though virtually all of the European countries frequently did so before and after the Great Depression.

FDR was undoubtedly the most popular and perhaps the most influential president since George Washington, yet even Roosevelt and his New Deal could be tripped up by that old devil, the separation of powers. This was especially apparent when Roosevelt hoped to use TVA as a way of conserving and rehabilitating the agriculturally depressed South. Despite Roosevelt's unprecedented landslide in 1936, Congress, in the very next year, defeated all of his efforts to conserve and reform the southern economy. Historian Barry Karl argues that that defeat was an even greater sign of presidential weakness than FDR's better-known rebuff at the hands of Congress over the court-packing bill of the same year.[14] And when in 1938 FDR tried to punish two senators of his own party who had opposed his policies by campaigning against them, local interest once again triumphed over party and president.

No European prime minister would have had to take such measures, but then the American people never had any intention of bringing the legislature and the executive into institutional agreement. The separation of powers may frustrate presidents and policies, but it surely assuages any danger from governmental power that may threaten the freedom which the American people have cherished from their beginnings. In fact, the New Deal itself would have been hamstrung if the Supreme Court had not finally agreed to interpret our eighteenth-century constitution to fit the needs of a twentieth-century integrated urban-industrial society. During the 1930s, when America's domestic problems were at their height, the Supreme Court finally discovered the Commerce Clause of the Constitution as a device for empowering Congress to deal with national issues like unemployment, agriculture, labor, and so forth, issues which the Constitution had not specified for Congressional action. That such power was available *only* on the sufferance of the Supreme Court became quite evident in the decision of *U.S. v Lopez* in the spring of 1995, when the Rehnquist court refused to recognize the Commerce Clause as the constitutional basis for a national ban against guns near schools. As Justice David Souter wrote in dissent, "it seems fair to ask whether the step taken by the Court today does anything but portend a return to the untenable jurisprudence from which the Court extricated itself almost sixty years ago. The answer," Souter concluded, "is not reassuring."[15]

Even the admittedly deep impact of the Great Depression did not convince Americans, once better times had arrived, that federal power should be kept in reserve in the event of large-scale unemployment in the future. Instead of a Full Employment Act of 1946, which was the early post-war approach for dealing with future depressions, the final act dropped the word "full" and provided little more authority than the creation of a Council of Economic Advisors for the President. Despite Franklin Roosevelt's popularity, not to mention adoration, even many of his admirers thought it was necessary to make sure that no other chief executive would have more than two terms. As one of the proponents of the Twenty-second Amendment, Senator Kenneth Wherry of Nebraska, said, "No man who has that persuasive power, such personal charm, should serve more than two terms. We've got to safeguard the American people."[16]

Reflect for a moment on the whole range of our history, which I have tried to sketch here. Over that span of time, there have been only three occasions during which Americans have been willing to accept the federal government as a primary agent of large policy. The first was the Civil War, where the Union split over the issue of who were Americans. The second instance was during the Populist era of the 1890s and the subsequent decade of the Progressive movement. The impetus to both came from the recognition that the United States was fast becoming an urban and industrial society, and from the impact of the depression of 1893. The third and most striking exercise of federal muscle came during the Great Depression and the Second World War. Since then, federal authority has been waning as memories of the Great Depression and the Second World War have faded. For a time those memories sustained Johnson's ill-fated Great Society and Nixon's environmental protection goals, while the Reagan-Bush years found the issue of national security in a world divided between Communism and the West some reason for a continued, if limited, employment of federal might. Since then, of course, the national and the international scenes have changed significantly, and the underlying American belief in a limited federal government has once again become a powerful rallying cry. The 1994 election thus offers almost a popular sigh of relief for a resumption of familiar political ways.

At the same time, it is clear that the American political system is not functioning as well as it did during the nineteenth century, though secession and Civil War could hardly be considered measures of political success. But when today more than half the electorate fails to vote, yet complains about the inadequacies of the federal establishment, something is clearly wrong, especially when the voters of the other western industrial democracies still maintain their high participation rates. Americans also complain about Congress and about the frequent conflicts between the parties and between Congress and the president. All of the European democracies manage to escape most of such conflict because governments are not divided between executive and legislature or between the two houses of the legislature. Europe's lower houses are always the dominant of the two.

Congress and the president are not the only elements of the political system that trace their beginnings to earlier times and circumstances. The parties, too, grew up in the midst of a common ideology, held by independent owners of property, who hoped to keep at a distance intrusions from the national government. European parties, which began later and developed within the milieu of an industrial and urban society, developed parties with more diverse ideologies. Because of that variety European voters could find an electoral basis for the diversity of their interests and concerns. Europeans continue to vote while Americans vote less and less. This is what political scientist Walter Dean Burnham refers to as the anachronistic nature of the American political system.

Aside from the fact that American governments operate on the undemocratic basis of less than half of the population participating, do these anachronisms make any practical difference? They make quite a bit of difference if you compare the life circumstances of Americans under their government with those of citizens of the European democracies, most of whom are considerably less wealthy. Take for example, national health care, for which Americans have been struggling, not to mention battling for an answer for some time. (Harry Truman first urged it forty years ago.) The European democracies have long maintained a decent health care system that meets the needs of their citizens. European democracies also have child care for working women, including paid leaves during pregnancy, while the United States, and only recently, offers working woman no more than limited and unpaid leave for pregnancy. Children, too, suffer severely in the United States when their situation is compared with that in Europe. A study of the income gap between rich and poor children among eighteen industrialized countries found the United States third from the bottom. The average household income of poor children in the United States in 1991 was $10,923 against $12,552 for poor children in Italy. Poor families with children in Germany and Belgium averaged almost $5,000 more than such families in the U.S.[17] Support for the unemployed in Europe is much more generous than that for Americans. Yet the United States is certainly among the richest countries in the world, if not itself the richest.

Certain issues that are contentious in America evoke no such response in Europe; that difference is to be traced again to long-held American values. Take abortion policy, for example, which in Europe is generally not a popularly disputed subject as it certainly is in the United States. Catholic countries like France and Italy permit abortion. The heart of the American difference from Europe is our emphasis upon individual rights, as Mary Ann Glendon of the Harvard Law School has shown.[18] Those who oppose abortion insist on a person's right to protect a fetus while those who favor abortion insist on a woman's right to control her body. The accommodations made in Europe do not seem possible for Americans. So-called "Rights Talk," Glendon has pointed out, derives from the rights the Founding Fathers defended against the intrusion of government. Yet that worthy beginning has today escalated to rights that any individual may insist upon.[19] Our heated contentions over gun control, which Europeans find hard to understand, also stem from the American belief that individual rights are being violated when the federal government controls the possession of guns.

Or take the American attitude toward taxes. Americans have long resonated with Chief Justice John Marshall's familiar dictum that "the power to tax involves the power to destroy." Most Americans apparently feel that they have been taxed to their eyebrows for years. Yet at the same time, as the British journal *The Economist* pointedly wrote, "Americans rail against their government's weakness, paralysis, venality, profligacy. Yet it is citizens who give their money and time to ensure that no changes can be made that are at the expense of their subsidy, their social-security cheque, their tax-break; it is mostly the voters' money that bribes the politicians; it is voters who insist that more needs to be done, but with lower taxes and without killing any existing programmes."[20] Among Europeans there seems to be a less strident approach toward ways and means. When Europeans expect health care, child support, and good unemployment benefits, they also expect to pay taxes. In 1994 twelve western European countries paid on average about 45 percent of their Gross Domestic Product for taxes as compared with the American proportion of only 31.6 percent. And while Americans these days are adamantly refusing to accept any new taxes, the German, French, and British governments all enacted fresh taxes during 1994.[21]

The point I am making here, of course, is that the American political system is not doing as well as expected or as it performed in its first century. That enduring system is not working when one measures the well-being of Americans against that of comparably wealthy societies. Nor is it working well by Americans' own measures, as the low level of voter participation and the low esteem in which Americans hold Congress and the federal government in general remind us.

Are Americans, then, about ready for deep and close analysis of their system with the intention of revising it drastically, such as separating the presidency into a chief of state and a chief of government as Europeans have done, or reducing the power of the Senate to make it comparable to the Bundesrat of Germany or the House of Lords of Britain? Very unlikely. Americans built these institutions and practices for good reasons: to protect their freedoms and to enhance their social welfare. And though these institutions may no longer meet our goals as well as they have in the past, history is not easy to repudiate. Despite the Civil War, the Depressions of 1893 and the 1930s, and World War II, Americans still see themselves as individualists, fearful of government intrusion and happy with a constitution in which checks and balances are embedded. After all, that constitutional system, these parties, and their historical practices are central elements in our identity as a people. To alter them fundamentally would mean another revolution. As Tocqueville recognized long ago, "although the Americans are constantly modifying or repealing some of their laws, they are far from showing any revolutionary passions. One can easily see, by the promptness with which they stop and calm themselves just when public agitation begins to be threatening and when passions seem most excited, that they fear a revolution as the greatest of evils, and that each of them is inwardly resolved to make great sacrifices to avoid one."[22]

Lacking that revolution, our politics will continue to be only partly democratic, frequently deadlocked, while our social well-being, as measured against that of countries less rich than ours, will continue to fall behind. Americans, in the end, like all peoples, must live with their past. For some people history can be a diabolical trap that swallows them, as happened to Germans in the 1930s; for others, like us, who may have loved freedom a little too much, our once fortunate history has now become the burden of American politics.

Notes

1. *New York Times*, August 10, 1995.

2. Quoted in *New York Times*, April 16, 1995.

3. A more extended presentation of the same point, developed culturally, psychologically, and politically, is in Lawrence Frederick Kohl's splendid book *The Politics of Individualism: Parties and the American Character in the Jacksonian Era* (New York, 1989).

4. Alexis de Tocqueville, *Democracy in America*, ed. J. P. Meyer and Max Lerner, trans. George Lawrence (New York, 1966), 614.

5. Quoted in Kohl, *Politics of Individualism*, 104.

6. Joel H. Silbey, " 'The Salt of the Nation': Political Parties in Ante-Bellum America," in Richard L. McCormick, ed., *Political Parties and the Modern State* (New Brunswick, N.J. 1984), 30.

7. Eric McKitrick, "Party Politics and the Union and Confederate War Efforts," in William Chambers and Walter Dean Burnham, eds., *American Party Systems* (New York, 1975), 117–51.

8. Quoted in Robert Higgs, *Crisis and Leviathan: Critical Episodes in the Growth of American Government* (New York, 1987), 83–84.

9. Morton Keller, *Affairs of State: Public Life in Late Nineteenth Century America* (Cambridge, Mass., 1977), 531.

10. Walter Dean Burnham, *The Current Crisis in American Politics* (New York, 1982), 12–13.

11. *The Economist*, June 1, 1995.

12. Cited in note 8 above.

13. William E. Leuchtenburg, "The Pertinence of Political History: Reflections on the Significance of the State in America," *Journal of American History* 73 (December 1986): 598.

14. Barry D. Karl, *The Uneasy State: The United States from 1915 to 1945* (Chicago, 1983), 168.

15. *New York Times*, April 27, 1995.

16. Quoted in Karl, *Uneasy State*, 233.

17. *New York Times*, August 14, 1995.

18. Mary Ann Glendon, *Abortion and Divorce in Western Law* (Cambridge, Mass., 1987).

19. Mary Ann Glendon, *Rights Talk: The Impoverishment of Political Discourse* (New York, 1991). See also Jean Bethke Elshtain's *Democracy on Trial* (New York, 1995).

20. *The Economist*, October 29, 1994.

21. *The New York Times*, February 16, 1995.

22. Tocqueville, *Democracy in America*, 614.

2

Women's History and Political History: Bridging Old Divides

Jane Sherron De Hart

An essay on bridging the divide between American women's history and American political history would not have been included in a volume such as this when Vincent De Santis began his scholarly career—or even some years later when I began my own. Women, historians assumed, had no separate history; their actions and experiences were encompassed in existing accounts of the past. Gender would have been deemed a concern of the English Department inasmuch as the word referred only to a grammatical distinction and the state of being one sex or the other.

Yet in the 1990s, books relating in some way to the history of women are second only to books published on the Civil War as the most popular historical subject in print. The definition of gender in the *Oxford English Dictionary* now includes its larger meaning: "the social and cultural, as opposed to the biological, distinctions between the sexes." Virtually every major scholarly press has in its list titles containing the word gender. Small wonder that women's historians, who started out a quarter century ago wandering, like Diogenes with a lantern, seeking to identify women and their activities—to "make the invisible woman visible"—are now charged with having traded in their lamps for telescopes and compasses. Christopher Columbus, it seems, may be a more appropriate role model for their imperial ambitions inasmuch as they now discover gender everywhere. Until relatively recently, however, many political historians have been as loath to acknowledge the relevance of gender to political history as women historians have been to focus on formal politics or the state.[1]

Old Divides and New Discoveries

While this long-standing opposition between "political" and "non-political" history antedated the emergence of women's history as a distinct field, there are various reasons why the divide between political history and women's history seemed so pronounced, especially in the 1970s and 1980s. If G. M. Trevelyan's much quoted definition of social history as "history with the politics left out" seemed to political historians to be applicable to the parent, it seemed even more appropriate to the child. Women's history, relying as much of it did on the methods and conceptions of social history, appeared to be not just the offspring of social history but an account primarily of the private sphere of family, sexuality, domestic labor, and female culture. Many women's historians saw the focus on nineteenth-century women's "sphere" and women's culture as both giving value to the differing experience of women that had been ignored (and devalued) and underscoring female agency (women as actors, rather than bystanders). But what a few feminists dubbed "her-story" as a play on "history" ("his-story") seemed to some traditionalists to be not word play, but truth-in-advertising. From their perspective, women's history had little to do with "real" history—no matter what challenges this new scholarship posed to received interpretations, conventional periodization, or established standards of historical significance. Others who were more favorably disposed scanned their checklist of nineteenth-century lecture topics—the Louisana Purchase, the Embargo and the War of 1812, the Monroe Doctrine, the Bank War, the Compromise of 1850, John Brown's Raid, the Civil War, Reconstruction, the Haymarket Riot, the Spanish-American War—and concluded that there was little in women's history that seemed relevant to the history they taught.[2]

There were, of course, some works that resonated with traditionalists. Biographies of reform politicians who happened to be female had begun to trickle in. Studies of the antislavery activists, Sarah and Angelina Grimke, Frances Wright, and Sojourner Truth, suffragist Elizabeth Cady Stanton, the WCTU's Frances Willard, and antilynching activist Jessie Daniel Ames, among others, demonstrated the impact of women in the political sphere. Of greater interest to political historians were the biographies of female politicians that emerged throughout the 1980s and 1990s. Most involved twentieth-century figures such as Belle

Moskowitz, who was a principal adviser to Al Smith, Governor of New York and presidential candidate in 1928; Molly Dewson, who as director of the Women's Division of the Democratic National Committee in 1936 had welded eighty thousand women into one of the most effective of all components of a newly revitalized Democratic Party; and Helen Gahagan Douglas, the three-term Congresswoman from California who became one of Washington's most outspoken liberals until defeated in her race for the Senate by Richard Nixon. And, of course, there was Eleanor Roosevelt, who, as the first volume of Blanche Cook's recent multivolume biography makes clear, was a passionate player in Democratic Party politics in her own right as early as the 1920s, despite her much repeated disclaimer that she was only acting as her crippled husband's surrogate. But for most readers outside the field of women's history, the innovations that distinguished feminist biographies from their more traditional counterparts—emphasis on female agency and the careful interweaving of public and private lives, for example—remained less significant than did the roles of these biographical subjects. As supporting actors—never the lead—most remained outside the limelight on the public stage of high politics.[3]

If, by the early 1980s, the rich and valuable analysis of private life that largely dominated feminist historical scholarship served also to underscore its marginality in the eyes of most political historians, change was underway. Focusing not on achieving individuals, but on women as a group and on the difference that gender made, historians of women had begun scrutinizing how women were affected by great political and social phenomena such as the American Revolution and industrialization. While practitioners of women's labor history investigated work and workers in the public sector, Linda Kerber and Mary Beth Norton examined that most significant of all political events, the American Revolution. They documented not only how women contributed to and experienced this critical development, but also probed its gendered political implications. The Revolutionary era, Kerber made clear in her pathbreaking study, was one in which male political leaders redefined the relationship of the individual to the state. But political theorists, assuming that women lacked full political identity and autonomy, said little about what the new relationship of women to the state might be. Excluded from the formal political world, women defined for themselves a political role that combined domesticity and republicanism. As good mothers functioning in the private sphere, they would inculcate civic virtue in their sons, thereby ensuring in the public sphere both national virtue and social order.[4]

The nineteenth century, framed by Republican Motherhood at one end and suffrage at the other, became the canvas on which dozens of new monographs traced the contours of female public activism. Invoking attributes of piety and domesticity associated with the pre-Civil War "cult of true womanhood" to justify their actions, thousands of white, mostly middle-class women in churches, clubs, and other voluntary associations maneuvered within a male-dominated polity between the domestic arena and formal governmental institutions. Black women, concerned with self-help and racial uplift (and ultimately, civil rights), were also involved. The starting place was the home, and the objects of concern were those women and children who were needy. But the home ultimately proved to be wherever women and children were located: slave cabins, factories, slums, even prisons, asylums, and brothels. Meeting the needs of the most vulnerable required involvement in a wide variety of actions designed to influence government. Before the century's end, women had participated in crowd actions, circulated petitions, formed organizations, founded institutions, and lobbied legislators. A few had even engaged in the actual writing of bills and staffed nascent governmental commissions *before* women could actually vote. Their efforts to influence government through non-electoral channels met with varying degrees of success. But this politics of domesticity (or maternalist politics, as it is sometimes called) became increasingly hard to ignore as it acquired an ever more public dimension, especially when large numbers of women concluded that the ballot would enhance their effectiveness as reformers.[5]

There were significant implications to this new scholarship. First, it alerted historians to the need to recognize women's historical agency. Women no less than men provided the energy that fueled nineteenth-century voluntary associations and reform movements, making even those organizations and charities without explicit political goals a training ground for citizenship and precursor of state-dispensed social welfare. The urge to participate in governance was clearly not gendered.

Second, the new scholarship on female public activism required enlarging the definition of politics. To limit what we call politics to activities within the electoral sphere would no longer do. An expanded definition now includes formal networks of influence working though non-electoral channels to shape public policy and affect the distribution of power and resources in a community. The presumption had been that those participating in informal networks were historically significant only if they were members of the polity. That presumption does not hold when we acknowledge that many of the nineteenth century's most ardent political practitioners were women. Denied the right to vote, hold office, or sit on juries, they hardly qualified as members of the polity.[6]

Third, these new studies called into question the old dichotomy of public and private. Tracing out the origins of Republican Motherhood and its evolution into the politics of domesticity demonstrated how those presumably fixed entities were continuously undermined. Knowledge of that subversion by publicly active women who were linked ideologically and experientially to domesticity challenges us to think anew about the relationship of private to public life, as Sara Evans has urged. At the very least, this new scholarship encourages recognition that these arenas, even if distinct, not only interpenetrate, but shape each other. Also underscored is the importance of spaces located between formal governmental institutions and the domestic sphere in which people can practice citizenship, thus learning skills needed for effective participation in a democracy.[7]

Finally, new information about public female activism led women's historians to begin using the analytical lens of gender to examine some of the most basic concepts with which political historians work: political culture, the state and state policy, citizenship, even nationalism. This work represents a new stage in feminist historical scholarship that Joan Scott anticipated in her influential article "Gender: A Useful Category of Historical Analysis," published in *The American Historical Review* in 1986. It is on this very recent work involving political culture, state formation, policy, citizenship, and finally nationalism that I wish to focus.[8]

Gendered Political Cultures and Policy Goals

First, the gendering of political culture. It is impossible to talk about this topic without reference to Paula Baker's important article, "The Domestication of Politics." Building on the ever-expanding literature on female political activism, Baker began with a broad definition of politics that includes "any action, formal or informal, taken to affect the course or behavior of government or the community." She then juxtaposed the new scholarship on the politics of domesticity next to our traditional understanding of nineteenth-century party politics, with its strong partisan loyalties and emphasis on party government. This juxtaposition gave rise to her central thesis that "gender, rather than other social or economic distinctions, [represented] the most salient political division" in nineteenth-century America.[9]

With the rise of the two-party system and the advent of universal male suffrage, Baker argued, a distinctly male political culture developed. This male political culture was rooted in male bonding across class—and ultimately even across racial lines—and in partisanship. Both were expressed and reinforced through the rituals of mass parties and public political behavior, all of which occurred in quintessential male spaces—the political meeting in the saloon, torchlight parades, and so on. Women might express political preferences, often participating in campaign rituals. If they were Whigs, they might even have participated at a level of partisanship that we have not previously appreciated. But party politics remained a stag affair. Legally, gender segregation became complete when the Fourteenth Amendment specifically inserted the word *male* as part of the criteria for political participation through exercise of the franchise.[10]

Counterposed to this male political culture of partisanship was a female political culture arising out of the politics of domesticity. Motherhood, in contrast to manhood, Baker notes, was the integrative force that allowed women to bond across barriers of class and race—although I would note that, more often than not, such cross-class and cross-racial efforts met with little success. While men focused on the ballot, women focused on social welfare, dispensing charity, building libraries and playgrounds, and improving schools, sanitation, and factory conditions. These deeply gendered subcultures ran along parallel tracks which partially converged only in the early twentieth century. Each was associated with a distinctly different method of shaping public policy.[11]

These subcultures were also associated with distinctly different policy goals. By the turn of century, members of both sexes had begun to acknowledge the inadequacy of laissez-faire liberalism. To solve the problems associated with a capitalist industrial economy required pressing for governmental action. The gendered character of those policy goals, William Chafe has argued, goes a long way toward explaining the contradictions and limitations we associate with Progressivism. Corporate rationalization and government modernization, Chafe has reminded us, were consistent with economic and political values traditionally associated with men. Women's focus was on local welfare programs and social-welfare institutions. For them, therefore, Progressivism was about securing humane, responsive government and laying the foundation of the welfare state: mothers' pensions, protective labor legislation, infant and prenatal health care, eradication of child labor, pure food and drug legislation, and, of course, suffrage.

Where these two highly gendered channels of political action tended to meet was on the common ground of prejudice against African Americans and the working class. Taking race and class as well as gender into account, Chafe insists, explains why some legislation associated with the Progressive Era seems outright regressive rather than progressive—immigration quotas and the disfranchisement of southern blacks, for example. Even those measures that were clearly progressive often reflected the limitations of their initiators and implementors. As other historians have made clear, legislation to protect maternal and infant health and provide assistance to needy mothers and children was undertaken in an inclusive spirit of gender solidarity. But implementation imposed a process of investigation by social workers and medical personnel which was intrusive, controlling, and reflective of the racial and class biases of the white middle-class.[12]

What contributed to the decline of these gendered political cultures? Certainly a factor was the demise of the single-sex institutions that had fostered both nineteenth-century notions of womanhood and manhood and the homosocial bonding so basic to highly gendered subcultures. More important factors, however, were suffrage and welfare. Suffrage, Baker argues, coincided with the shift from mass politics to interest group politics. This shift made the vote less important, which explains, in part, why women got the franchise when they did. As the ballot became less important, so too did the partisanship and the campaigning associated with a male political culture. Instead, I would argue, other forms of collective activity, particularly spectator sports, became more critical to the formation of male gender identity.

An equally critical factor in the demise of these deeply gendered political cultures was the emergence of the welfare state. If Progressivism

marked the domestication of politics and the weakening of the nineteenth-century divide between domestic and political spheres, the New
Deal made welfare too important to be left to women. Recall Robin
Muncy's account of the struggle by women to stake out turf in the newly
professionalized and bureaucratized world of reform. Her climactic
chapters on the history of the Sheppard-Towner Maternity and Infancy
Act are paradigmatic. Her analysis of the struggle between the female
bureaucrats of the Children's Bureau and the male doctors in the Public
Health Service is complex and nuanced. The outcome, however, was
clear: when child welfare became bureaucratic turf worth struggling for,
men won. And they consolidated their victory when the Social Security
Act put its largest children's program, Aid to Dependent Children,
under the auspices of the male-controlled Social Security Board rather
than the female-controlled Children's Bureau. This seminal episode
alerts us to the fact that state formation, a field of inquiry once assumed
to be gender-neutral, clearly is not. Women too contributed to state formation, populating bureaucracies such as the Children's Bureau, even
battling for control of policy, as the history of Sheppard-Towner suggests. Indeed, when one looks at welfare-state formation comparatively,
American women were both central and crucial to an extent unrivaled
elsewhere. Their preeminence, according to Kathryn Sklar, lies in the
fact that women's activism served as a surrogate for working-class
social-welfare activism, for complex historical reasons having to do
partly with American political culture generally and partly with the
political culture of middle-class women.[13]

   While the feminizing of suffrage and the masculinizing of welfare
both help to explain the demise of gendered political cultures, that
demise has been a longer time coming than Baker acknowledged.
Evidence of distinctly gendered political cultures can be found well past
the midcentury, as my own study of more recent politics suggests. Many
of the women active on behalf of ratification of the Equal Rights
Amendment were exemplary legatees of a style of politics in which
political efficacy resided in influencing those who held power. As pro-
ERA lobbyists, they excelled at compiling information on legislators,
collecting evidence of sex discrimination in law, and mastering legal
implications of the amendment. They learned about the Supreme Court,
the Fourteenth Amendment, "suspect classification," and legislative
intent. They supplied information packets to lobbying groups and the

press, disseminated newsletters and fact sheets, and staged debates and rallies—all actions designed to mobilize public support and influence state legislators. But when narrow defeats in the handful of states essential to ratification dictated a shift from mobilization politics to electoral politics, many found themselves unable to make the shift from lobbyist to politician.[14]

Engaging in the nuts and bolts of electioneering required more than a change in tactics. It meant letting go of what Madeleine Kunin, former governor of Vermont, termed "a surrogate system" in which "men represent our views and needs. . . ." It also meant functioning in a different political culture, one in which ambition, aggressiveness, toughness, and even ruthlessness were privileged. For the candidate, it meant owning ambition and power and incorporating both into one's self-image—a departure from traditional notions of sorority, non-partisanship, and service characteristic of predominantly female organizations engaged in interest group politics. Some women elected to major offices as late as the 1980s found power itself to be such a gendered concept that a politically effective Connecticut Congresswoman confessed, "It is a word I don't like." That Diane Feinstein chose the much repeated slogan "tough *and* caring" for her 1990 California gubernatorial campaign suggests the continuing effort of female candidates to bridge these two political cultures on the eve of the twenty-first century.[15]

The deeply gendered policy priorities that emerged from these two political cultures have also enjoyed a persistence too little appreciated. Consider the current practice known as "legislative typecasting," the frequent assignment of women in elective office to legislative committees dealing with what have traditionally been labeled "women's concerns." For legislators who got their start in politics as members of local boards and organizations concerned with child care, education, health, human service, reproductive rights, even domestic violence, such areas are those in which they have policy expertise. For these women, assignments to committees dealing with "women's issues" are often assignments of choice. But legislative typecasting also stereotypes female legislators who have expertise in other areas. Perhaps more important, it allows male legislators (and special interest groups) to retain control over policy areas long identified with male interests and in which "real" power is perceived to reside: taxes and budgets, for example. The problem, considered sufficiently serious for women state legislators to devote a full session to it at their 1991 meeting, serves as yet another reminder that, even as legislative bodies sexually integrate and even as women legislators extend their range of committee involvement, policy priorities remain strikingly gendered.[16]

Policy itself can be a site in which gender is formed and contested, as a look at the Social Security Act reveals. Verbatim accounts of meetings that hammered out the language of the 1939 amendments involving Old Age Insurance provide a case in point. Policy makers, Alice Kessler-Harris discovered, justified a lower social security stipend for elderly women than for men on the grounds that, as grandmothers, women would live with one of their children and would help with housework and child care. Assumptions about male and female behavior that were racialized also permeated the legislative process. The resulting system of benefits not only perpetuated inequities with regard to race and class, Kessler-Harris notes, but sent powerful messages about existing gender norms.[17]

The two-tiered welfare state, as feminist scholars have revealed, is itself a demonstration of the power of gender to shape policy and of policy to reinforce gender norms. In the upper tier are contributory social insurance programs; the lower tier is composed of non-contributory social assistance programs which are means-tested. Upper-tier beneficiaries, usually retired wage earners, may receive relatively generous benefits, while citizens dependent on lower-tier programs, mainly non-widowed single women and their children, thus remain impoverished. The differentiation has to do with the basis of claims. Almost all men make their claims on the basis of their labor in the paid labor force, while most women—although a declining proportion—make their claims on the basis of family status as widows of covered men or mothers of needy children.[18]

Gender is no less present in the origins of such programs, as feminist scholars in political science as well as history have demonstrated. Recall those middle-class practitioners of the politics of domesticity. When they sought to protect needy women and children in the early years of the twentieth century, they argued for governmental support for the most vulnerable, i.e., children. They also used children as rhetorical surrogates for women: aid, likely to be withheld for women, might be made available for those women's children. In the Progressive era, Mothers' Pensions, the predecessor of our present program of Aid to Families with Dependent Children (AFDC), were finally established. Needy women received Mothers' Pensions because they were good mothers, a designation that, as Linda Gordon has pointed out, required them to conform to a model of motherhood that was culturally specific, i.e., middle-class. Eligibility standards thus encompassed a variety of variables, many of which were qualitative, reflecting the judgment of caseworkers; duration of benefits was uncertain.[19]

Men became recipients of benefits via a different route, as Barbara Nelson has explained. When industrial workers argued for workmen's compensation and employers signed on, they did so in order to replace a tort liability system with a standardized insurance program that was based on the paid labor of white men. As common law legal defenses weakened, leaving employers less protected against damage suits from injured workers, reform-minded businessmen, reformers, and ultimately union leaders agreed to set up standardized rules for determining the extent of injuries and the amount and duration of payment. The fact that the recipients received their benefits as deserving breadwinners through formulaic, routinized, and non-intrusive measures reinforced the legitimacy of their claim.[20]

Architects of these two legislative innovations were not intentionally discriminatory. But in separating welfare state beneficiaries into child-bearers and wage-earners, and in creating programs where women received non-contributory social assistance that was means-tested while men received non-means-tested contributory social insurance, they created gendered prototypes. As such, these early programs laid the foundation for different and unequal channels of social provision, also reinforcing traditional divisions of labor and racial privilege. Beneficiaries, for example, were overwhelmingly white. At the very least, feminist scholars insist, the emergence of a two-tiered welfare state demonstrates that scholarship on the welfare state that neglects gender—or fails to explore how gender, race, and class interact—provides at best a partial picture of social policy, and at worst, a badly distorted one.

Indeed, the racialized gender dynamics of welfare policies and politics have been hard to escape of late. When Congress was debating the 1995 Personal Responsibility Act, part of the Republican Contract with America, we had only to flip the pages of the newspapers to accounts of debate over AFDC recipients to discover that the stereotypic image of the black welfare mother unwilling to work or wed has supplanted any notion of social citizenship—the right to economic security and welfare, to use T. H. Marshall's classic definition. My example is not meant to deny the salience of adolescent pregnancy, out-of-wedlock childbirth, and budget deficits as national issues. But it does serve to underscore the extent to which welfare politics, long gender coded, have, especially since the 1960s, been racially coded as well.[21]

Such coding alerts us to the need to explore the boundaries of welfare provision: who is included and who is not? How do categories of inclusion and exclusion develop and what do they tell us about constructions of citizenship? Citizenship as a status that carries with it generic rights and obligations incumbent on all citizens presumably overrides other identities particular to those who are citizens of the state: we pay taxes, for example, whatever our sexual, racial, or ethnic identity. But social citizenship may be more gendered and racialized than we initially assumed. The same may be true for other forms of citizenship.[22]

Gendering of Citizenship

Until recently, most of us have not thought much about citizenship as gendered, in part because women have always been citizens of the republic. Rights and obligations of citizenship—voting, paying taxes, bearing arms, serving on juries—are described by the Constitution in generic terms as incumbent on all citizens. Yet gender, like class, race, and ethnicity, continues to matter in constructions of citizenship. In the new republic, Carroll Smith-Rosenberg has argued, the virtuous and independent white male citizen was constructed on a conceptual basis that "fused masculinity and republicanism as the defining characteristics of the new American subject," describing him in part by what he was not—the feminine and racialized other. In an impressive analysis of various kinds of evidence, including the political iconography of the early republic, Smith-Rosenberg points out how subjugated unruly figures of women, blacks, and American Indians signified the superiority of the white male citizen.[23]

Within this context, claiming space for a woman citizen was, as Linda Kerber has pointed out, a formidable undertaking. At the heart of the problem was the old English law of domestic relations, coverture, which transferred a woman's civic identity to her husband upon marriage. The resulting restrictions on women—their inability to hold property, to sue and be sued, to enter into contracts—all are matters of which we are well aware. But coverture had implications for citizenship as well. Under the old law of domestic relations, Kerber reminds us, a woman's only chosen obligation was to her husband. So long as married women were understood to owe all of their obligation to their husbands they had, as one prominent lawyer in the nineteenth century put it, no more "*political* relationship to the *state* than . . . an alien." Or, to put the matter somewhat differently, women served the state by serving their husbands and, by extension, their households.[24]

Within that ideological framework, women's initial exclusion from both the rights and obligations of citizenship seemed "rational, realistic and wise." What we still have not fully appreciated, Kerber argues, is the lingering impact of this old law of domestic relations upon more recent constructions of citizenship. Naturalization laws provide a case in point. Caucasian alien women who married U.S. citizens were automatically granted citizenship; it was assumed that their allegiance to the new state was contingent on the oath they took to their husbands. The same logic cost American-born women who married alien husbands their citizenship, as the Supreme Court affirmed in 1915 (*Mackenzie v Hare*). Independent citizenship for women, a part of the suffragists' agenda, was secured with the Cable Act of 1922, with some notable exceptions that owed their existence to racism. American-born women who married "an alien ineligible to citizenship" (an immigrant from China, Japan, or India) continued to forfeit their American citizenship upon marriage.[25]

One way of tracing the political history of women in the U.S., Kerber notes, is to observe the "redirection of a series of obligations from husbands and households to oneself as an individual or to the state." Voting and jury service provide prime examples of that evolution. Suffragists emphasized rights claims as autonomous citizens. Antisuffragists responded that a husband's ballot sufficed for both and that the ballot would upset "the present relationship of men and women in the home," as an Illinois antisuffragist so delicately put it. While suffragists prevailed with the ratification of the Nineteenth Amendment, the meaning of citizenship had not been resolved. Racism and poll taxes in the South prevented black and poor white women, as well as their male counterparts, from voting until the 1960s. Morever, the argument that duties to husband and families "trump duties to the the public and to the state" continued to permeate the controversy over a woman's civic obligation, as Kerber makes clear.

The debate over jury service is a case in point. Although some states added women's names to the jury pool in the immediate aftermath of suffrage, others did not. Many discovered that they could maintain the practice of virtually all-male juries by permitting a wide range of exemptions which women happily utilized. When feminists opposed permissive jury service, defenders inevitably reiterated the argument that women had household obligations that should take precedence. As late as 1961 when Gwendolyn Hoyt appealed her conviction for second-degree murder by an all-male jury on the grounds that the jury had not been drawn from a full cross-section of the community, the state of Florida responded true to form. If only ten of the 3,000 names in the pool were the names of women, attorneys for the state of Florida argued, it was because obligation to family outweighed obligations to fellow citzens. Kerber relates a telling incident: during the oral argument before the Supreme Court, the assistant attorney general of Florida was asked to explain why it was logical to excuse women from jury service so easily. Caught off guard by a question from Earl Warren, he blurted out, "Well, Mr. Chief Justice . . . they have to cook the dinners!"[26]

Nowhere is the dynamic of gender more evident than in definitions of military obligation. The right to protection by the state has never entailed for women the reciprocal obligation to bear arms in its defense. By the 1970s, congressional passage of the Equal Rights Amendment by an overwhelming majority seemed to imply that full citizenship required equal responsibility—a position strongly endorsed by the growing numbers of women in the military who resented the way the system of rewards penalized noncombatants. But the subsequent rejection by Congress of President Jimmy Carter's proposal to register young women, should there be another draft, suggested otherwise. While the Supreme Court in the *Rostker* decision upheld Congress's position with respect to registration, it is worth remembering that the Court was divided. In his dissent, Justice Thurgood Marshall noted that in requiring males, but not females, to register for the draft, women were being "excluded from a fundamental civic obligation." The presence of military women in the invading forces in Panama and Iraq is evidence that in the all-volunteer army the combat exemption is being eroded. But that erosion, as Kerber cautions, "does not necessarily or directly measure

Americans' understanding of whether *all* women, like all men, have an obligation to bear arms. . . ."[27]

My point, however, is not simply that citizenship is gendered. Nor is it that rights and obligations have been continuously negotiated, although they have been—so much so, in fact, that citizenship is coming to be understood less as a mark of fixed status and more as a practice. Rather, it is the extent to which our most fundamental political concepts and institutions are sites in which gender is inscribed, shaped, and contested. One last example suffices.

Gendering of Nationalism

Nationalism and national identity, much discussed by political historians in the past, have once again become a focus of attention. The period in which "the first real models of nationhood" emerged, which later generations would borrow and transform, is of course the late eighteenth and early nineteenth century. Taking a cue from Benedict Anderson, who suggests that nation-states are made not just through force but through loyalties, scholars in a variety of disciplines, myself included, have begun to look at how social differences are deployed to define—and redefine—the "imagined community."[28]

Historians customarily think of nationalism in relation to ethnicity or race, recalling old connections of family, kinship, and ethnicity embedded in claims of nationhood. Yet even in mature, multi-ethnic nation-states, the need to create a "fictive ethnicity" persists, often taking a racialized form in which ethnicity and race are equated, as Etienne Balibar reminds us. In the United States, for example, individuals of European origin first identified as "swarthy," such as the Irish and Italians, gradually became "white." In the face of reason and historical evidence, these recent arrivals even insisted that white Americans were the only true Americans and that other Americans (American Indians, African Americans, and Hispanic Americans), some of whom had resided within U.S. territorial boundaries far longer, were marginalized "others."[29]

Ethnicity and race are not the only constituent categories of nationalism. George Mosse's pioneering study, *Nationalism and Sexuality*, makes clear that in the nation-states of Western Europe he examined, sexuality was also fundamental. Certain sexual attitudes, desires, and practices came to be perceived as allied with nationalism, while others, which had been tolerated in earlier eras, were deemed threatening, demanding control. It is no coincidence, he argues, that with the emergence of modern nationalism in the late eighteenth century, homoeroticism had to be purged from the male bonding that was endemic in wars of liberation. Nor was it a coincidence that in the nineteenth century, people who preferred having sexual relations with persons of their own sex were for the first time defined as (pathologically deviant) homosexuals and lesbians. Marked as abnormal not merely by virtue of individual sexual acts but also in terms of psychological make-up, bodily structure, and appearance, they were "outsiders" from whom "insiders" could set themselves apart.[30]

Like sexuality, gender too is embedded in constructions of national identities, serving as a marker of difference around which to define the "imagined community." Although gender norms within and among nations may be as varied as nations themselves, the model of the independent national state developed in the West within a patriarchical context. Women supported and participated in early nationalist movements. A few even disguised themselves as boys in order to fight in wars of liberation, as did Deborah Sampson, who enlisted in the Fourth Massachusetts Regiment. But female patriots were of use primarily as symbols of the nation—Germania, Britannia, and Columbia come immediately to mind. Usually depicted as idealized, static figures with a classical quality, they represented quiet strength rather than active political engagement, thereby signaling women's place in the nation that these female images personified. Since wars for nationhood are often cast as battles for manhood, the agents of national formation were (and are) male. In the new United States, arms-bearing men in the thirteen colonies bonded across barriers of ethnicity, religion, and class to make a revolution and write the constitution and laws that shaped a new nation in North America. The point is not that the Founding Fathers were men—we have always known that. Nor is it that patriarchy shaped the constitution and laws they wrote. How could it be otherwise in a patriarchal society? Rather, the point is the enduring affinity of nationalism and particular forms of masculinity. In the late twentieth century, struggles of national liberation continue to be masculine affairs with women relegated to national service as mothers, even when they prove themselves to be skilled guerrilla fighters, as did the female soldiers of Eritrea.[31]

Given the fusion of nationalism and particular gender forms, it is not suprising that the sharply demarcated gender roles and norms associated with nineteenth-century bourgeois society during the formative period of nation-building have became firmly, if tacitly, identified with the nation. To be sure, gender, like ethnicity, race, and sexuality, is always in the process of reformulation in the modern nation-state, as is national identity itself. (The continual reconfiguration of separate European ethnicities in the American context has long preoccupied students of immigration, as historians are well aware.) But these formative configurations of gender and nationhood, while subject to change at the margins, are also remarkably persistent in their core. During moments of crisis, when social cohesion seems precarious, they are often reasserted, sometimes coercively. The recognition that national identity is defined in part through the shaping of particular forms of gender and sexuality against other forms allows us to view these historical moments with new insight. We can better understand why, in the United States, traditional gender norms, roles, and hierarchies have survived the demise of colonialism and the emergence of feminism.

Consider the representations of the Vietnam War contained in American films, fiction, personal accounts, and political and social analyses. The images not only reaffirm male bonding, as literary and film analyst Susan Jeffords has demonstrated. Even more clearly, they posit a homosocial community transplanted from battlefield to homefront from which, according to Jeffords, women are eliminated from considerations of value. Because warfare is not separate from society, such representations are not "created" by war, Jeffords has argued. Rather, they reveal preexisting social tensions, among them the strain of changing gender relations. More importantly, these representations of masculinity reinforce and renegotiate contested relations of dominance by reasserting male authority.[32]

Consider also an earlier historical moment, the "long fifties" (from 1945 to around 1965), which was also a time of intense anxiety about the nation's security. How do we explain the exaggerated domesticity and highly politicized homophobia that many scholars have identified as distinguishing features of the Cold War era? Salient factors were the extraordinary stresses placed on the American family by the Great Depression and World War II. A depressed economy meant delayed marriage, deferred children, unemployed heads of household; war further challenged traditional gender arrangements and removed restraints on deviant sexual behavior. But while a desire to return to "normalcy" was understandable, the key factor, according to Elaine May, was the Cold War. In *Homeward Bound*, her influential study of white middle-class family life, May argued that rigid heterosexuality and strict adherence to traditional gender roles constituted a domestic version of containment. Just as anticommunism required the containment of Sino-Soviet expansion abroad, so gender revolution (feminism) and deviant expressions of sexual desire and practice (homosexuality) had to be effectively contained at home.[33]

Although May's thesis is insightful, it does not explain why that linkage predated the Cold War or, more important, why it has remained so powerful and persistent after the demise of communism in Europe and the breakup of the Soviet Union. Proponents of gay and women's rights, in an effort to underscore the ideological dimension of national identity, argued as early as the 1950s that the most compelling demonstration of Americanism would be achieved by living up to the American creed and according full freedom and equality to all minorities. Yet a substantial number of people in this country continue to reject that argument. What was—and remains—at issue, not merely for those on the political Right but for millions of Americans of all political persuasions, becomes clearer when we keep in mind two factors: first, that these founding paradigms of gender and nationhood continue to be reasserted, and second, that the human body, as Michel Foucault has instructed us, is a reflection of and the central metaphor for the implicit order that prevails in a civilization. According to anthropologist Mary Douglas, the human body "can stand for any bounded system." Its boundaries, she explains, can "represent any boundaries which are threatened and precarious." Not surprisingly, many people are inclined to conflate the human body and the body politic, to fuse sex with gender, and to assume anatomy dictates heterosexuality. For such people during the Cold War years, the linkages so basic to domestic containment—anticommunism, traditional gender norms, and heterosexual, marital sex—were fundamental. In that symbolic universe, gender ambiguity, homosexuality, and communism itself were assaults on the body. It is no accident that communism was likened to a disease that disfigured and destroyed, and that undetected Communist cells were seen as analogous to diseased cells spreading within the human body, as historian Geoffrey Smith has noted. To prevent the spread of contagion within the national body required that strict boundaries be erected to contain not only communism, but gender revolution, non-marital sexuality, especially homosexuality, and, for some, even race mixing.[34]

But what of the present? How do we explain the continuing battles over gender and sexuality that we encounter in issues as recent as women in military academies and as enduring as sex education in the schools? How are we to understand the gender and sexual agenda of conservative politics? Are pronouncements about the end of the Cold War premature? Perhaps they are, if by the Cold War we mean a densely woven web of relationships and ideas that has sustained not only a large and lethal military structure but also ideas about national identity. Yet in many respects the end of the Cold War has blurred national identity, just as it has called into question America's international military role. As a result, we are witnessing recurrent efforts to reaffirm and reconfigure founding paradigms of gender, sexuality, and nationhood, as groups within the nation-state seek to redefine "the people" versus "the other" in much the same way as states themselves do in relation to each other. The culture wars of recent years provide a case in point. Key societal groups, deeply divided by conflicting values and ideals, battle over a wide range of social policy issues from abortion and affirmative action to gays in the military, welfare reform, and national history standards. Behind this discord, scholars have noted, is a single overriding concern: national identity. At issue are competing visions of what this nation stands for, what it has been and aspires to be, and who we are as a people.[35]

To probe the politics of national identity, whether with respect to the contemporary culture wars, as I am now doing, or in terms of the conflicting discourse of other eras in our nation's past, is surely the task of the political historian. Yet it requires not only grounding our history empirically but also understanding the ways in which gender and sexuality, as well as ethnicity and race, are deployed, often unconsciously, in the construction and production of national identity. We need to understand as well that gender, race, sexuality, ethnicity, and even national identity are not timeless "natural" entities but social constructions. Hardly static, they can best be understood, women's historians insist, as "highly interactive, fluid formations, historically and spatially located."[36]

If the language seems unfamiliar, the insights involved lead to what is most familiar—politics and power. In examining how social differences in specific times and places are constructed, reproduced, and deployed in both the private and public arenas, how public and private interpenetrate, and whose interests are served, women's historians have enlarged both our definition of politics and our understanding of power. Political historians, especially, are beneficiaries.

What, then, can we conclude? If normative U.S. history can no longer be understood to be male, and if gender intrudes into regions of the political narrative where it was conventionally thought to play no part, saturating many of our most basic political concepts, then both our existing historical accounts and traditional analytical practices are challenged. We can respond by marginalizing the new scholarship, pointing to the weakest examples, and dismissing it as particularistic or imperialistic. (The inconsistency of the charges is no deterrent to critics.) Or we can take advantage of what historians of women and historians of politics have in common, bridging old divides. Both share a scholarly preoccupation with politics and power. Citizenship, national identity, political culture, and, most especially, the state are increasingly subjects of mutual interest. Both aspire to write the most accurate accounts possible of human relationships in the past. Building on these commonalities poses the greater challenge. But it also offers greater rewards—a political history that is enriched and invigorated by the new scholarship, one that is more compelling, probably more critical, and certainly more complete.[37]

Notes

I am especially grateful to Laura Kalman, Linda K. Kerber, and William E. Leuchtenburg for their careful and constructive reading of an earlier draft of this essay.

1. *Oxford English Dictionary*, 2d ed. (Oxford: Clarendon Press, 1989), s.v. "gender." The much used phrase, "making the invisible woman visible," is the title of a collection of essays. See Anne Firor Scott, *Making the Invisible Woman Visible* (Urbana: University of Illinois Press, 1984).

2. There are numerous accounts of the emergence of women's history as a field. For example, see Joan Wallach Scott, *Gender and the Politics of History* (New York: Columbia University Press, 1988), pp. 16–27, and her "Women's History," in *New Perspectives on Historical Writing*, edited by Peter Burke (University Park: The Pennsylvania State University Press, 1992), pp. 42–66.

A dissenting voice calling for greater attention to formal politics was that of Ellen Du Bois, whose own work has focused on suffrage. On Du Bois and her critics, see "Politics and Culture in Women's History," *Feminist Studies* 6 (1980): 26–64. Du Bois's concern was that the focus on women's agency in a separate female culture obscured the reality of patriarchy. Her critics argued that the focus on politics as electoral and governmental activities accepted a traditional model of historical significance that obscured and undervalued women's actions.

3. On significant women in reform politics, see, for example, Gerda Lerner, *The Grimke Sisters of South Carolina: Pioneers for Women's Rights and Abolition* (Boston: Houghton Mifflin, 1966); Celia Morris Eckhardt, *Fanny Wright: Rebel in America* (Cambridge: Harvard University Press, 1984); Carlton Mabee, *Sojourner Truth: Slave, Prophet, Legend* (New York: New York University Press, 1993); Elisabeth Griffith, *In Her Own Right: A Life of Elizabeth Cady Stanton* (New York: Oxford University Press, 1984); Ruth Bordin, *Frances Willard: A Biography* (Chapel Hill: University of North Carolina Press, 1986); Jacquelyn Dowd Hall, *Revolt Against Chivalry: Jessie Daniel Ames and the Women's Campaign against Lynching* (New York: Columbia University Press, 1974).

Biographies of female politicians include Elizabeth Israels Perry, *Feminine Politics and the Exercise of Power in the Age of Alfred E. Smith* (New York: Oxford University Press, 1987); Susan Ware, *Partner and I: Molly Dewson, Feminism, and New Deal Politics* (New Haven: Yale University Press, 1987); Ingrid Scobie, *Center Stage: Helen Gahagan Douglas, A Life* (New York: Oxford University Press, 1992); Blanche Weisen Cook, *Eleanor Roosevelt: Volume One, 1884–1933* (New York: Viking, 1992). See also Christie Mille, *Ruth Hanna McCormick: A Life in Politics, 1880–1940* (Albuquerque: University of New Mexico Press, 1992).

4. Linda K. Kerber, *Women of the Republic: Intellect and Ideology in Revolutionary America* (Chapel Hill: University of North Carolina Press, 1980), and Mary Beth Norton, *Liberty's Daughters: The Revolutionary Experience of American Women, 1750–1800* (Boston: Little, Brown, 1980).

5. The literature is extensive; the following citations are by no means inclusive, even of monographs, much less of the voluminous journal articles. For an overview of women's organizations and activism at the national level, see Anne Firor Scott, *Natural Allies: Women's Associations in American History* (Urbana: University of Illinois Press, 1991). See also *Visible Women: New Essays in American Activism*, edited by Nancy Hewitt and Suzanne Lebsock (Urbana: University of Illinois Press, 1993). For the history of women's reform activities within a single city, see Nancy Hewitt, *Women's Activism and Social Change: Rochester, New York, 1822–1872* (Ithaca, N.Y.: Cornell University Press, 1984). Lori Ginzberg, *Women and the Work of Benevolence: Morality, Politics, and Class in the Nineteenth-Century United States* (New Haven: Yale University Press, 1990), ably examines reformers' tactics and underlying ideologies. Religion, particularly Protestant Evangelicalism, both motivated and shielded from criticism many women, black and white, who worked to extend the boundaries of home and sisterhood throughout the nineteenth century. See, for example, Evelyn Brooks Higginbotham, *Righteous Discontent: The*

Women's Movement in the Black Baptist Church, 1880–1920 (Cambridge: Harvard University Press, 1993); Jean E. Friedman, *The Enclosed Garden: Women and Community in the Evangelical South, 1830–1900* (Chapel Hill: University of North Carolina Press, 1985); and Peggy Pascoe, *Relations of Rescue: The Search for Female Moral Authority in the American West, 1874–1939* (New York: Oxford University Press, 1990). The increasing public presence of pre-Civil War women is the focus of Mary Ryan, *Women in Public: Between Banners and Bullets, 1825–1880* (Baltimore: Johns Hopkins University Press, 1990).

For black women, commitment to race and community underlay activism. See, for example, Paula Giddings, *When and Where I Enter: The Impact of Black Women on Race and Sex in America* (New York: Bantam Books, 1984), and Jacqueline Rouse, *Lugenia Burns Hope: A Black Female Reformer in the South, 1871–1942* (Athens: University of Georgia Press, 1989). Scholarly articles on black women's activism are increasingly evident. See Anne Firor Scott, "Most Invisible of All: Black Women's Voluntary Societies," *Journal of Southern History* 56 (1990): 3–22; Darlene Clark Hine, " 'We Specialize in the Wholly Impossible': The Philanthropic Work of Black Women," in *Lady Bountiful Revisited*, edited by Kathleen D. McCarthy (New Brunswick, N.J.: Rutgers University Press, 1990); Cheryl Towsend Gilkes, "Building in Many Places: Multiple Commitments and Ideologies in Black Women's Community Work," in *Work and the Politics of Empowerment*, edited by Ann Bookman and Sandra Morgen (Philadelphia: Temple University Press), pp. 53–76; Anne Meis Knupfer, "Toward a Tenderer Humanity and a Nobler Womanhood: African-American Women's Clubs in Chicago, 1890 to 1920," *Journal of Women's History* 7 (Fall 1995): 58–76. See also Stephanie J. Shaw, "Black Club Women and the Creation of the National Association of Colored Women"; Linda Gordon, "Black and White Visions of Welfare: Women's Welfare Activism, 1890–1945"; and Lillian S. Williams, "And Still I Rise: Black Women and Reform, Buffalo, New York, 1900–1940," all in *We Specialize in the Wholly Impossible: A Reader in Black Women's History*, edited by Darlene Clark Hine, Wilma King, and Linda Reed (New York: Carlson, 1995), pp. 433–86, 521–42. Gordon's essay, which is a comparative study of black and white women's welfare activism, is particularly informative on the socio-economic profile of leaders in both groups and the differences in emphasis with respect to welfare reforms such as mother's pensions. Important dissertation literature includes Glenda Elizabeth Gilmore, "Gender and Jim Crow: The Politics of White Supremacy in North Carolina, 1896–1920" (Ph.D. diss., University of North Carolina, 1992).

On Jewish women's activism, which, like other aspects of Jewish women's history, has been relatively neglected, see Faith Rogow, *Gone to Another Meeting: The National Council of Jewish Women, 1893–1993* (Tuscaloosa: University of Alabama Press, 1993).

On specific reform movements, see, for example, Jean Fagen Yellin, *Women and Sisters: Antislavery Feminists in American Culture* (New Haven: Yale University Press, 1990); Dorothy Sterling, *Ahead of her Time: Abby Kelley and the Politics of Antislavery* (New York: W. W. Norton, 1991); Estelle Freedman, *Their Sisters'*

Keepers: Women's Prison Reform in America, 1830–1930 (Ann Arbor: University of Michigan Press, 1981); Ruth Bordin, *Women and Temperance: The Quest for Power and Liberty, 1873–1900* (Philadelphia: Temple University Press, 1980); Barbara Epstein, *The Politics of Domesticity: Women, Evangelism, and Temperance in Nineteenth-Century America* (Middletown, Conn.: Wesleyan University Press, 1981).

Studies focusing on some of the extraordinary reformers revolving around Hull House for most or part of their careers include: Allen Davis, *American Heroine: The Life and Legend of Jane Addams* (New York: Oxford University Press, 1973); *Alice Hamilton: A Life in Letters*, edited by Barbara Sicherman (Cambridge: Harvard University Press, 1984); and Kathryn Kish Sklar, *Florence Kelley and the Nation's Work: The Rise of Women's Political Culture, 1830–1900* (New Haven: Yale University Press, 1995). The linkage of the Hull House women as well as other women activists to the creation of the Children's Bureau is skillfully traced in Robyn Muncy, *Creating a Female Dominion in American Reform, 1890–1935* (New York: Oxford University Press, 1991).

The increasing involvement of the women activists in formal politics is documented for the Hull House women in Kathryn Kish Sklar's "Hull House in the 1890s: A Community of Women Reformers," *Signs* 10 (1985): 658–77. See also S. Sara Moonson, "The Lady and Tiger: Women's Electoral Participation in New York City before Suffrage," *Journal of Women's History* 2 (Fall 1900): 100–135. The relationship of reform activism to suffrage has long been recognized. See, for example, Anne Firor Scott, *The Southern Lady: From Pedestal to Politics* (Chicago: University of Chicago Press, 1970). The standard history of suffrage is still Eleanor Flexner, *Century of Struggle: The Women's Rights Movement* (Cambridge: Harvard University Press, 1958). See also Ellen Carol Du Bois, *Feminism and Suffrage: The Emergence of an Independent Women's Movement in America, 1848–1869* (Ithaca, N.Y.: Cornell University Press, 1978).

The term "maternalist" has been used to describe women activists, black and white, who used the rhetoric of motherhood to justify their political activism. Among the more prominent examples of its usage are Theda Skocpol, *Protecting Soldiers and Mothers: The Political Origins of Social Policy in the United States* (Cambridge: Harvard University Press, 1992), and Sonya Michel and Seth Koven, "Womanly Duties: Maternalist Politics and the Origins of the Welfare State in France, Great Britain and the United States, 1880–1920," *American Historical Review* 95 (October 1990): 1076–1108. The concept has come under increasing scrutiny from historians of women for a variety of reasons, among them: (1) loose parameters which result in its application to women's groups that range from feminist to antifeminist, from radical to conservative; (2) the conflation of women and mothers which obscures recognition of women as workers; (3) cultural specificity which obscures the differing meaning maternalism held for black activists. For a fuller discussion, see Molly Ladd-Taylor, "Toward Defining Maternalism in U.S. History," and Eileen Boris, "What About the Working Mother," both in *Journal of Women's History* 5 (Fall 1993): 110–13 and 104–9.

6. For a discussion of the need for a broader definition of politics, see Louise A. Tilly and Patricia Gurin, "Women, Politics, and Change," in *Women, Politics, and Change*, edited by Tilly and Gurin (New York: Russell Sage Foundation, 1990), pp. 3–32.

7. See Evans, "Women's History and Political Theory," in *Visible Women*, Hewitt and Lebsock, eds., pp. 101–39.

8. The most systematic effort to develop gender as a category of historical analysis and to bring women's history into a criticial relationship with so-called traditional history has been made by Joan Wallach Scott. Her article in the *American Historical Review* is reprinted in Scott's *Gender and the Politics of History*, pp. 28–50.

9. This and the following paragraphs are based upon Paula C. Baker, "The Domestication of Politics: Women and American Political Society, 1780–1920," *American Historical Review* 89 (June 1984): 620–48. See also Baker, *The Moral Frameworks of Public Life: Gender, Politics, and the State in Rural New York, 1870–1930* (New York: Oxford University Press, 1991).

10. For work done since the publication of Baker's article on the Whig Party's incorporation of women, see Elizabeth Varon, "Tippecanoe and the Ladies, Too: White Women and Party Politics in Antebellum Virginia," *Journal of American History* 82 (September 1995): 494–521, and " 'We Mean to be Counted': White Women and Politics in Antebellum Virginia" (Ph.D. diss., Yale University, 1993). For other recent scholarship on antebellum women and politics, see Michael E. McGerr, "Political Style and Women's Power, 1830–1930," *Journal of American History* 77 (December 1990), 864–86. On the late nineteenth and early twentieth centuries, see Rebecca Edwards, "Gender and American Political Parties, 1880–1900" (Ph.D. diss., University of Virginia, 1995), and Sarah Wilkerson-Freeman, "Women and the Transformation of American Politics: North Carolina, 1898–1940 (Ph.D. diss., University of North Carolina, 1995).

11. Motherhood was the operative term inasmuch as it was women's common capacity for motherhood that created the shared responsibility for the nation's children. That motherhood was often not sufficient to overcome differences of race, ethnicity, and class has been frequently documented by historians of women. See, for example, Rosalyn Terborg-Penn, "Discontented Black Feminists: Prelude and Postscript to the Passage of the Nineteenth Amendment," in *Decades of Discontent: The Women's Movement, 1920–1940*, edited by Lois Sharf and Joan M. Jensen (Westport, Conn.: Greenwood Press, 1983), pp. 261–78; Giddings, *When and Where I Enter*; Elisabeth Lasch-Quinn, *Black Neighbors: Race and the Limits of Reform in the American Settlement House Movement, 1890–1945* (Chapel Hill: University of North Carolina Press, 1993); and Nancy Schrom Dye, "Creating a Feminist Alliance: Sisterhood and Class Conflict in the New York Women's Trade Union League, 1903–1914," *Feminist Studies* 2 (1975): 24–36.

Recent scholarship has demonstrated that the problems of racial and class differences were often more complex than was initially assumed. For example, the charge that Southern suffragists were racists has been much modified by recent work that demonstrates the wide range of views on race held by white suffragists. Compare Aileen Kraditor, *The Ideas of the Woman Suffrage Movement, 1890–1920* (New York: Columbia University Press, 1965), chap. 7, with Marjorie Spruill Wheeler, *New Women of the New South: Leaders of the Woman Suffrage Movement in the Southern States* (New York: Oxford University Press, 1983), and especially Suzanne Lebsock, "Woman Suffrage and White Supremacy: A Virginia Case Study" in *Visible Women*, pp. 62–100, and Elna Green, *Southern Strategies: Southern Women and the Suffrage Question* (Chapel Hill: University of North Carolina Press, forthcoming).

12. William H. Chafe, "Women's History and Political History: Some Thoughts on Progressivism and the New Deal," in *Visible Women*, pp. 101–18. Chafe's point about the element of social control that inhered in female-inspired reforms is based on a number of studies, among them those of Muncy and Gordon cited in notes 5 and 19. Gwendolyn Mink provides an especially nuanced analysis of the effort of women's reform organizations to uplift and regulate. She argues that maternalist efforts to educate poor women and racial minorities to middle-class American cultural practices were based on liberal rather than essentialist premises, with equality as the ultimate goal. The effect, however, was to strengthen ideological and institutional forms of subordination. See Gwendolyn Mink, *The Wages of Motherhood: Inequality in the Welfare State, 1917–1942* (Ithaca, N.Y.: Cornell University Press, 1995).

13. Muncy, *Female Dominion*, pp. 93–157. See also Molly Ladd-Taylor, *Women, Child Welfare, and the State, 1890–1930* (Urbana: University of Illinois Press, 1994). The argument that women's activism served as a surrogate for working-class social-welfare activism has been elaborated in much of Sklar's recent work. See for example, Kathryn Kish Sklar, "The Historical Foundation of Women's Power in the Creation of the American Welfare State, 1830–1930," in *Mothers of a New World: Maternalist Politics and the Origins of Welfare States*, edited by Seth Koven and Sonya Michel (New York: Routledge, 1993), pp. 43–93.

14. For a more detailed account, see my "Rights and Representation: Women, Politics, and Power in the Contemporary United States," in *U.S. History as Women's History: New Feminist Essays*, edited by Linda K. Kerber, Alice Kessler-Harris, and Kathryn Kish Sklar, pp. 214–42, 403–14, and also Donald G. Mathews and Jane Sherron De Hart, *Sex, Gender, and the Politics of ERA: A State and the Nation* (New York: Oxford University Press, 1990).

15. Kunin is quoted in "Talk of the Town," *The New Yorker*, August 3, 1992, p. 24. Congresswoman Nancy Johnson of Connecticut is quoted in Dorothy Cantor and Toni Bernay with Jean Stoess, *Women in Power: The Secrets of Leadership* (Boston: Houghton Mifflin, 1992), p. 51. Cantor and Bernay indicate that Johnson's feelings were shared by other high-level female politicians whom they interviewed, many of whom talked less about their ambivalence toward political power than their desire to redefine it. Ruth Mandel, Director of the Eagleton Institute for Politics, reports that this discomfort with power is less apparent among women politicians in the 1990s. Conversation with author, June 12, 1993. On the Feinstein gubernatorial

campaign, see Celia Morris, *Storming the Statehouse: Running for Governor with Ann Richards and Dianne Feinstein* (New York: Scribner, 1992), pp. 77–78. The difficulties inherent in making the transition from a female political culture to a male political culture are also evident in Linda Witt, Karen M. Paget, and Glenna Matthews, *Running as a Woman: Gender and Power in American Politics* (New York: Free Press, 1994).

16. CAWP Forum for Women State Legislators, November 14–17, *Program* (New Brunswick, N.J.: Center for the American Woman and Politics, 1991).

17. Alice Kessler-Harris, "Designing Women and Old Fools: The Construction of the Social Security Amendments of 1939," in *U.S. History as Women's History*, pp. 87–106.

18. Mary Jo Bane, "Politics and Policies in the Feminization of Poverty," and Margaret Weir, Ann Shola Orloff, and Theda Skocpol, "The Future of Public Policy in the United States: Political Constraints and Possibilities," in *The Politics of Social Policy in the United States*, edited by Margaret Weir, Ann Orloff, and Theda Skocpol (Princeton: Princeton University Press, 1986), pp. 381–96, 421–25.

19. It is worth noting that, increasingly, sociologists and political scientists have joined historians in exploring the gendered historical origins of social policy, among them Theda Skocpol, Ann Orloff, and Barbara Nelson, whose works are cited elsewhere in this essay. There is also considerable effort on the part of political scientists to move beyond the kind of institutional studies of the welfare state that dominated during the 1980s to recognize interactions among the institutions of state, market, and family. Consideration of the range of outcomes involving the family allows for the introduction of gender relations, thus making possible a convergence between mainstream and feminist welfare state scholarship in political science. See *Gendering Welfare States: Combining Insights of Feminist and Mainstream Research*, edited by Diane Sainsbury (Thousand Oaks, Calif.: Sage Publications, 1994).

On mothers's pensions, see Linda Gordon, "Putting Children First: Women, Maternalism and Welfare in the Early Twentieth Century," in *U.S. History as Women's History*, pp. 63–86, and *Pitied But Not Entitled: Single Mothers and the History of Welfare, 1890–1935* (New York: Free Press, 1994); Skocpol, *Protecting Soldiers and Mothers*, chap. 8; Mink, *The Wages of Motherhood*, esp. chap. 2; and Joanne Goodwin, "An American Experiment in Paid Motherhood: The Implementation of Mothers' Pensions in Early Twentieth-Century Chicago," *Gender & History* 4 (Autumn 1992): 323–42.

20. See Barbara J. Nelson, "The Origins of the Two-Channel Welfare State: Workmen's Compensation and Mothers' Aid," in *Women, the State, and Welfare*, edited by Linda Gordon (Madison: University of Wisconsin Press, 1990), 123–51, and, for a slightly different interpretation, Ann Shola Orloff, "Gender in Early U.S. Social Policy," *Journal of Policy History* 3 (1991): 249–81.

21. T. H. Marshall, *Citizenship and Social Class and Other Essays*, edited by Seymour Martin Lipset (Garden City, N.Y.: Doubleday, 1964), pp. 71–72. See also Nancy Frasier and Linda Gordon, "Contract Versus Charity: Why Is There No

Social Citizenship in the United States," *Socialist Review* 22 (July–September 1992): 45–67. On the role of race in welfare politics, see Jill Quadagno, *The Color of Welfare: How Racism Undermined the War on Poverty* (New York: Oxford University Press, 1995), and Gwendolyn Mink, "The Lady and the Tramp: Gender, Race, and the Origins of the Welfare State," in *Women, the State, and Welfare*, ed. Gordon, pp. 92–122. Mink makes clear that race intruded into social policy prior to the 1960s.

22. Eileen Boris, "The Racialized Gendered State: Constructions of Citizenship in the United States," *Social Politics: International Studies in Gender, State, and Society* 2 (Summer 1995): 160–80. The racialization of citizenship is also considered in Mink, "The Lady and the Tramp," in *Women, the State, and Welfare*, pp. 92–122.

23. Carroll Smith-Rosenberg, "Dis-Covering the Subject of the 'Great Constitutional Discussion,' 1786–1789," *The Journal of American History* 79 (December 1992): 841–73.

24. For a lengthy discussion of coverture relative to citizenship and the Blake quotation, see Linda K. Kerber, "The Paradox of Women's Citizenship in the Early Republic: The Case of *Martin vs. Massachusetts*, 1805," *The American Historical Review* 97 (1992): 349–78.

25. For the quotation, see "Introduction," *U.S. History as Women's History*, eds. Kerber, Kessler-Harris, and Sklar, p. 28. Information on citizenship in this and the following paragraphs is based on Linda K. Kerber, "A Constitutional Right to Be Treated Like American Ladies: Women and the Obligations of Citizenship," in *U.S. History as Women's History*, pp. 17–35. A much more extensive treatment is available in Kerber's *The Obligations of Citizenship: Women, Men and the Law in the United States* (forthcoming). On married women and nationality, see Candice Dawn Bredbenner, "Toward Independent Citizenship: Married Women's Nationality Rights in the United States, 1855–1937" (Ph.D. diss., University of Virginia, 1990), and *MacKenzie v Hare*, 239 U.S. 299 (1915).

26. Quoted in Kerber, "A Constitutional Right to be Treated Like American Ladies," p. 31. The Supreme Court upheld the ruling of the Florida Supreme Court, acknowledging women's "special responsibilities" to the family. See *Hoyt v Florida*, 368 U.S. 57 (1961). *Hoyt* was ultimately reversed by the Supreme Court in *Taylor v Louisiana*, 419 U.S. 522 (1975).

27. Thurgood Marshall, in *Rostker v Goldberg*, 101 Sup. Ct. 2646 (1981). See also Kerber, "A Constitutional Right to be Treated Like American Ladies," in *U.S. History as Women's History*, p. 34.

28. Benedict Anderson, *Imagined Communities: Reflections on the Origin and Spread of Nationalism*, (London: Verso, 1983), pp. 49, 66. *Imagined Communities* has become one of the most cited works in the field. Other important studies include Ernest Gellner, *Nations and Nationalism* (Oxford: Basil Blackwell, 1983), and E. J. Hobsbawm, *Nations and Nationalism since 1780: Programme, Myth, Reality* (Cambridge: Cambridge University Press, 1990). While much of the work of social scientists on this topic relies on modernization theory, the subaltern studies move-

ment has brought the perspective of cultural studies to bear on problems of post-coloniality, nationalism, and national identity. These issues have not attracted the attention of historians of the United States in recent years; however, Lawrence Levine and Robert Wiebe are at work on new studies.

29. Etienne Balibar, "The Nation Form: History and Ideology," translated by Immanuel Wallerstein and Chris Turner, *Review, Fernand Braudel Center* 13 (Summer 1990): 392–461; also Etienne Balibar and Immanuel Wallerstein, *Race, Nation, Class: Ambiguous Identities* (London: Verso, 1991). Balibar's use of the adjective "fictive" is not meant to imply that ethnicity is not grounded in lived experience or that it does not have real consequences. Rather, the emphasis is on the social construction over time of what seems to be a "natural" and timeless category. For an important statement on ethnicity as social construction by leading U.S. scholars, see Kathleen Neils Conzen, David A. Gerber, Ewa Morawska, George E. Pozetta, and Rudolph J. Vecoli, "The Invention of Ethnicity: A Perspective from the U.S.A.," *Journal of American Ethnic History* 12 (Fall 1992): 4–32.

For the process by which various European immigrant groups underwent a kind of trans-ethnic, racial homogenization that enabled them to claim whiteness, see David Roediger, "Whiteness and Ethnicity in the History of 'White Ethnics' in the United States," in Roediger, *Towards the Abolition of Whiteness: Essay on Race, Politics, and Working Class History* (London: Verso, 1994), and *The Wages of Whiteness: Race and the Making of the American Working Class* (New York: Verso, 1991); also Noel Ignatiev, *How the Irish Became White* (New York: Routledge, 1995), and Arnold R. Hirsch, *Making the Second Ghetto: Race and Housing in Chicago, 1940–1960* (New York: Cambridge University Press, 1983). A superb analysis of the process by which Euro-Americans in the eighteenth century established a sense of national identity that imagined white Americans as the only true Americans is provided by Carroll Smith-Rosenberg, "Captured Subjects / Savage Others: Violently Engendering the New American," *Gender & History* 5 (Summer 1993): 177–95.

30. George L. Mosse, *Nationalism and Sexuality: Respectability and Abnormal Sexuality in Modern Europe* (New York: Howard Fertig, 1985). See also *Nationalisms and Sexualities*, edited by Andrew Parker, Mary Russo, Doris Sommer, and Particia Yaeger (New York: Routledge, 1992).

31. For new historical scholarship that explores gender and nationalism in an international context, see the special issue of *Gender & History* 5 (Summer 1993). On the intersection of gender and race in the production of the new American national, see Smith-Rosenberg, "Dis-Covering the Subject of the 'Great Constitutional Discussion,' 1786–1789." Apart from Smith-Rosenberg, U.S. historians have been far less active with respect to this topic than have literary scholars. An example of scholarship by the latter is *Subjects and Citizens: Nation, Race, and Gender from Oroonoko to Anita Hill*, edited by Michael Moon and Cathy N. Davison (Durham: Duke University Press, 1995).

On women as symbols of the nation, see Mosse, *Nationalism and Sexuality*, chap. 5.

32. Susan Jeffords, *The Remasculinization of America: Gender and the Vietnam War* (Bloomington, Ind.: Indiana University Press, 1989), esp. chaps. 2–3, 6.

33. Elaine Tyler May, *Homeward Bound: American Families in the Cold War Era* (New York: Basic Books, 1988). Scholars in gay and lesbian studies have further documented the stringent efforts to contain homosexuality in the new national security state. See John D' Emilio, "The Homosexual Menace: The Politics of Sexuality in Cold War America" in *Passion and Power: Sexuality in History*, edited by Kathy Peiss and Christina Simmons (Philadelphia: Temple University Press, 1989), pp. 226–40, and Allan Berube and John D' Emilio, "The Military and Lesbians During the McCarthy Years," *Signs: Journal of Women in Culture and Society* 9 (1984): 759–75. These episodes are contextualized within the larger history of homosexuality in the U.S. in Lillian Faderman, *Odd Girls and Twilight Lovers: A History of Lesbian Life in Twentieth-Century America* (New York: Columbia University Press, 1993), and John D'Emilio, *Sexual Politics, Sexual Communities: The Making of a Homosexual Minority in the United States, 1940–1970* (Chicago: University of Chicago Press, 1983).

34. On the efforts of women's and gay rights groups to use Cold War rhetoric and appeals to the American creed for inclusive purposes, see Joanne Meyerwitz, "Gender, Sex, and Cold War Language of Reform" (paper presented at the 1994 Landmarks Conference on the Cold War and American Culture, Washington, D.C.). With respect to civil rights for African Americans, see Mary L. Dudziak, "Desegregation as a Cold War Imperative," *Stanford Law Review* 14 (May 1992): 246–67.

On the body as metaphor, see Michel Foucault, *The History of Sexuality*, vol. 1 (New York: Vintage, 1990). On the body and boundaries, see Mary Douglas, *Purity and Danger: An Analysis of Concepts of Pollution and Taboo* (London: Routledge and Kegan Paul, 1966), p. 67. On communism as a disease, see Geoffrey S. Smith, "National Security and Personal Isolation: Sex, Gender and Disease in the Cold-War United States," *International History Review* 14 (May 1991): 307–37.

35. See, for example, James Davidson Hunter, *Culture Wars: The Struggle to Define America* (New York: Basic Books, 1991), p. 50.

36. Jane Sherron De Hart, *Defining America: Gender, Sexuality, and the Politics of National Identity*, forthcoming. I am indebted to Alice Kessler-Harris for this characterization of social constructions which is contained in her contribution to *New Viewpoints in Women's History: Working Papers from the Schlesinger Library 50th Anniversary Conference*, edited by Susan Ware (Cambridge: The Schlesinger Library, 1994).

37. For characterizations of women's history as imperialistic and particularistic respectively, see Robert Darnton, "Cherchez la Femme," *New York Review of Books* 62 (August 10, 1995): 22–24, and Peter D. Novick, *That Noble Dream: The "Objectivity Question" and the American Historical Profession* (New York: Cambridge University Press, 1988), pp. 496–510 passim.

3

The Politics of Reconstruction

Michael Les Benedict

Vincent De Santis published his first book, *Republicans Face the Southern Question*, in 1959.[1] It was his doctoral dissertation, begun and completed under the direction of C. Vann Woodward, then on the faculty of Johns Hopkins University. *Republicans Face the Southern Question* was quintessential political history. But it did something that all too few political histories do. Because De Santis was describing how Republicans sought to expand their political appeal in the South, he of necessity had to link the development of public policy to the political structures of the later nineteenth century—that is, to party organization, patronage, and other party institutions. And then he had to link both to voter behavior. *Republicans Face the Southern Question* is one of the few studies we have that attempts to show how politicians' desire to achieve political success, the structure of political institutions themselves, and public opinion combine to determine public policy.

Few historians have discussed the way politics *worked* during the Reconstruction era that preceded the period Vincent wrote about, and then related the system to changes in Reconstruction policy. Joel Silbey has linked grass-roots politics and Democratic policy towards Reconstruction in his study of Democrats from 1860 to 1868, *A Respectable Minority*.[2] But no one has done the same for the Republicans. In fact, few historians have written much at all on the politics of the period I intend to discuss—the years that followed the establishment of Republican Reconstruction policy. Until recently, most general studies of Reconstruction slighted national policy in the 1870s, shifting attention to developments in the southern states. William Gillette's *Retreat from Reconstruction*, published in 1979, was the first book-length study of post-1868 national Reconstruction politics since volumes 6 and 7 of James Ford Rhodes's *History of the United States from the Compromise of 1850*, which appeared in 1906.[3]

It remains so. However, Eric Foner's magisterial *Reconstruction: America's Unfinished Revolution* broke the usual pattern among general histories by attending as much to later as to earlier national Reconstruction policy.[4]

The paucity of histories linking public policy to the political system and grassroots voting behavior reflects a general problem in political history—political historians have had a difficult time making the connection. Professor Foner has told the story of how Reconstruction policy changed in the 1870s at a very high level of abstraction—tensions between employers and labor in the North led powerful northern interests to sympathize with southern conservatives instead of black southern workers and their Republican allies. He has described the macropolitics of Reconstruction, but he has not described the actual politics—the way public opinion was translated into public policy.

Eschewing discussion of the political system, Foner neither cites nor incorporates what was once called the "new political history," whose practitioners utilized statistical methods to analyze mass voting behavior during the Civil War era. Their conclusions don't fit very well into his story. Where Foner sees the clash of a free-labor and slave-labor society, a battle about moral issues that divided rival economic systems, they perceived a clash of ethnic and religious cultures. Republicanism permitted voters of New England heritage and evangelical Protestants to vent their hostility towards southerners, immigrants, Catholics, and "liturgical" Protestants.[5] Although most of the ethnocultural political studies have concentrated on the origins of the Republican party, at least one—Paul Kleppner's *The Third Electoral System*—assesses the whole Civil War and Reconstruction era, continuing on to 1892.[6] Archetypical of ethnocultural studies, Kleppner's work sharply challenged the notion that the issues debated by the political elites motivated the voting of the masses. "That assumption ignores the enormous differences in kind between mass and elite cognitions," he wrote.[7] So while elite intellectuals, newspaper editors, and politicians debated about the nature of the Union, slavery, and the place of the freedmen in American society, Kleppner inferred that ordinary voters voted their cultural antipathies, with local elections, which raised such issues, more important than national ones. The Republican party originated in nativism and anti-Catholicism, expressed anti-southernism during the Civil War era, and turned back to nativism and anti-Catholicism in the 1870s.

This darker view of the motivations of rank-and-file Republican voters coincides with doubts other historians have expressed about the degree of Republican commitment to racial justice. Scholars studying antebellum race relations and the origins of the Republican party have argued that Republicans shared the racism endemic in American society.[8] This conclusion led De Santis's mentor to describe racism as the deepest rooted of the "Seeds of Failure in Radical Race Policy" during Reconstruction.[9] It informs Gillette's work as well. Having attributed the passage of the Fifteenth Amendment to Republicans' need for black votes rather than commitment to racial justice in an earlier work, he concluded in his study of Reconstruction in the 1870s that a racist reaction in the North led Republicans to abandon Reconstruction.[10]

The purpose of this paper is to link the shifts in Reconstruction policy more closely to the political system of both North and South than these excellent works have done. Mid-nineteenth-century public policy was driven more directly by public opinion and election concerns than we may realize from our late-twentieth-century perspective. Despite reformers' complaints, there were few well-organized interest groups; lobbying was primitive.[11] A campaign like Tom Scott's effort to get government funding for the Texas and Pacific Railroad—a forerunner of modern lobbying—was a thing of wonder, and like most nineteenth-century lobbying it was an effort to get a benefit—a charter, a land grant, and subsidy—from an essentially distributive system of public policy. It was not an effort to determine the direction of general public policy; in fact, Scott failed to secure his subsidy at least in part because public opinion had come to oppose such subsidies as a whole.[12]

Money was growing more important in politics, but levies on office-holders and cash syphoned from public projects accounted for more of it than the donations of organized interest groups—which hardly existed.[13] There were influential individual donors who had important economic interests, but when one looks at the correspondence of congressmen, one finds such men trying to cajole or persuade their legislators much like any other correspondent. And the common currency of such lobbying was the claim that the correspondent reflected a public opinion which would affect the political fortunes of the party and the individual politician. As Joel Silbey put it in his study of the nineteenth-century political system, "Independent party leaders were rarely the puppets of the new economic elites. They had other masters."[14]

When it came to Reconstruction, the most important factor affecting immediate policy decisions was their perceived impact on public opinion and politics. Elections seemed never-ending in mid-nineteenth-century America. Congressional elections were held at various times of the year, rarely at the same time as the presidential election in November. States reelected governors every year, or every second or third year. The elections rarely coincided with presidential or local elections, although often with congressional elections. Observers regarded these rolling elections as an ongoing public opinion poll. Historians may think that local issues were more important than national ones in these canvasses. But in an era of intense partisanship, contemporary politicians and other analysts regularly found in them portents of great meaning for national politics. The state and local elections of 1867, in which Republican setbacks were accounted a repudiation of radicalism on Reconstruction issues, were a classic example.[15]

Like all polls, those implicit in local and state elections could be self-fulfilling. Thus politicians watched the results of the elections of the fall of 1875 in Ohio, Pennsylvania, and other northern states with intense interest. Another loss after the shellacking of 1874 was held to doom Republican chances for the presidency in 1876. On the other hand, Republican victories would mean that the Democrats had frittered their great chance away.[16]

It was in this environment that President Grant in 1875 refused to accede to Governor Adelbert Ames's plea to intervene to stop violence in Mississippi's elections. Grant's decision on that occasion probably did more than any other single decision to seal the fate of Republican Reconstruction. Grant made it in direct response to warnings from Republican leaders that intervention would cost the party crucial elections in the North in 1875 and consequently the presidency in 1876.[17] The Republicans did win in 1875, and the predicted consequence—a victory in 1876—followed.

It is usual to think that such a decision reflected a broad change in public opinion in the North—that out of some combination of racism, economic and class interest, and the revival of ethnocultural issues, northerners in the 1870s turned their backs on the commitments that had sustained Reconstruction. A closer look makes the political process by which that happened—if it happened at all—more understandable.

But before we take that look, one must pay particular attention to the politics of Reconstruction in the South. After all, had southern

Republicans succeeded in creating a viable party there, there would have been no need for national intervention, no occasion for northern Republicans to retreat from their commitments. Indeed, throughout the Reconstruction era, the chief goal of Republicans North and South was to create a competitive Republican party in the South. At all times, national Republicans relied on southen Republicans for information and advice about how to do it. Southern Republicans presented alternative strategies for achieving that goal. These alternative strategies provided the context for the determination of national policy throughout Reconstruction.

From the vantage of one hundred years, the failure of Republicans to create a multiracial party in the South and the subsequent collapse of the party there seem to have been fore-ordained. As Eric Foner has pointed out, no emancipation effort had ever attempted to empower newly freed people to the degree that Republicans had empowered them in the South.[18] The social and economic implications of racial equality in basic rights were so radical and the Republicans' black constituency so poverty-stricken and inexperienced, that in retrospect success seems to have been impossible. North Carolina carpetbagger Albion Tourgée conceded years later that he had been on *A Fool's Errand*.[19] The final end to federal intervention to protect southern Republicans seems to have been, as one historian of Reconstruction titled his last chapter, "The Only Possible Ending."[20]

But that had not been the perception when Tourgée and others enlisted in the southern Republican party. Black politicians may have had no choice, some white Republicans may have been idealists and others short-term opportunists, but none of them expected to be political martyrs. Such savvy and experienced southern politicians as Joseph E. Brown and William Woods Holden knew what they were doing. Both had been powers in Democratic politics since the 1850s (Holden, in fact, since the 1840s). Many other newly-enlisted Republicans were experienced, if not so eminent, Whig and Democratic politicans.[21] The fact was that these men had weighed the chance of success and found it attainable. Indeed, at the time Grant ascended to the presidency, southern Republicans were confident that their party would attract widespread support from *white* southerners, assuring its legitimacy, its competitiveness, and even, they believed, its dominance.

Although they expected massive support from the freedmen, these Republicans knew that they needed white support as well to create viable parties in the southern states. Brown saw this clearly. "[T]he negro vote will not do to rely on . . . ," he wrote Georgia's Republican Governor Rufus Bullock. "[I]t is impossible to maintain the [Republican party] . . . in the South, without a division of the white vote."[22] In the early years of Reconstruction they were sure that they would be able to attract such white support, and this confidence led many of them to eschew the proscriptive, disfranchising policies radical unionists had advocated ever since the war broke out.

The confidence of southern Republicans was based on assumptions that most Americans held about the relationship between politics and social and economic institutions, as well as their own understanding of the southern political heritage. They shared the Republican ideology of free labor, according to which the equal opportunity of all men to bargain freely for goods and services, in an environment where education and enterprise were encouraged, promised general liberty and prosperity.[23] To Republicans, North and South, their party was as surely a manifestation of a modern, progressive society as were enlightened Protestant churches, schools, temperance, and industry. "Wherever railroads, telegraphs, and common schools are plenty, democrats are very soon to be in a minority," a California Republican wrote a colleague in a typical statement of his party's faith. "[W]hen you get away from these civilizing and enlightening influences democratic majorities are often enough to swamp the whole."[24]

Republicans were convinced that the slavery system was responsible for the general economic and social stagnation that they thought characterized the South. Frederick Law Olmsted, the most influential prewar critic of the economics of slavery, had put it simply: "[T]he average progress in happiness and wealth, which has been made by the people of each State, is in almost exact ratio to the degree in which the democratic principle has been radically carried out in their constitution, laws, and customs."[25] "Freedom has given to the North unexampled prosperity and constantly increasing wealth and power," Republicans believed. "[F]reedom and free institutions will secure for the South the same results."[26]

Since economic and social progress and Republicanism were inextricably linked, emancipation inevitably would lead southerners to revise their policial perceptions. Already many white southerners conceded that the abolition of slavery was a blessing. Republicans were confident that "[t]he day is not far distant when the [same] men . . . will be equally free to confess that Reconstruction, with its common schools, Republican newspapers, Northern capital, and universal suffrage, was even more salutary and effective in the great work of southern redemption."[27] In the wake of Ulysses S. Grant's inauguration, many Republicans thought they saw clear signs of the expected change. As early as 1869 both the *New York Tribune* and *New York Times* were referring to "the New South."[28] The political consequence was clear. Southern Republicans were confident that "[t]he progressive element is destined, sooner or later, to shape the policy of every Southern State."[29]

Republicans thought they had a fertile field from which to harvest white recruits. They believed that there had been an undercurrent of hostility to slavery among nonslaveholding whites before the war and that their party inevitably would be its beneficiary. They were well aware of the intrastate sectionalism that in nearly every southern state had pit slaveholding regions against regions where nonslave agriculture predominated. They knew that slave agriculture had priced fertile land beyond the reach of ordinary farmers, that underrepresented yeomen farmers had protested tax policies, that entrepeneurs wanted state support to develop railroads, that reformers had urged expenditures on education, and that slaveholder-dominated legislatures had resisted.[30] They were convinced that the majority of white southerners would have opposed secession in 1860–1861, had not slaveholders so completely controlled the media and pulpit, and had they not utilized violence to suppress opposition.[31] Moreover, southern Republican leaders were acutely aware of the unionist resistance to the Confederacy during the war itself, since many of them had been active in it.[32]

Republicans believed that these antislavery materials were still at hand—what Wendell Phillips called "the labor, the toil, the muscle, the virtue, the strength, the democracy, of the Southern States . . .—the poor white, a non-slaveholder, deluded into rebellion for a system which crushes him. . . ."[33] To build their party with these materials, southern Republicans regularly tried to fan resentment against the old slaveholding elite while stressing the issues they believed had divided slaveholder from nonslaveholder. Some of the rhetoric was aimed directly at poorer whites and suggested class-based appeals. However, most Republicans stressed the benefits to all sure to follow good-faith adoption of the free-labor system. "Roast Beef and good times ahead, boys. That's the talk," the aptly named Atlanta *New Era* advised Republican campaigners. That was the way to overcome antipathy to the party's northern origins. "I tell you Yankees and Yankee notions are just what we want in this country . . . ," a North Carolina Republican declaimed. "We want some of those same Yankee tricks played down here that have covered the North with rail roads and canals."[34]

As they organized from 1867 to 1869, southern Republicans worked to enact the policies that would secure their political future. They promised to reform "the iniquitous and unequal taxation and assessments which, discriminating against labor and laborers, have born so unjustly and unequally upon the people."[35] In Louisiana and South Carolina, they explicitly promised to frame policies that would break up large estates and make small landholdings available to ordinary citizens.[36] And in South Carolina, at least, they tried to carry through, attempting to force redistribution through high taxation of uncultivated farm land. The tax laws established by the state constitutional convention called under the Reconstruction Acts "are the death blow to the large plantation system," a leading black delegate exulted.[37]

Republicans wrote ad valorem and equal taxation provisions into nearly every southern state constitution they framed in 1867 and 1868. Some Republican state constitutions allowed for slightly progressive taxation, establishing exemptions for certain amounts of property or income. Some banned poll taxes as well.[38] In most, Republicans liberalized homestead exemptions.[39] Republican state legislatures gave workers prior liens upon employers' property to guarantee fulfillment of employment contracts. They gave merchants priority over employers in liens on the property of employees, enabling workers to secure credit from merchants rather than having to borrow from their employers.[40] All these provisions were designed to demonstrate a common interest between white and black workers. "The real issue is not over a 'white man's party,' but the *poor-man's party*, and of equal rights to all," the Vicksburg (Miss.) *Republican* urged.[41]

Throughout the South, Republicans placed special emphasis on promoting free public education. Education was the handmaiden of progress. It promoted intelligence, moderation, discipline, thrift, energy, and morality, all of which bred Republicanism, unlike the Democratic party, which drew its support from "the ignorance and vice of mankind," from "the old slave-owner and slave-driver, the saloon-keeper, . . . the criminal class of the great cities, [and] the men who cannot read and write."[42] Education would solve the central problem for Republicans—to break the influence of the old elite "over the poor, illiterate class, who never had a political opinion of their own, but have always voted as their *masters* dictated," as one Mississippi activist put it.

Moreover, the establishment of free public schools would provide tangible evidence of Republican concern for ordinary white men and women. State-supported education was an area of public policy where their interests coincided with those of the freedmen and ran contrary to those of the old planter elite. Once public schools for their children were established, surely white southerners would rally against a party that threatened to dismantle them. Republicans were sure that "[a] schoolhouse . . . is an argument for the new order of things . . . that cannot be resisted."[43]

Republicans placed even greater reliance on their ability to use government to promote prosperity and spread it to a larger proportion of the population than ever before. Economic development was crucial to the success of their party. Southern Republicans were well aware that nascent hostility to slavery among small farmers and laborers had included a large component of hostility to the black slaves themselves. Confident that emancipation would lead to increased prosperity for all southerners, Republicans would demonstrate that emancipation was not what economists now would call a zero-sum game, in which the economic gains of freedmen had to come at the expense of whites. The exhortation of the Republican provisional governor of Texas was typical: "To have a successful Republican party in Texas," he wrote a party worker, "it . . . must . . . advance the material interests of the whole people."[44]

An ambitious effort to extend railroad facilities was central to the Republican program in nearly every state. Railroads would bring every part of a state into the national and international economy. They would permit farmers to exchange subsistence farming for cash crops; they would increase land values; they would end intellectual and cultural isolation; they would bring in capital investment and immigration. Moreover, railroad legislation would appeal to those elements of the southern electorate—many Whigs and some dissident Democrats—that had worked futilely for similar legislation before the war. It was impossible to overstate the importance to the Republicans of a successful transportation policy. "[T]he *success* & the *prudence* with which our policy of internal improvement is carried out will realize or defeat our hopes," a North Carolina state legislator exhorted Holden.[45]

Southern Republicans argued that only an activist national government could augment state internal improvement programs. They were quick to point out that theirs was the party of broad construction of the Constitution, the party that had already expended millions of federal dollars to develop transportation throughout the North and West. "When a large appropriation is asked for the North, let us ask a million of dollars to improve the harbor of Savannah, and another for Charleston," Brown urged on the Georgia campaign trail. "When a Pacific railroad is to be built for the West, let us ask a few millions to rebuild the levees on the Mississippi river."[46]

Even more important to the southern economy than federal aid for internal improvements was the distribution of the currency. The South was desperately cash- and capital-short because the distribution of the currency was closely linked to the distribution of national banks established during the War, which had the sole right to issue United States bank notes. The South, out of the Union and then destitute, had been able to secure hardly any national banks. There were none at all in Mississippi, two each in Alabama, Arkansas, and Louisiana. Of nearly $318,000,000 in national bank notes circulating in 1869, only $7,160,000 had been issued by southern banks—less than the amount issued in Maine alone.[47] Since a national capital market had not yet developed, money did not flow easily from North to South to fill the void. To secure capital, southerners had to pay a premium in high interest rates.

Desperately, southerners sought direct northern investment. "There has never been a time when so much general good could be done with so little capital at so small a risk," they pleaded.[48] The same conviction impelled the influx of the "carpetbaggers" who southerners would later condemn so bitterly. Carpetbaggers originally came not to fatten off of politics but in hopes of making a killing with the investment of modest amounts of capital. But these minimal amounts were not enough to revitalize the southern economy. Only action in Washington could secure national banks and national bank notes for the South, Republicans pointed out. Conservative / Democratic[49] representatives could not hope for sympathetic consideration from the Republican government in Washington. "We want . . . government aid and sympathy in a hundred things—not one of which a Democrat could control if he were elected and sent to Congress," southern Republicans insisted.[50]

Convinced that securing white support was critical to the survival of their party, many southern Republicans believed it essential to make overtures to white southerners, to signal that they were welcome in the party and that they need not worry about proscriptive public policies. Thus they advocated the repeal of laws disfranchising Confederates that borderstate Republicans had passed during the war. They success-fully blocked such provisions in most of the new constitutions ratified under the Reconstruction Acts and were appalled at their inability to do so in Texas, Virginia, and Mississippi. They urged Congress to remove the officeholding disqualification the Fourteenth Amendment imposed on many who had held office under the Confederacy. Such proscrip-tions could only alienate the very population Republicans so desper-ately needed to recruit. Those who advocated it were proposing government by a small white population of die-hard unionists and a large former-slave population over what would be a large and certainly alienated and restive population of whites—in many cases a majority of the population as a whole. No economic policies could overcome the hostility thus engendered. No success could legitimize the resulting governments.

Not only was proscription inconsistent with a Republican appeal for southern white support, many southern Republicans warned, but too much attention to the interests of black southerners was also counter-productive. Conservative southern Republicans recognized the ineluctable fact of southern white racism. Appeals to white resentment of the planter elite and to hopes for economic development would work only if the race issue were muted, they worried. As the Republicans' issue was the promise of prosperity; the Democrats' issue was race.

Therefore, from the beginning both southern and northern Republicans urged restraint on the southern party's black rank and file.[51] "The black man . . . must win over to his side, if not through sym-pathy or humanity, then through interest, enough of the whites to give him . . . the opportunity of influencing the government," the *Nation* cau-tioned. "The way to do this is to refrain as far as possible from stimulat-ing white prejudices and arousing white passions, to avoid every step or measure that is likely to unite the whites *as whites* against the blacks."[52] The Louisiana Republican leader, Henry Clay Warmoth, told a black audience that he hoped significant numbers of freedmen would vote Democratic. "Race conflicts are sure to ensue if party lines are based on race," he warned. "[M]ore negroes becoming Democrats will bring whites into the Republican party and in that is the safety of the Republic and the prosperity of the people." Years later Warmoth recalled how he had campaigned for white votes.[53]

Such advice was easy for white Republicans to give, but hard for black Republicans to take. While the freedmen and their leaders were as anxious for economic prosperity as the next man, and equally hostile to the planter "aristocracy," they had essential interests as black people and as laborers. If aspiring Republican politicians took radical positions to appeal to those interests, was it realistic to think that the freedmen would withhold their support in order to expand the appeal of the Republican party? In essence, many white Republicans were counting on the freedmen to sacrifice short-term to long-term interests. It would have required a discipline that few groups of white American voters have ever displayed.

There is little evidence that black workers expected to secure land through confiscation. What was crucial for them was to have local courts and law-enforcement officials that would enforce contracts fairly and protect the right of workers to move freely from job to job.[54] With those rights protected, the freedpeople could hope for significant economic gains. As planters universally complained, the freedwomen and children quickly withdrew from the full-time agricultural work force. Many freedmen moved to towns to seek work unassociated with slavery. In a free-labor system, the remaining agricultural workers could not be forced to work the long hours extorted from them under slavery. The result was a severe labor shortage which promised higher wages or, as southerners moved towards sharecropping, greater independence and a larger share of the profits for the croppers. In a society with a shortage of labor, it was not labor organization that was crucial to workers, it was freedom from laws restricting mobility and freedom of contract, as well as enforcement of the common-law rules that secured these freedoms. The result would be a radical redistribution of the product of labor away from the planter and to the laborer.[55] Clearly, such an evenhanded legal regime would alienate both large and small planters, who relied on black labor. Republicans would have to choose. No Republican who endorsed legislators who might be soft on this issue, or who advocated the appointment of "intelligent" judges who might favor planters in employment disputes, could expect black support.

Much of the leadership of the black community came from those who had been free before the war or who immigrated from the North. The interests of these people, a professional class influential far out of proportion to their numbers, went beyond those of the mass of black workers. They wanted equal access to transportation and entertainment facilities, to higher education, and to the professions.[56] For some black men politics was the only way they could earn enough money to sustain a middle-class living, or to raise capital for other investments.[57] When Republicans asked such men to surrender their interests and ambitions for the sake of their party and their race, they were asking for sacrifices few people would have been willing to make. Nonetheless, the desire to attract white southern support was so strong that the argument could be made, and men who advocated such conservatism could hope to win support from party activists.

Disfranchisement, the role of African Americans in the party, and civil-rights legislation immediately became the focal points for factional conflict within the southern Republican party—an illustration of how a key part of the political system, intraparty factionalism, affected public policy. The winner-take-all American political system channels aspiring public servants into two parties—in some states and localities into one party—where they must compete for nominations and appointive positions. As I have discussed elsewhere, in the nineteenth century it was usual for politicians to form intraparty alliances of varying durations.[58] In the South, rival factions of ambitious Republican politicians identified with one position or the other, trying to win support from party activists and the rank and file. The rivalries were the more bitter for the fact that Republican leaders often were ostracized by white southerners and unable to earn livings equal to their education and social positions outside the public arena.[59] More radical Republicans, in many cases northern immigrants to the South, agreed that economic development was crucial to winning white support, but they argued that conciliation would not work. Instead, both the state and federal governments had to demonstrate that there was no alternative for southern whites but to accept the new situation. Southern whites would become reconciled, and even enthusiastic, as freedom brought economic prosperity. Until then southern Republicans had to rely on black voters.

Naturally, black southerners responded to the courtship of politicians who were prepared to recognize their interests. We "were up to be knocked down to the highest bidder," a local black leader made clear. The freedmen might not yet have enough educated leaders to govern, a Republican reported, but they knew enough to choose representatives "from among our white friends who were to be depended upon . . . to look after their interests." White Republicans had better get the message. As a black politician in Memphis told them, "We want candidates to stand by principles and their friends. . . . If you leave the principles of the Republican party, we shall leave you."[60]

Futilely, conservative southern Republicans urged caution. The potential of securing white votes in the South was clear. White unanimity had broken down after the passage of the Reconstruction Act in 1867. Important white leaders openly urged their people to accept the situation or privately began to negotiate with conservative Republicans. The adhesion of such politicians as Brown and Holden, who had made their careers through anti-aristocratic politics, suggested the potential of the Republicans' own anti-aristocratic appeal. Large numbers of whites, concentrated in the old nonslaveholding regions, had voted to hold constitutional conventions under the Reconstruction Acts—about 30 percent of the registered white voters in North Carolina, Alabama, and Georgia, and about 10 percent in Virginia, Florida, and Texas.[61] If they wanted to turn these floating voters into Republicans, conservatives argued, the party must avoid alienating them with disfranchisement, racially progressive legislation, or African-American nominations to office. Frustrated southern conservatives complained to northern Republicans that a tiny minority of no more than three thousand white radicals was alienating tens of thousands of white, potentially Republican voters. Efforts to secure this white support were being defeated by "a small set of men who fancied that by appealing to the ignorance & prejudice of the freedmen they could monopolize the offices of the state."[62] Of course, the reality was quite different. African Americans had interests and they backed politicians who served them. As a South Carolina Conservative perceived, "The negroes have been accused of being easily led by demagogues; but they really rule the demagogues, not the demagogues them. Let the politicians do anything which is distasteful, and opponents spring up in every quarter."[63]

Conservative and radical Republicans cooperated uneasily. In most, but not all southern states, Republicans at first nominated more moderate leaders for the top state offices, while more radical Republicans were elected to the Senate and the House of Representatives. Since congressional delegations, and especially senators, had the strongest influence over federal appointments, federal officeholders often formed the backbone of more radical southern Republican factions, while state appointees backed more moderate policies. The complaint of a North Carolina native Republican was typical: "[O]ur Federal office holders, composed almost entirely of the carpet bag class, are utterly inefficient, politically worthless and intensely selfish. . . . Deserving men . . . and first rate politicians of our own people are thrust aside to keep these men in power."[64] Moderates were continually weakened in the party by the desertion of allies, who bolted party nominations to nominate rival tickets backed by the Democrat / Conservatives. Where such bolting tickets were successful, as in Virginia and Tennessee in 1869 and West Virginia and Missouri in 1870, they led not to stronger, conservative Republican parties but to Democratic / Conservative supremacy.

Northern Republicans and the administration of Ulysses S. Grant, inaugurated in 1869, wavered over whom to support. They continued to vacillate even in the face of growing violence in the South, manifest in the rise of the Ku Klux Klan. By spring of 1870 this violence was already growing serious, and it exacerbated southern Republican divisions. Those who were committed to conciliating white southerners tended to deny that it was as pervasive as more radical Republicans alleged, and they especially denied that it had the support of the conservative, business-minded southerners whose support they were courting. To concede otherwise would have serious political ramifications; it would mean a diminution of their own influence and the rise of that of their hard-line rivals. Although there were exceptions, as a whole Republican governors of the southern states, responsible for maintaining the peace, tended towards conciliation, while Republican senators, responding to appeals from frightened local activists and black Republicans, criticized their caution. Of crucial importance to southern Republican factional politics, the violence and the failure of conciliationist Republicans to deal with it led black Republicans, who made up the overwhelming majority of the party's rank and file in the Deep South, to swing decisively towards the southern hard-liners. By 1871 the more radical factions—often led by northern immigrants to the South—were ascendant there, with their leaders taking over the top state offices. As Mississippi Senator Adelbert Ames explained to a colleague, "The Carpetbagger . . . has a hold on the hearts of the colored people that nothing can destroy. He is the positive element of the party and if the South is to be redeemed from the ways of Slavery it must be done by him."[65] African-American leaders secured larger numbers of official positions, and they demanded that Republicans support new state and federal civil-rights acts to secure equal access to public educational institutions, hotels and transportation facilities, theaters, and places of amusement.[66]

More conservative southern Republicans fumed at the support black Republicans gave the hard-liners. "The trouble is, that they will vote for any man who makes a noisy demonstration of devotion to their rights, without the slightest regard to his past public career, or his private character," a disillusioned southern unionist lamented. "Life-long devotion to the Union . . . went for nothing."[67] Black voters "were not disposed . . . to take counsel from *leading high-minded Union men*," another southern Republican echoed, "but only from irresponsible white adventurers who pandered to their wishes."[68]

The politics of Reconstruction in the South had led to hard-line Republican ascendancy in the region, and it was this ascendancy that made federal intervention in the South necessary. Eschewing conciliation, promoting the interests of their mostly black constituency, nominating African-American aspirants to important political offices, southern Republicans had slight hope for southern white support in the short term. When the depression of 1873 dashed prospects for the economic prosperity all Republicans had counted on to win southern whites over to the party of progress, the Republican position in the South was dire indeed.[69] White electoral support eroded. Table 1 indicates how completely the racial distribution of the electorate predicted opposition to Republicanism in most of the southern states. Only in Tennessee and Texas did the proportion of white voters fail to correlate highly with opposition to Republicanism.

Denying the legitimacy of the governments imposed by federal action, the overwhelming majority of whites perceived the Republican party as an engine of class legislation. As Republicans provided public services to African-American constituents, southern Conservatives

Table 1
Correlations between Republican Voting Patterns and the
Distribution of White Voters, 1868–1876

	1868	1869–1871	1872	1873–1875	1876
ALABAMA	–.74	–.71	–.69	–.81	–.57
ARKANSAS	–.46		–.79		–.86
FLORIDA			–.82		–.90
GEORGIA	–.55		–.44		–.39
LOUISIANA	–.56		–.76		–.67*
MISSISSIPPI		–.81	–.89	–.80	–.43
NORTH CAROLINA	–.61		–.83		–.75
SOUTH CAROLINA	–.73	–.79	–.81	–.60	–.91
TENNESSEE	.32	.02	–.17	–.25	–.04
TEXAS		.23	.26	.26 / .19**	.13
VIRGINIA		–.89	–.81	–.82	–.83

Note: Correlations for 1868, 1872, and 1876 based on presidential election returns; correlations for off-year elections based on gubernatorial returns. As yet unreconstructed, Mississippi, Texas, and Virginia cast no votes for president in 1868. Florida's electoral vote was determined by the state legislature in 1868, without a popular vote.

* The correlation between Democratic voting patterns and the distribution of white voters was .84.
** Gubernatorial elections in 1873 and 1875.

charged that corrupt politicians were enriching themselves with government offices, bribery, and theft, retaining power by supporting legislation that transferred resources from white taxpayers to venal African-American voters. Judges who attempted to provide impartial justice were denounced as showing favoritism to black workers.[70] Where whites made up a significant majority of the population, Democrats returned to power, often aided by dissident conservative Republicans and utilizing some degree of intimidation and violence. In states where African Americans were a majority or so close to it that Republicans needed few white votes to win, more and more Democrat / Conservatives turned to leaders who advocated violence. Only the willingness of the federal government to intervene—that is, the resolve of northern Republicans—inhibited them. As long as forceful federal action demonstrated that violence was counter-productive, more moderate Democrats could argue that appeals to conservative southern Republicans were more likely to succeed, especially if national Republican leaders could be persuaded to use their influence to bolster them rather than the dominant radicals.[71] When the Grant administration failed to counteract the Democrats' open use of intimidation in the state elections of 1874 in Alabama and 1875 in Mississippi, it cut the ground from under Democratic moderates, opening the way for the violent campaigns of 1876 in South Carolina and Louisiana. As we all know, the Republican regimes of the South collapsed before the onslaught.

How and why did northern Republican resolve dissipate? That question takes us back to the politics of Reconstruction in the North. When one looks at the voting behavior of the northern electorate, some key facts stand out. First, there almost certainly was an ethnocultural aspect to the voting alignments of the Civil War era. Tables 2A and 2B show the correlation between Democratic and Republican voting patterns from 1864 to 1868 and different ethnocultural variables in a number of northern states.[72] They indicate that anywhere from about 25 to 85 percent of the variance in Republican voting patterns can be explained by the distribution of ethnic and religious groups within the states.

Charts 1, 2 and 3 tell a similar story. They indicate the dramatic shift in election behavior that took place in counties of Ohio, Indiana, and Illinois with high concentrations of voters of New England/upstate New York, or "Yankee," heritage. The emergence of the Republican party clearly energized these voters. German-dominated counties, in contrast, remained Democratic. But one does not see the dramatic shift in voting that characterized the Yankee counties. In Ohio and Indiana the German counties remained safely Democratic but only slightly more so than during the 1840s and 1850s. In Illinois, where the Republicans aimed a powerful appeal at Germans, they were far more competitive in predominantly German counties than the Whigs had been. (Note, too, that Table 1 shows that while the pattern of German settlement correlated negatively with Republican voting in several northern states, it did not in Illinois or Indiana.)

These charts certainly say something about the Republican appeal to Yankee voters and the continued appeal of Democrats to German and Irish immigrants. But despite significant ethnic polarization, it is not so certain that the basis of the Republican appeal was hostility to immigrants and Catholics. Democratic voting by Germans in Illinois, Indiana, and Ohio persisted, but it did not increase. This suggests a continuation of a prior allegiance established during the second, Whig-Democratic party system or perhaps during the Know-Nothing agitation

Table 2A

Republican Voting Patterns and Ethnocultural Variables

	N.Y.	Pa.	Ohio	Ind.	Mich.	Ill.	Wis.	Iowa	Minn.
Austria	-.62	x	x	x	x	x	x	x	x
Baptist	.61	.32	.41				.43**		
Canada								-.38	
Congregationalist	.41	x	.38**	x		.33	.46(.60)**		
Dutch Reformed	-.38	-.32**						x	x
England & Wales						.34		-.51	
Episcopalian	-.61		x	x		x		x	
France		-.36***		-.41					
German Reformed	-.39**						x		x
Germany	-.64	-.44	-.61		-.39		-.48		
Indiana	x	x	x	x	.39		x		
Ireland	-.71	-.30			-.63				
Lutheran			-.43	-.36					-.47 (-.62)
Maryland	-.55***			x	x	x	x	x	x
Methodist	.38								
New Jersey	-.45***	-.32	x	x	x	x	x	x	x
New York	x	.33(.50)	.33(.50)	x	.70	.51	.66	x	.60

Ohio	x		x						
Pennsylvania	x	x	x		.56		.37(.53)	.37	
Presbyterian		.36			.43				.37
Quaker	x	x	x	.36	x	x	x	-.47	x
Roman Catholic	-.60	-.30	-.50	-.33	-.60		-.37		-.50
Scandinavia		x			-.41				
Scotland						.33		-.34	
Switzerland	-.35								
Universalist	.35**		x				x		
Vermont / Mass.	.46*	x	x	x	.60	x	.71	x	
Wisconsin	x	x	x	x	x	x	x	x	.54
Total explained variance (R²)	87%	35%	62%	26%	66%	27%	82%	44%	59%

Note: The figures are simple Pearsonian correlations (*r*). The figures in parentheses are partial correlations, with the relationships among all other enthocultural variables controlled; they are given when they indicate a relationship clearly stronger than that indicated by simple *r*. An x means that the census records did not provide data on the variable for the given state; a blank means that the variable did not correlate with the partisan division at more than .30 or was not significant at the .01 level.

*Massachusetts
**1850
****1880

Table 2B

Democratic Voting Patterns 1864–1868 and Ethnocultural Variables

	N.Y.	Pa.	Ohio	Ind.	Mich.	Ill.	Wis.	Iowa	Minn.
Austria		x	x	x	x	x	x	x	.38
Baptist	-.36	-.38	-.47	-.33(.44)	-.53	-.51	-.58(-.70)	-.33	
Canada	-.39	x	-.42*		-.33	-.62		-.63	
Congregationalist		x	x						
Dutch Reformed		x	x	x	x	x		x	x
England & Wales	.48			-.53		-.58	.44	-.32	
Germany							.66	-.45	.54
Illinois	x	x	x	x	x	x	-.34		
Kentucky	x	x		.32	x	.49	x	.57**	x
Lutheran	.40	.30	.42				.46(.75)*		
Massachusetts	-.36	-.54**	x	x	x	x		x	
New York	x	-.42	-.58	-.51		-.75	-.36	-.65	
Ohio	x	-.33	x	-.33					
Pennsylvania	x	x		-.41			-.37		
Quaker	x	x		-.32(.47)		x	x	x	
Roman Catholic							.32	.36(.52)	x
Scandinavia		x			-.58	-.41	-.51(-.70)	-.34	.51
Scotland		-.35	-.43		-.43	-.57		-.43	
Switzerland								.31(.46)	
Vermont	-.49	x	x	x		x		x	x
Total explained variance (R²)	45%	42%	61%	40%	49%	65%	81%	62%	37%

Note: The figures are simple Pearsonian correlations (*r*). The figures in parentheses are partial correlations, with the relationships among all other enthocultural variables controlled; they are given when they indicate a relationship clearly stronger than that indicated by simple *r*. An x means that the census records did not provide data on the variable for the given state; a blank means that the variable did not correlate with the partisan division at more than .30 or was not significant at the .01 level.

*1850
**1880

Chart 1

Ohio Counties and Voting Shifts, 1840s to 1860s

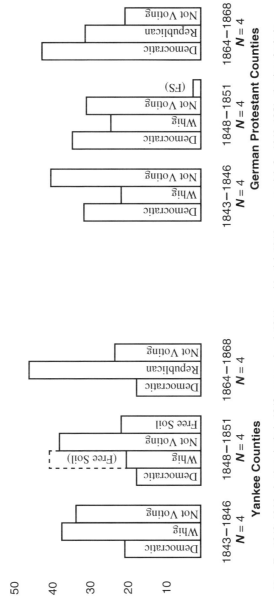

Note: For 1843–1846, elections include 1843 congressional, 1844 presidential, 1846 gubernatorial; for 1848–1851, elections include 1848 presidential, 1850 and 1851 gubernatorial; for 1864–1868, elections include 1864 presidential, 1865 gubernatorial, 1866 congressional, 1867 gubernatorial, 1868 presidential. *N* refers to the number of counties included in the analysis.

Chart 2

Indiana Counties and Voting Shifts, 1840s to 1860s

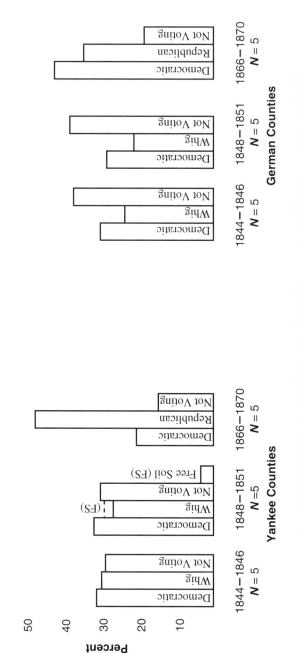

Note: For 1844–1846, elections include 1844 presidential, 1845 congressional, 1846 gubernatorial; for 1848–1851, elections include 1848 presidential, 1849 gubernatorial, 1851 congressional; for 1866–1870, elections include 1866 congressional, 1868 presidential, 1870 congressional. *N* refers to the number of counties included in the analysis.

Chart 3

Illinois Counties and Voting Shifts, 1840s to 1860s

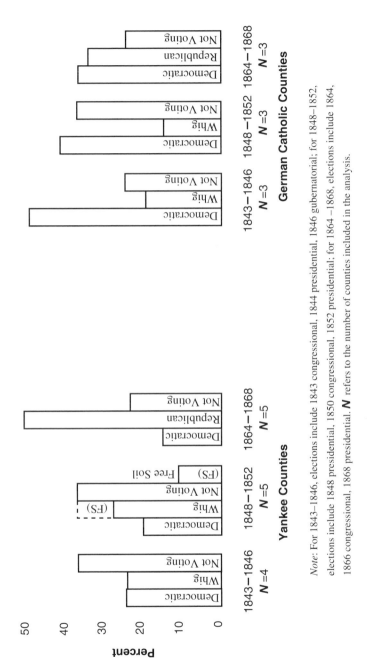

Note: For 1843–1846, elections include 1843 congressional, 1844 presidential, 1846 gubernatorial; for 1848–1852, elections include 1848 presidential, 1850 congressional, 1852 presidential; for 1864–1868, elections include 1864, 1866 congressional, 1868 presidential. *N* refers to the number of counties included in the analysis.

that preceded the Republican party's emergence as the second party in a new two-party system.

There are clear indications that the Republican appeal was based more on antislavery than nativism. Table 3 shows the correlations between Republican voting and a variety of statewide referenda that related to either issues of race or to one of the leading issues separating ethnocultural groups—prohibition and liquor license. They indicate that race-related issues almost completely displaced the prohibition issue during the 1860s and that the prohibition issue revived after the ratifica-

Table 3
Correlations for Referenda and Elections

	Republican	Democratic
Pre-War		
Illinois, black exclusion, 1848		
1856 presidential vote	.65	.53
1858 congressional vote	.40	.53
Michigan, black suffrage, 1850		
1856 presidential vote	.61	.47
1858 congressional vote	.56	.64
Indiana, black exclusion, 1851		
1856 presidential vote	.59	.52
1858 congressional vote	.48	.29
Ohio, license, 1851		
1856 presidential vote	.16	.56
1858 congressional vote	.32	.57
Michigan, prohibition, 1853		
1856 presidential vote	.51	.55
1858 congressional vote	.69	.65
Rhode Island, license, 1853		
1856 presidential vote	.88	.54
1858 congressional vote	.75	.73*
Wisconsin, prohibition, 1853		
1856 presidential vote	.43	.48
1858 congressional vote	.26	.48
Pennsylvania, prohibition, 1854		
1856 presidential vote	.34	.43
1860 presidential vote	.48	.38
Illinois, prohibition, 1855		
1856 presidential vote	.76	.81
1858 congressional vote	.70	.74

Table 3 *Continued*

	Republican	Democratic
Iowa, prohibition, 1855		
1854 congressional vote	.95	.84
1856 presidential vote	.36	.56
1858 congressional vote	.15	.42
Wisconsin, black suffrage, 1857		
1857 gubernatorial vote	.80	.98
1858 congressional vote	.44	.37
Iowa, black suffrage, 1857		
1857 gubernatorial vote	.25	.50
1858 congressional vote	.33	.50
1860 congressional vote	.51	.58
Oregon, black exclusion, 1857		
1858 gubernatorial vote	.76**	.75
1860 presidential vote	.78**	.27
New York, black suffrage, 1860		
1860 presidential vote	.88	.90
Post-War		
Connecticut, black suffrage, 1865		
1865 gubernatorial vote	.86	.98
1864–68 mean party vote	.86	.93
Minnesota, black suffrage, 1865		
1865 gubernatorial vote	.81	.89
Wisconsin, black suffrage, 1865		
1865 gubernatorial vote	.92	.95
1864–68 mean party vote	.83	.92
Minnesota, black suffrage, 1867		
1867 gubernatorial vote	.78	.86
Kansas, black suffrage, 1867		
1868 presidential vote	.76***	.87
1864–68 mean party vote	.69***	.76
Ohio, black suffrage, 1867		
1867 gubernatorial vote	.98	.99
1864–68 mean party vote	.92	.97
Iowa, black suffrage, 1868		
1868 presidential vote	.94	.97
1864–68 mean party vote	.92	.96
Michigan, prohibition, 1868		
1868 presidential vote	.79	.73
1864–68 mean party vote	.84	.57
Minnesota, black suffrage, 1868		
1868 presidential vote	.98	.98

Table 3 *Continued*

	Republican	Democratic
Minnesota, black suffrage, 1865–68 mean vote		
1865–68 mean party vote	.90	.95
New York, black suffrage, 1869		
1864–68 mean party vote	.90	.82
Michigan, black suffrage, 1870		
1864–68 mean party vote	.84	.51
Ohio, license, 1874		
1870–73 mean party vote	.56	.40
Michigan, license, 1876		
1872–76 mean party vote	.61	.21
Kansas, prohibition, 1880		
1880 presidential vote	.47	.62

Note: Voting patterns were based on proportion of the total eligible electorate. This gave individual correlations for Republican and Democratic patterns with both support and opposition for black rights and prohibition. The highest correlation is reported on the table, without signs. The highest Republican correlation was always with support for the pro-black rights or prohibition position—either a positive correlation with support for those positions or a negative correlation with opposition. The opposite held true for Democrats.

*Also correlated with anti-license position at .48
**Also correlated with anti-black rights position at .41 in 1858 and .64 in 1860
***Also correlated with the anti-black rights position at .47 in 1868 and at .60 for the mean 1864–68 vote

tion of the Fifteenth Amendment appeared to take African-American voting rights out of northern state politics. There was an extraordinarily high correlation between Republican voting patterns and voting patterns on African-American suffrage referenda as early as 1860, significantly higher than correlations between party and ethnocultural issues.

Of course, by the mid-1860s African-American suffrage had become a party issue, inclining Republicans to support it out of party loyalty. But if so, Republican politicans had succeeded in making it so. One wonders why they would do that, if northern white racism was as overwhelming a force as some historians have said. The answer lies in the fact that politicians do not merely respond to public opinion, they attempt to shape it—hopefully to promote the public good and certainly to promote their political careers. Like modern politicians, Reconstruction-era politicians tested issues, molded them, abandoned them, and revived them in a delicate dance with public opinion.

Naturally, they chose issues and tried to present them in a form that they thought promised political success for themselves and (more than today) their party.

Despite the racism endemic in North as well as South, Republicans chose to stress the slavery and civil-rights issue rather than prohibition, Sabbatarianism, immigration restriction, and similar ethnoculturally charged issues that might have appealed to much of their constituency. That is certainly apparent in the issues they chose to raise in Congress. Table 4 indicates the types of legislation both parties proposed in the House of Representatives between 1869 and 1880. Moral regulation made up less than one-half percent of the total. Of course, the nineteenth-century federal system lodged authority to regulate morals in the state rather than federal government. But Republicans generally avoided such issues in state campaigns as well, and for good reason. They divided Republicans more than they united them. They might energize part of the party's rank and file, but in most states the losses exceeded the benefits. When Republicans raised such issues, they always seemed to lose votes.[73] Therefore, as Table 5 shows, only about 7 percent of the planks of Republican state platforms from 1869–1880 were directed to what we may call "social issues," such as prohibition, church-state relations, and immigration restriction.

Because local issues could be dangerous, Republicans tried to keep voters focused on national issues. Even during years where no national officer was up for election, more Republican platform planks referred to Civil War issues than any other single issue. Moreover, planks dealing with economic development and regulation, taxation and retrenchment, and civil-service reform rarely pertained to state government alone. Even some social issues, such as foreign immigration, inherently involved national action. Although it will take further research to demonstrate conclusively, if one excludes the *pro forma* endorsement of state and national candidates and administrations, Table 4 suggests that at all times well over half of the planks were devoted to national issues.

Analysis of electoral behavior seems to confirm that voters found national issues more salient than local ones. Chart 4 graphs the median estimated voter turnout in presidential and gubernatorial elections at the state level from 1855 to 1880. Not only was the median turnout in presidential elections higher than the median gubernatorial election turnout in any year but 1868, but gubernatorial turnout also consistently peaked

Table 4
Proposed Legislation in the House of Representatives, 1869–1880

	Congress						
	41	42	43	44	45	46	Total
Economic Promotion	674 (19%)	533 (13%)	512 (10%)	421 (9%)	508 (8%)	383 (5%)	3031 (9%)
Reconstruction and Civil Rights	583 (16%)	425 (10%)	290 (6%)	268 (6%)	322 (5%)	305 (5%)	2193 (7%)
Economic Regulation	169 (5%)	213 (5%)	257 (5%)	146 (3%)	244 (4%)	331 (4%)	1360 (4%)
Financial Legislation	122 (3%)	133 (3%)	215 (4%)	165 (3%)	299 (5%)	219 (3%)	1153 (4%)
Moral Regulation	15 (.4%)	11 (.3%)	16 (.3%)	13 (.2%)	20 (.3%)	41 (.5%)	116 (.4%)
Other (primarily pension appropriations)	2060 (57%)	2961 (69%)	3761 (75%)	3889 (79%)	5301 (79%)	6342 (83%)	24,314 (76%)
Total	3623	4276	5051	4902	6694	7621	32,167

Table 5

Issues in Northern Republican Platforms, 1869–1880

	Presidential Election Years		Congress-Only Election Years		Odd Election Years		Total
War Issues	78 (22%)		63 (22%)		83 (29%)		224 (24%)
(Reconstruction & Civil Rights)		(56)		(53)		(59)	
(National Sovereignty)		(13)		(5)		(13)	
(Veterans' Legislation)		(9)		(5)		(11)	
National Finances	27 (8%)		38 (13%)		30 (10%)		105 (11%)
Economic Development and Regulation	19 (5%)		27 (10%)		52 (18%)		98 (11%)
Taxation and Economy in Government	17 (5%)		13 (5%)		27 (9%)		57 (6%)
Civil Service Reform and Honesty in Government	21 (6%)		11 (4%)		25 (9%)		57 (6%)
Social Issues	18 (5%)		23 (8%)		27 (9%)		68 (7%)
(Prohibition)		(1)		(5)		(4)	
(Church-State Relations)		(2)		(1)		(6)	
(Immigration Restriction)*		(2)		(3)		(4)	
Other (principally endorsements of candidates and administrations)	181 (50%)		110 (39%)		47 (16%)		328 (35%)
Total	361		285		291		937

*Includes 3 anti-Chinese immigration planks

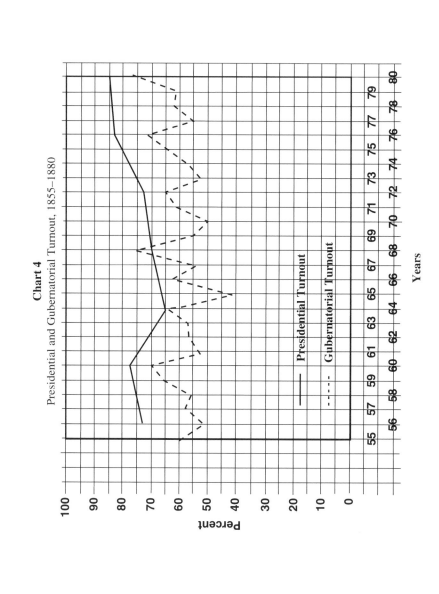

Chart 4

Presidential and Gubernatorial Turnout, 1855–1880

in presidential-election years. Table 6 demonstrates that—to different degrees—voting patterns were more consistent in presidential elections than in elections for state officers, even though most states elected governors every year or every other year. (The correlations in parentheses are those for non-presidential years four years apart.) These stable voting patterns and higher turnouts in presidential elections led to Republican victories, while more volatile elections for state officers led to losses if not outright defeats.

The voting pattern in the congressional elections of 1866, familiar to all students of Reconstruction, is most illustrative. Despite the fact that congressmen were national officers, voting patterns in off-year congressional elections varied much more than those in presidential-year elections, which closely resembled the pattern of the vote for president. Democrats always seemed to do better in off-year than on-year elections. The exception was the election of 1866, which Andrew Johnson turned into a referendum on Reconstruction when he broke with the Republican party, orchestrated the formation of an anti-Republican alliance, and launched an ambitious speaking tour through the North—

Table 6

Median Correlations between Republican Voting Patterns in Succeeding
Elections in Various Northern States, 1855–1880

	Presidential Election Years	Non-Presidential Election Years
Illinois	.83	*
Indiana	.89	*
Iowa	.74	.72 (.65)
Kansas	.63	.47 (.58)
Maine	.91	.83 (.65)
Massachusetts	.69	.58 (.61)
Michigan	.83	.77 (.58)
Minnesota	.63	.35
New Jersey	.89	.88
New York	.95	.95 (.91)
Ohio	.95	.90
Pennsylvania	.92	.90
Vermont	.90	.44 (.39)
Wisconsin	.83	.74

*Gubernatorial elections in Illinois and Indiana took place only in presidential years.

the "Swing Around the Circle."[74] That off-year election galvanized voters almost as effectively as a presidential canvass, and the high correlation between its voting pattern and those of presidential elections between 1860 and 1880 showed it, as did the highest turnout in an off-year congressional election between 1858 and 1874.[75] Table 7 gives the correlation between presidential elections and succeeding, off-year congressional elections. Compare the correlations among the elections of 1864, 1866, and 1868 to the others. If only all off-year elections could look like that one, Republicans lamented. In 1866 they hardly lost a congressman, following a huge gain in 1864. In most other off-year elections they lost twice as many or more, often from smaller pools.[76]

Throughout the 1870s, Republicans would do best when they could convince voters that the South was resurgent and again brutalizing its African-American people. That consideration was one of the main reasons that the Grant administration and northern Republicans finally endorsed the hard-liners rather than the conciliationists in the South. In 1871 they ended a dangerous period of drift by uniting on the Ku Klux Klan act; they carried the elections of 1872 on the southern issue. In 1876 they did it again. Georgia Republican and former Attorney General Amos T. Ackerman wrote that year, Rutherford B. Hayes "will

Table 7

Median Correlations between Republican Voting Patterns in Succeeding Presidential and Congressional Elections in Northern States, 1855–1880

1856–1858	.72
1858–1860	.71
1860–1862	.70
1862–1864	.77
1864–1866	.83
1866–1868	.84
1868–1870	.67
1870–1872	.70
1872–1874	.58
1874–1876	.63
1876–1878	.66
1878–1880	.70

Note: Northern states included are Illinois, Indiana, Iowa, Kansas, Maine, Massachusetts, Michigan, Minnesota, New Jersey, New York, Ohio, Pennsylvania, Vermont, and Wisconsin. Not included: California, Connecticut, Nevada, New Hampshire, Oregon, and Rhode Island.

be elected, if the people can see that the old issues are not settled, particularly in the South." Southerners intended that the extension of rights to African Americans "shall be only nominal. Let the North know this, and the battle is won."[77] Democrats knew it too. Furiously, they denounced Republicans for waving the "bloody shirt"—cynically keeping the old war issues alive. "What they want now is the very thing they constantly shed tears over—a first-class 'southern outrage,'" the Richmond *Dispatch* editorialized scornfully.[78] But when southern whites provided it—in the form of the bloody Hamburg Massacre in South Carolina—the *Dispatch* recognized the consequences. "We know as well as any one else that it would take only a few such affairs to . . . make HAYES's election sure," it wrote.[79] As anyone familiar with the election of 1876 knows, southern outrages did not quite make Hayes's election sure. But they made it possible.

Professor De Santis has described how, on becoming president, Hayes ostentatiously repudiated Republican intervention in the South, dividing and demoralizing his party.[80] How then did the Republicans manage to recover and win the presidential election of 1880? In 1879, having gained control of both the House and Senate in off-year elections, the Democrats tried to force the repeal of the Reconstruction-era election laws. The Democrats attached the repeal to the military appropriations bill, guessing that Hayes would not veto so essential a piece of legislation. They guessed wrong, and they paid for it. The independent but Democratic-leaning *New York Herald* knew it from the beginning. "[T]he republican leaders have not until within a few weeks entertained any confident expectation of carrying the Presidential elections next year. . . . Then came the Democratic idiocy. . . . The democrats could hardly do better if they received their orders directly from the other side."[81]

Given the potency of the Civil War issues, it should not surprise us that many Democrats urged that the party end its die-hard opposition to the extension of equal civil and political rights to African Americans and turn to other issues instead.[82] Republicans had succeeded in linking equal civil and political rights for African Americans with the triumph of loyalty and Unionism in the war. Despite northern racism, the civil-rights issue, presented the right way, was a winner, not a loser.

By 1871 Democrats advocating a "New Departure" were gaining strength. Their problem was that the war issues united the Democratic minority as thoroughly as they united the Republican majority. On most other issues—finances, banking, even the protective tariff—they were as divided as their opponents. They could unite on the "corruption" of the Grant administration and the well-oiled state Republican party machines. But that hardly seemed a winner, because the "outs" always charged the "ins" with corruption. If they could convince northerners that they really meant to concede civil and political rights to the freedmen, they could appeal to a widespread desire in the North for peace and reconciliation—a sentiment that persisted despite distrust of southern intentions. In those circumstances, moreover, Democrats could give their own spin to the race issue. Echoing the charges of their southern white allies, northern Democrats insisted that black southerners, now protected in their civil and political rights, were being duped into supporting the political ambitions of white adventurers and thieves. Sustained blindly by a constituency with no property to lose, carpetbaggers and scalawags were plundering the South. In this form, one that did not explicitly challenge the freedmen's civil and political rights, Democratic appeals to Republican racial prejudice could be effective.

What made these appeals credible was that they were echoed by important elements within the Republican party itself—another illustration of how intraparty factionalism affected public policy. In the fluid circumstances surrounding the organization of the new Republican party, there had been an immense amount of jockeying among these factions, with none securing too much control for too long a time. But by the late 1860s and early 1870s, most party organizations had stabilized. The Tenure of Office Act of 1867 had the unintended effect of strengthening the influence of Republican United States senators within their state parties.[83] Senators such as Roscoe Conkling of New York, Zachariah Chandler of Michigan, and Oliver P. Morton of Indiana slowly emerged as the heads of formidable "machines" that controlled local political patronage and nominations, just as southern Republican senators had gained predominant influence in their states.[84]

The process is an example of what the great political scientist Robert Michels called the "iron law of oligarchy"—the inevitable institutionalization of political movements into bureaucratized political parties, with a concomitant loss of internal democracy and openness.[85] There were a large number of losers, among them not only the members of declining factions but also Republican newspaper editors, who had exercised a great deal of independent influence on the party in its formative years, and intellectuals, whose role as articulators of antislavery ideals had been crucial in broadening the party's appeal but whose skills were less important than those of party hacks, who got out the vote now that partisan identifications had solidified.

Members of these groups howled in protest as mere machine politicians took over the party. But how could they oust the dominant leaders from power and regain their old influence? One thing was certain. They could not do it as long as the main issue dividing Republican from Democrat continued to be the antislavery, Civil War, civil-rights issue that riveted rank-and-file Republicans to their party and made the key political skill the simple ability to turn out voters at election time. The simple fact was that the dominant leaders—even reluctant warriors, who like Morton had sought to stem the tide of radical Republicanism—were now firmly associated with that issue. No one was going to wave the bloody shirt better than they. E. L. Godkin, the disgruntled editor of *The Nation*, articulated the situation clearly. "[P]eople came to look upon fidelity to the antislavery cause . . . as the one test of statesmanship, and under cover of this feeling a large number of gentlemen have won their way to places in public life." But now, "the circumstances have . . . so changed, and the problems presented for solution are so different, that they are fit to fill them no longer."[86]

But this argument could carry weight only if Republicans agreed that the great moral issue was settled. So it was that after the southern states were restored to normal relations in the Union, after Grant was elected president in 1868, and after Congress sent the Fifteenth Amendment to the states for what was expected to be certain ratification, dissident Republicans launched a great campaign to convince Republican voters that it was time to close the Civil War with amnesty and to turn to new issues of finances and reform.

When the regular Republican leadership proved surprisingly resilient, dissidents perceived the machinations by which they retained power—the patronage, the distribution of governmental largesse to sympathisers, the appeal to dead issues—to be essentially corrupt. Claiming the mantle of "reform," they linked this corruption to what they feared was a growing tendency to exercise governmental power to redistribute resources, by giving tariff protection to manufacturers and their workers at the expense of consumers and less developed regions of the country, passing Granger legislation to serve the interests of farmers and shippers at the expense of railroad investors, making huge public-works expenditures in the cities at the expense of property-owning tax-payers, and manipulating the money supply to benefit farmers and entrepeneurs at the expense of creditors. They were easily persuaded by southern Democrats that Republican programs to benefit the freedmen in the South at the expense of white taxpayers constituted another example.

The combination of their desire to move away from Civil War issues and their opposition to redistributive government economic policies—what they called "class legislation"—led Republican "reformers" into a de facto alliance with Democrats. Occasionally this alliance took on a concrete form, as in the Liberal Republican and Democratic nomination of Horace Greeley for the presidency in 1872. But generally it was limited to parallel attacks on the leadership of the Republican party—accusations of corruption and of ignoring the real issues facing Americans while making demagogic appeals to the settled ones surrounding slavery, race, and the war.[87] At the same time, both reform Republicans and Democrats had an interest in portraying white southerners as reconciled to the results of the war, including the extension of basic civil and political rights to the freedmen, and in fact now the victims of cynical carpetbaggers and scalawags. Finally, both dissident Republicans and Democrats pointed to the stress placed on government institutions, especially the federal system, by the intervention in the South to protect civil and political rights.

The constant reiteration of these themes in the dissident-controlled journals of the northern press, whose influence was enhanced by the claim that the reformers' independence of both party orgnizations made them reliable and neutral observers, did undermine the appeal of the Civil War issues to the rank and file.[88] The effect was especially apparent after 1870 and in non-presidential year elections, when it was more difficult for Republicans to keep their voters focused on national issues. Table 7 shows the correlations between Republican voting patterns in succeeding national elections. The trend down from the Republican heyday of 1864 through 1868 is clear.

Foner links this trend to growing class tensions in the North. With labor unrest growing, "consciousness of being members of a separate capitalist class . . . spread within the business community. . . . [I]n the face of agrarian unrest and working-class militancy, metropolitan capitalists united as never before," he writes. Capitalists and businessmen, now identifying more with white southern property-owners than the black southern working class and fearful of an activist state, turned against Reconstruction.[89]

There is a good deal of truth to this portrayal of the reaction of many businessmen (and financiers—a group to which Foner gives too little attention) to Reconstruction in the South. But there is no evidence that their distaste for Republican Reconstruction policy determined the result. Although the sharp sectional divisions among business interests were slowly giving way to greater harmony in the 1870s, the business community was by no means united. And its influence was clearly limited; the passage of Granger legislation demonstrated either that business interests could not control policy in states like Wisconsin, Illinois, and Iowa, or that their class consciousness was not so well developed after all. As Joel Silbey has observed, when businessmen came to perceive their common interests, they turned against the nineteenth-century political system because they could *not* exercise enough influence within it to secure them.[90]

Moreover, the business community as a whole had *never* sympathized with radical Reconstruction. Many businessmen and financiers were Democrats. Others clearly favored conservative Republicans rather than radicals. The few who had been ostentatious radicals, such as Boston textile manufacturer Edward Atkinson, turned towards conservatism as early as 1867.[91] The real damage was done by the reform Republicans, who articulated a philosophy of laissez-faire moralism that appealed not only to businessmen and capitalists, but which resonated with the tenets of free-labor ideology to which nearly all northerners adhered.[92] It was they who lent credibility to the charge that the Republican regimes of the South were violating basic American norms in an orgy of plunder and class legislation.

Still, we must be careful about what we mean by the "abandonment" of Reconstruction by northern voters. The problem for Republicans was not that their rank and file had turned against the freedmen or against Reconstruction. The reaction to southern outrages demonstrated that. The problem was that in spite of southern outrages, the reformers convinced a large enough minority of Republican voters that the fruits of the antislavery victory were secure, making elections doubtful.

Republicans had always been divided on issues unrelated to slavery. If that glue weakened, the party's base was bound to erode.

The party leaders' difficulty was exacerbated by the fact that an even smaller minority of Republicans did actually turn against further intervention in the South as a matter of political and constitutional principle. Republicans not only faced the problem that their best issue was losing its salience; in some important states, such as New York and Ohio, reformers hostile to Reconstruction might hold the balance of power between the parties. In those states an appeal to Civil War issues, while energizing the rank and file, might alienate enough dissidents to lose the election. Recognizing these facts, Republican leaders searched desperately for an issue that would augment or replace Reconstruction without putting their own party positions in jeopardy. They tried combinations of anti-Catholicism and hard money between 1873 and 1875 and an early version of anticommunism in 1877 and 1878. Later they would try the protective tariff.

But nothing could replace the Civil War issues when it came to martialing ordinary Republican voters. So Republicans turned to an expedient that had tragic results for the freedmen of the South. They did raise the Civil War issues, but in a way that avoided driving dissidents to the Democrats. The potential of this approach first became clear in the great Amnesty debate of 1876. Having recently persuaded President Grant not to send troops to Mississippi for fear of losing the elections of 1875 in the North, the Republican leader in the House, former Speaker James G. Blaine, moved to exclude Jefferson Davis from a bill designed to give him amnesty. Southern Democrats rose in a bitter defense of Davis and the Confederate South and an equally bitter attack on Republican Reconstruction policy; Blaine's response and that of James A. Garfield electrified the party's rank and file. "Hundreds of thousands of ardent, oppressed hearts responded with a battle-cry of joy," Garfield's friend Albert Gallatin Riddle recalled a few years later.[93]

Republicans considered the Amnesty debate, which followed closely upon the Republican victories in the 1875 state elections, to have been the turning point in the remarkable recovery from the disastrous congressional elections of 1874. The lesson was not lost upon Republican leaders. The best political course was to raise the war issues that excited the majority of Republicans without proposing to do anything that might alienate the minority. One way to do that was to shift the issue from the rights of freedmen in the South to the behavior of the Democrats during the war. Blaine had done that successfully in the Amnesty debate, and it became more and more the pattern afterwards—although southern racial outrages did continue to reinforce the partisan allegiance of many northern Republicans as well.

The Republican strategy was tragic for African Americans. It broke the crucial link Republicans had so carefully crafted among African-American civil and political rights, loyalty, moral progress, unionism, and patriotism. It eliminated the counter-weight that held northern racism in check among Republicans, allowing southern Democrats to shape the race issue as they wished. Thus it was not increased racism that led to the erosion of northern support for Reconstruction, it was the erosion of support for Reconstruction that led to increased racism.

The new Republican strategy converted the living issue of equal rights into the dead one of Democratic perfidy in the Civil War. Although such a constricted waving of the bloody shirt triggered a host of associations binding Republicans to their party, it could not last forever. In the late 1880s, as fading memories of the war undermined the effectiveness of merely rhetorical attacks on Democrats' wartime sins, Republicans tried to revitalize bloody-shirt rhetoric by again linking it to the civil and political-rights issue, bringing forward the Force Act of 1890. But by then the Republican strategy had done its damage. As their leaders allowed the issue of equal rights to atrophy, too many northern Republicans had become indifferent to the fate of African Americans.[94] In light of that indifference it is no suprise that Republican politicians did little to protest the open violation of African-American rights in the 1890s and after. That was no longer the way to energize their voters; it was certainly not the way to attract new ones. The politics of Reconstruction was over.

Notes

1. Vincent P. De Santis, *Republicans Face the Southern Question: The New Departure Years, 1877–1897* (Baltimore: Johns Hopkins University Press, 1959).

2. Joel H. Silbey, *A Respectable Minority: The Democratic Party in the Civil War Era, 1860–1868* (New York: W. W. Norton, 1977).

3. William Gillette, *Retreat from Reconstruction, 1869–1879* (Baton Rouge: Louisiana State University Press, 1979); James Ford Rhodes, *The History of the United States from the Compromise of 1850 to the Final Restoration of Home Rule*

at the South in 1877, vol. 6: *1866–1872* and vol. 7: *1872–1877* (New York: Macmillan, 1906). The revisionist studies of the 1960s barely attended to the subject. See for example, John Hope Franklin, *Reconstruction: After the Civil War* (Chicago: University of Chicago Press, 1961); Rembert W. Patrick, *The Reconstruction of the Nation* (New York: Oxford University Press, 1967); Kenneth M. Stampp, *The Era of Reconstruction, 1865–1877* (New York: Alfred A. Knopf, 1965).

4. Eric Foner, *Reconstruction: America's Unfinished Revolution, 1863–1877* (New York: Harper & Row, 1988).

5. Ronald P. Formisano, *The Birth of Mass Politics: Michigan as a Case Study* (Princeton: Princeton University Press, 1971); Michael F. Holt, *Forging a Majority: The Formation of the Republican Party in Pittsburgh, 1848–1860* (New Haven: Yale University Press, 1969); Holt, *The Political Crisis of the 1850s* (New York: Wiley, 1978).

6. Paul Kleppner, *The Third Electoral System, 1853–1892: Parties, Voters, and Political Cultures* (Chapel Hill: University of North Carolina Press, 1979).

7. Ibid., 8.

8. For works stressing the racist elements of the antislavery movement and Republicanism, see Robert F. Durden, "Ambiguities in the Anti-Slavery Crusade of the Republican Party," in Martin Duberman, ed., *The Antislavery Vanguard: New Essays on the Abolitionists* (Princeton: Princeton University Press, 1965), 362–94; Eric Foner, "Politics and Prejudice: The Free Soil Party and the Negro, 1849–1852," *Journal of Negro History* 50 (October 1965): 239–56; Eugene Berwanger, *The Frontier Against Slavery: Western Anti-Negro Prejudice and the Slavery Extension Controversy* (Urbana: University of Illinois Press, 1967); Larry Gara, "Slavery and the Slave Power: A Crucial Distinction," *Civil War History* 15 (March 1969): 5–18.

9. C. Vann Woodward, "Seeds of Failure in Radical Race Policy," in Woodward, *American Counterpoint: Slavery and Racism in the North-South Dialogue* (Boston: Little, Brown, 1971), 163–83.

10. William Gillette, *The Right to Vote: Politics and the Passage of the Fifteenth Amendment* (Baltimore: Johns Hopkins University Press, 1965); Gillette, *Retreat from Reconstruction, 1869–1879* (Baton Rouge: Louisiana State University Press, 1979).

11. Margaret S. Thompson, *The "Spider Web": Congress and Lobbying in the Age of Grant* (Ithaca, N.Y.: Cornell University Press, 1985).

12. C. Vann Woodward, *Reunion and Reaction: The Compromise of 1877 and the End of Reconstruction*, rev. ed. (New York: Oxford University Press, 1991); Michael Les Benedict, "Southern Democrats in the Crisis of 1876–1877: A Reconsideration of *Reunion and Reaction*," *Journal of Southern History* 46 (November 1980): 508–509.

13. Foner, *Reconstruction*, 486–87; Keith Ian Polakoff, *The Politics of Inertia: The Election of 1876 and the End of Reconstruction* (Baton Rouge: Louisiana State University Press, 1973), 127–30, 134–40.

14. Joel Silbey, *The American Political Nation, 1838–1893* (Stanford: Stanford University Press, 1991), 194. See also Foner, *Reconstruction*, 486–87.

15. Michael Les Benedict, "The Rout of Radicalism: Republicans and the Elections of 1867," *Civil War History* 18 (December 1972): 334–44.

16. *New York Tribune*, July 6, 1875, p. 4; New York *Nation*, July 15, 1875, p. 33; Alfred Yapla[?] to William Allen, March 30, 1875, Allen Mss., Library of Congress (hereafter L.C.); Charles Francis Adams, Jr., to Carl Schurz, Aug. 14, 1875, Schurz Mss., L.C.; Zachariah Chandler to James G. Blaine, Aug. 15, 1875, Blaine Mss., L.C.; Samuel J. Randall to George W. Morgan, Aug. 17, 1875, Vertical File, Western Reserve Historical Society, Cleveland, Ohio.

17. Gillette, *Retreat from Reconstruction*, 159; Foner, *Reconstruction*, 562–63.

18. Eric Foner, *Nothing But Freedom: Emancipation and Its Legacy* (Baton Rouge: Louisiana State University Press, 1983), 45–47.

19. Albion W. Tourgée, *A Fool's Errand* (New York: Fords, Howard and Hulbert, 1880).

20. James E. Sefton, *The United States Army and Reconstruction, 1865–1877* (Baton Rouge: Louisiana State University Press, 1967), 236.

21. Holden's fellow North Carolina Republicans Oliver H. Dockery, John Pool, Tod R. Caldwell, and others were experienced Whig politicians. Edgar Estes Folk, "W. W. Holden and the North Carolina Standard, 1843–1848: A Study in Political Journalism," *North Carolina Historical Review* 19 (January 1942): 22–47; Folk, "W. W. Holden and the Election of 1858," ibid. 21 (October 1944): 294–318; James L. Lancaster, "The Scalawags of North Carolina, 1850–1868" (Ph.D. diss., Princeton University, 1974); Horace W. Raper, *William W. Holden: North Carolina's Political Enigma* (Chapel Hill: University of North Carolina Press, 1985). So were Alabama ex-Congressman Alexander White and Lewis E. Parsons, whom Andrew Johnson had appointed Alabama's provisional governor in 1865. Robert M. Patton, whom Alabamans had elected to replace Parsons, Republican Governor David P. Lewis, and Samuel F. Rice had been active Democrats. Alabama's Republican Senator Willard Warner had been a Republican legislator in Ohio. William M. Cash, "Alabama Republicans During Reconstruction: Personal Characteristics, Motivations, and Political Activity of Party Activists, 1867–1880" (Ph.D. diss., University of Alabama, 1973); Sarah Woolfolk Wiggins, *The Scalawag in Alabama Politics, 1865–1881* (Tuscaloosa: University of Alabama Press, 1991); Richard N. Current, *Those Terrible Carpetbaggers: A Reinterpretation* (New York: Oxford University Press, 1988), 34–35, 68–69. James Lusk Alcorn of Mississippi and William G. Brownlow of Tennessee, both of whom would serve as Republican governors and senators, were experienced Whigs; Andrew Jackson Hamilton, who joined the Republicans while serving as provisional governor in Texas, had been an active Democratic ally of unionist Sam Houston. Lillian A. Pereya, *James Lusk Alcorn: Persistent Whig* (Baton Rouge: Louisiana State University Press, 1966); Thomas B. Alexander, "Whiggery and Reconstruction in Tennessee," *Journal of Southern History* 16 (August 1950): 291–305; John L. Waller, *Colossal Hamilton of Texas: A Biography of Andrew Jackson Hamilton, Militant Unionist and Reconstruction Governor* (El Paso: Texas Western Press, 1968).

22. Brown to Bullock, December 3, 1868, Hargrett Collection, University of Georgia.

23. Eric Foner, *Free Soil, Free Labor, Free Men: The Ideology of the Republican Party Before the Civil War* (New York: Alfred A. Knopf, 1970), 11–39; Louis Gerteis, "Slavery and Hard Times: Morality and Utility in American Antislavery Reform," *Civil War History* 29 (December 1983): 316–31; Donald K. Pickens, "The Republican Synthesis and Thaddeus Stevens," *Civil War History* 31 (March 1985): 57–73. See also Gabor S. Boritt, *Lincoln and the Economics of the American Dream* (Memphis: Memphis State University Press, 1978).

24. Frederick F. Low to Cornelius Cole, October 25, 1871, Cornelius Cole Mss., U.C.L.A. Library, Los Angeles, Calif.

25. Frederick Law Olmsted, *A Journey in the Seaboard Slave States, in the Years 1853–1854 with Remarks on Their Economy*, 2 vols. (New York: G.P. Putnam's Sons, 1904; originally published in 1856), 1:239.

26. Union Congressional Republican Committee, *The Policy of Congress in Reference to the Restoration of the Union*, printed in the Boston *Evening Journal*, May 29, 1867 (supplement), 4. For the general antislavery conviction that slavery condemned society to economic and cultural backwardness, see Richard N. Current, *Northernizing the South* (Athens: University of Georgia Press, 1983), 33–35, 40–41, 54–57; Robert William Fogel and Stanley L. Engerman, *Time on the Cross: The Economics of American Negro Slavery*, 2 vols. (Boston: Little, Brown, 1974), 1:158–90; Foner, *Free Soil, Free Labor, Free Men*, 40–51; Ronald G. Walters, *The Antislavery Appeal: American Abolitionism After 1830* (Baltimore: Johns Hopkins University Press, 1976), 111–28.

27. "Occasional" (John W. Forney) in the Philadelphia *Press*, February 4, 1870, p. 4.

28. *New York Tribune*, March 11, 1869, p. 4; *New York Times*, August 17, 1869, p. 4.

29. Wilmington (N.C.) *Post*, July, 1867, quoted in James A. Padgett, ed., "Reconstruction Letters from South Carolina," *North Carolina Historical Review* 20 (January 1943): 81. For other examples, see the Little Rock *Republican*, November 3, 1868, p. 2; April 2, 1869, p. 2; April 6, 1869, p. 2.

30. There is a large literature on intrastate sectionalism in the South, stressing a variety of sources of conflict and an important although smaller literature on conflict over taxation. See Charles S. Sydnor, *The Development of Southern Sectionalism, 1819–1848* (Baton Rouge: Louisiana State University Press, 1948), 275–93; Ralph A. Wooster, *Politicians, Planters, and Plain Folk: Courthouse and Statehouse in the Upper South, 1850–1860* (Knoxville: University of Tennessee Press, 1975), 2–21; George Ruble Woolfolk, "Taxes and Slavery in the Ante Bellum South," *Journal of Southern History* 26 (May 1960): 180–214; Jonas Viles, "Sections and Sectionalism in a Border State," *Mississippi Valley Historical Review* 21 (June 1934): 3–22; Charles Henry Ambler, *Sectionalism in Virginia from 1776 to 1861* (Chicago: University of Chicago Press, 1910); Alison Freehling, *Drift Toward Dissolution: The Virginia Slavery Debate of 1831–1832* (Baton Rouge: Louisiana State University, 1982), 36–81, 122–69, 235–41; Freehling, "Editorial Revolution, Virginia, and the Coming of Civil War: A Review Essay," *Civil War History* 16 (March 1969): 64–72; Stanley John Folmsbee, *Sectionalism*

and Internal Improvements in Tennessee, 1796–1845 (Philadelphia: n.p., 1939), passim and especially 54–56, 116–19, 148–53, 162–76, 208–9, 216–35; Mary Emily Robertson Campbell, *The Attitude of Tennesseans Towards the Union, 1847–1861* (New York: Vantage Press, 1961), 34–35, 38–40, 175, 198–212 passim; Eric Russell Lacy, *Vanquished Volunteers: East Tennessee Sectionalism from Statehood to Secession* (Johnson City, Tenn.: East Tennessee State University Press, 1965); Thomas E. Jeffrey, "National Interests, Local Issues, and the Transformation of Antebellum North Carolina Politics," *Journal of Southern History* 50 (February 1984): 43–74; Joseph Carlyle Sitterson, "Economic Sectionalism in Ante-Bellum North Carolina," *North Carolina Historical Review* 16 (April 1939): 134–46; Marc W. Kruman, *Parties and Politics in North Carolina, 1836–1865* (Baton Rouge: Louisiana State University Press, 1983), 88–103, 189–96; John L. Inscoe, *Mountain Masters, Slavery and the Sectional Crisis in Western North Carolina* (Knoxville: University of Tennessee Press, 1989); William A. Schaper, "Sectionalism and Representation in South Carolina, A Sociological Study," *Annual Report of the American Historical Association for 1900*, 2 vols. (Washington, D.C.: Government Printing Office, 1901), 1:237–464; Laura A. White, "The National Democrats in South Carolina, 1852–1860," *South Atlantic Quarterly* 28 (October 1929): 374–76; Lucien E. Roberts, "Sectional Factors in the Movements for Legislative Reapportionment and Reduction in Georgia, 1777–1860," in James C. Bonner and Lucien E. Roberts, eds., *Studies in Georgia History and Government* (Athens: University of Georgia Press, 1940), 94–122; Peter Wallenstein, " 'More Unequally Taxed than any People in the Civilized World': The Origins of Georgia's Ad Valorem Tax System," *Georgia Historical Quarterly* 69 (Winter 1985): 459–87; Michael P. Johnson, *Towards a Patriarchal Republic: The Secession of Georgia* (Baton Rouge: Louisiana State University Press, 1977), 85–90; Lewy Dorman, *Party Politics in Alabama from 1850 to 1860* (Wetumpka, Ala.: Alabama State Department of Archives and History, 1935), 96–98, 222; Percy Lee Rainwater, *Mississippi: Storm Center of Secession, 1856–1861* (Baton Rouge: Louisiana State University Press, 1938), 6–12; Edwin Arthur Miles, *Jacksonian Democracy in Mississippi* (Chapel Hill: University of North Carolina, 1960), 18–32; Richard Aubrey McLemore, ed., *A History of Mississippi*, 2 vols., (Hattiesburg: University and College Press of Mississippi, 1973), 1:249–50, 266–74, 284–85, 295–96, 369–71; James Byrne Ranck, *Albert Gallatin Brown: Radical Southern Nationalist* (New York: Appleton-Century, 1937), 4–10; Roger Wallace Shugg, *Origins of Class Struggle in Louisiana: A Social History of White Farmers and Laborers . . . 1840–1875* (University, La.: Louisiana State University Press, 1939), 121–34; Carl H. Moneyhon, *Republicanism in Reconstruction Texas* (Austin: University of Texas Press, 1980), 12–16; Weston J. McConnell, *Social Cleavages in Texas: A Study of the Proposed Divison of the State* (New York: Columbia University Press, 1925), 15–39; D. W. Meinig, *Imperial Texas: An Interpretive Essay in Cultural Geography* (Austin: University of Texas Press, 1969), 38–62 passim; Roger A. Griffin, "Intrastate Sectionalism in the Texas Governor's Race of 1853," *Southwestern Historical Quarterly* 76 (Fall, 1972): 142–60.

31. David M. Potter, *Lincoln and His Party in the Secession Crisis* (New Haven: Yale University Press, 1942), 235–39; Potter, "Why the Republicans Rejected Both Compromise and Secession," in George Harmon Knoles, ed., *The Crisis of the Union: 1860–1861* (Baton Rouge: Louisiana State University Press, 1965), 99–102. The conviction that southern unionists were duped or dragged into war is evident in the histories of secession that appeared during and immediately after the war—for example, Horace Greeley, *The American Conflict: A History of The Great Rebellion in the United States of America, 1860–'64*, 2 vols. (Hartford, Conn.: O.D. Case & Co., 1864), 1:350–51; Benson J. Lossing, *Pictorial History of the Civil War in the United States of America*, vol. 1 (Philadelphia: George W. Childs, 1866), 36–40; Henry Wilson, *The Rise and Fall of the Slave Power in America*, 3 vols. (Boston and New York: Houghton Mifflin Co., 1872–77), 1:127–46.

32. Paul D. Escott, *Jefferson Davis and the Failure of Confederate Nationalism* (Baton Rouge: Louisiana State University Press, 1978), 94. See ibid., 94–134, 196–225; Stephen E. Ambrose, "Yeoman Discontent in the Confederacy," *Civil War History* 8 (September 1962): 259–68; Georgia Lee Tatum, *Disloyalty in the Confederacy* (Chapel Hill: University of North Carolina Press, 1934); Charles W. Ramsdell, *Behind the Lines in the Southern Confederacy* (New York: Greenwood Press, 1944), passim; Charles H. Wesley, *The Collapse of the Southern Confederacy* (New York: Russell and Russell, 1937), 47–73 passim, 74–104; Richard E. Beringer, "The Unconscious 'Spirit of Party' in the Confederate Congress," *Civil War History* 18 (December 1972): 315–23; Wilfred Buck Yearns, *The Confederate Congress* (Athens: University of Georgia Press, 1960), 71–83; Hugh C. Bailey, "Disaffection in the Alabama Hill Country, 1861," *Civil War History* 4 (June 1988): 183–93; Yearns, "North Carolina in the Confederate Congress," *North Carolina Historical Review* 29 (July 1952): 359–78; Raper, *Holden*, 45–58; Martha L. Turner, "The Cause of the Union in East Tennessee," *Tennessee Historical Quarterly* 40 (Winter 1981): 366–80; Henry T. Shanks, "Disloyalty to the Confederacy in Southwestern Virginia, 1861–1865," *North Carolina Historical Review* 21 (April 1944): 118–35.

33. Wendell Phillips, "The State of the Country," in Phillips, *Speeches, Lectures, and Letters* (Boston: Lee & Shepard, 1884), 532–33.

34. Atlanta *New Era*, March 13, 1868, quoted in Mark W. Summers, *Railroads, Reconstruction, and the Gospel of Prosperity: Aid Under the Radical Republicans, 1865–1877* (Princeton: Princeton University Press), 26; see Thomas B. Settle, Notes of a Speech Delivered in Rockingham County, . . . March, 1867, in the Thomas Settle Papers, Southern Historical Collection, University of North Carolina, Chapel Hill; Charles D. Drake, *Immediate Emancipation in Missouri*, in Drake, *Union and Antislavery Speeches* (Cincinnati: Applegate & Co., 1864), 282–88; Richard G. Lowe, "The Republican Party in Antebellum Virginia," *Virginia Magazine of History and Biography* 81 (July 1973): 266, 269–70; E. Russ Williams, Jr., "John Ray: Forgotten Scalawag," *Louisiana Studies* 13 (Fall 1974): 244, 246; Roger P. Leemhuis, *James L. Orr and the Sectional Conflict* (Washington: University Press of America, 1979), 107–108; Ross A. Webb, *Benjamin Helms Bristow* (Lexington: University Press of Kentucky, 1969), 72–73, 87–88.

35. Mississippi Republican platform of 1869, in Edward McPherson, comp., *Political History of the United States During the Period of Reconstruction ...* (Washington, D.C.: Solomons & Chapman, 1875), 481. From 1867 to 1869, equal taxation planks appeared in Republican platforms in Alabama, Arkansas, Mississippi, South Carolina, and Virginia: ibid., 251, 253, 481, 485; *Appleton's Annual Cyclopedia* (1867), 26, 695, 758. For examples of Republican use of the tax issue in Arkansas, see E. W. Gantt's and Thomas Boles's election speeches published in the Little Rock *Republican*, September 4, 1868, p. 2 and November 2, 1868, p. 2, respectively, and the *Republican*'s editorial of June 15, 1869, p. 2.

36. *Appleton's Annual Cyclopedia* (1867), 460, 695.

37. Francis L. Cardozo, *Address Before the Grant Council of the Union Leagues ... July 27, 1870*, published as "Document—The Union Leagues and the South Carolina Election of 1870," ed. Edward F. Sweat, *Journal of Negro History* 41 (April 1976): 209; Joel Williamson, *After Slavery: The Negro in South Carolina during Reconstruction* (Chapel Hill: University of North Carolina Press, 1965), 148–59.

38. Constitution of Alabama (1868), Art. 9, sec. 1; Const. of Arkansas (1868), Art. 10, sec. 2; Const. of Florida (1868), Art. 13, sec. 1; Const. of Louisiana (1868), Title 6, art. 118; Const. of Mississippi (1869), Art. 7, sec. 20; Const. of North Carolina (1868), Art. 5, sec. 1, 3, Art. 7, sec. 9; Const. of South Carolina (1868), Art. 2, sec. 33; Const. of Virginia (1869), Art. 10, sec. 1, 4.

39. Const. of Alabama (1868), Art. 14; Const. of Arkansas (1868), Art. 12, sec. 1, 3; Const. of Florida (1868), Art. 10; Const. of Georgia (1868), Art. 7, sec. 5135; Const. of North Carolina, Art. 10, sec. 1, 3; Const. of South Carolina, Art. 2, sec. 32; Const. of Virginia (1869), Art. 11, sec. 1. See Kenneth Edson St. Clair, "Debtor Relief in North Carolina During Reconstruction," *North Carolina Historical Review* 18 (July 1941): 215–35; Robert J. Haws and Michael V. Namorato, "Race, Property, and Economic Consequences of Reconstruction," *Vanderbilt Law Review* 32 (January, 1979): 319–22; Jack B. Scroggs, "Carpetbagger Constitutional Reform in the South Atlantic States, 1867–1868," *Journal of Southern History* 27 (November 1961): 479–80.

40. Harold Woodman, "Post-Civil War Southern Agriculture and the Law," *Agricultural History* 53 (January 1979): 318–37; Joel Williamson, *After Slavery: The Negro in South Carolina During Reconstruction, 1861–1877* (Chapel Hill: University of North Carolina Press, 1965), 171–72.

41. Vicksburg (Miss.) *Republican*, April 28, 1868, quoted in Summers, "Radical Reconstruction and the Gospel of Prosperity: Railroad Aid Under the Southern Republicans" (Ph. D. diss., University of California, 1980), 73.

42. Philadelphia *Press*, October 9, 1869, p. 4; George Frisbie Hoar, "Are the Republicans in to Stay?" *North American Review* 149 (November 1889): 621.

43. Little Rock *Republican*, May 25, 1869, p. 2.

44. Elisha M. Pease to James G. Tracy, May 24, 1869, Pease papers, Austin Public Library.

45. George M. Welker to William W. Holden, May 11, 1869, Holden Mss., Duke University.

46. Joseph E. Brown, *Speech of Ex-Gov. Joseph E. Brown, of Georgia, Delivered in Milledgeville, Ga., June 6th, 1867, on the Present Situation and Future Prospects of the Country* (n.p., [1867]), 1.

47. *Banker's Magazine* 24 (January 1870): 547. For general information about banking, currency, credit, and finances in the postwar period, see William J. Schultz and M. R. Caine, *Financial Development of the United States* (New York: Prentice-Hall, 1937), 312–62 passim; Milton Friedman and Anna Jacobson Schwartz, *A Monetary History of the United States, 1867–1960* (Princeton: Princeton University Press, 1963), 15–88 passim; Edward C. Kirkland, *Industry Comes of Age: Business, Labor, and Public Policy, 1860–1897* (New York: Holt, Rinehart and Winston, 1961), 13–42; John A. James, *Money and Capital Markets in Postbellum America* (Princeton, Princeton University Press, 1978), 22–29; Richard Sylla, "Federal Policy, Banking Market Structure, and Capital Mobilization in the United States, 1863–1913," *Journal of Economic History* 29 (December 1969): 657–86. For the banking and financial situation in the South, see George L. Anderson, "The South and the Problem of Post-Civil War Finance," *Journal of Southern History* 9 (May 1943): 181–85; Roger L. Ransom and Richard Sutch, *One Kind of Freedom: The Economic Consequences of Emancipation* (Cambridge, England: Cambridge University Press, 1977), 106–25. Notes of credit, with slaves as collateral, were a central form of circulating financial media in the South. Emancipation depreciated their value and eliminated this form of collateralized note in the future. See Richard Holcombe Kilbourne, Jr., *Debt, Investment, and Slaves: Credit Relations in East Feliciana Parish, Louisiana, 1825–1885* (Tuscaloosa: University of Alabama Press, 1995). Modern financial experts recognize that deposits in commercial banks augment currency in the nation's money supply. Sixty percent of these deposits were in the national banks and therefore, like currency, concentrated in the northeast and mid-Atlantic states. Friedman and Schwartz, *Monetary History of the U.S.*, 17.

48. Theodore C. Peters, *A Report Upon Conditions of the South, with Regard to Its Need for a Cotton Crop and Its Financial Wants in Connection Therewith as Well as the Safety of Temporary Loans* (Baltimore: H. A. Robinson, 1867), 8 and passim; Montgomery *Alabama State Journal*, March 11, 1869, p. 2.

49. Until the mid-1870s, Republicans' opponents in the South often referred to Republicans as "Radicals" and to themselves as "Conservatives," rather than Democrats. The custom reflected the fact that southerners of both Whig and Democratic backgrounds organized the opposition to Republican Reconstruction policy from 1865 to 1868.

50. Montgomery *Alabama State Journal*, June 24, 1869, p. 2.

51. For examples, see Henry Wilson's speech at New Orleans in May, 1867, Boston *Evening Journal*, May 30, 1867, p. 2; Horace Greeley's address at Richmond, Va., *New York Tribune*, May 17, 1867, p. 1; ibid., May 20, 1867, p. 4; May 28, 1867, p. 4; Cincinnati *Commercial*, July 5, 1867, p. 5; Daniel R. Goodloe, *Letter of Daniel R. Goodloe to Hon. Charles Sumner, on the Situation of Affairs in North Carolina* (n.p., [1868]), 14–15; Wiggins, *The Scalawag in Alabama Politics*, 27–34.

52. New York *Nation*, October 15, 1868, p. 304.

53. Henry Clay Warmoth, *War, Politics and Reconstruction: Stormy Days in Louisiana* (New York: Macmillan, 1930), 75.

54. For insight into the importance of fairly administered legal institutions to enforce contracts, see Donald G. Nieman, *To Set the Law in Motion: The Freedmen's Bureau and the Legal Rights of Blacks, 1865–1868* (Millwood, N.Y.: KTO Press, 1979), 179–89, and Nieman, "Black Jurors and Reconstruction Justice: The Case of Washington County, Texas," unpublished paper delivered at the annual meeting of the American Society for Legal History, November, 1989, Charleston, S.C.

55. Although historians generally have recognized that planters were desperate to maintain their recourse to compel the freedpeople to labor, they have been slow to recognize what is clear from planters' own complaints—that they would be forced to pay what they considered to be impossibly high wages if they competed for black labor. The result of the new ability of African Americans to resist coercion was the establishment of the sharecropping system, which provided important advantages over wage labor until Democrats altered its legal context after regaining power in the 1870s. Harold D. Woodman, *New South, Old South: The Legal Foundations of Credit and Labor Relations in the Postbellum Agricultural South* (Baton Rouge: Louisiana State University Press, 1995); Robert Higgs, *Competition and Coercion: Blacks in the American Economy, 1865–1914* (Cambridge, England: Cambridge University Press, 1977), 40–53; Roger L. Ransom and Richard Sutch, "The Impact of the Civil War and Emancipation on Southern Agriculture," *Explorations in Economic History* 12 (January 1975): 1–28; Michael S. Wayne, *The Reshaping of Plantation Society: The Natchez District, 1860–1880* (Baton Rouge: Louisiana State University Press, 1983), 45–52, 110–40; Ronald L. F. Davis, *Good and Faithful Labor: From Slavery to Sharecropping in the Natchez District, 1860–1890* (Westport, Conn: Greenwood Press, 1982), 78–115; Charles L. Flynn, *White Land, Black Labor: Caste and Class in Late Nineteenth-Century Georgia* (Baton Rouge: Louisiana State University Press, 1983), 57–83; Ralph Shlomowitz, "'Bound' or 'Free'? Black Labor in Cotton and Sugarcane Farming, 1865–1880," *Journal of Southern History* 50 (November 1984): 569–96; Thavolia Glymph, "Freedpeople and Ex-Masters," in Glymph and John J. Kushma, eds., *Essays on the Postbellum Southern Economy* (College Station, Tex.: Texas A. & M. University Press, 1985), 48–72.

56. William C. Hine, "Black Politicians in Reconstruction Charleston," *Journal of Southern History* 49 (November 1983): 555–84; Thomas C. Holt, *Black Over White: Negro Political Leadership in South Carolina during Reconstruction* (Urbana: University of Illinois Press, 1977), 43–71; Holt, "Negro State Legislators in South Carolina during Reconstruction," in Howard N. Rabinowitz, ed., *Southern Black Leaders of the Reconstruction Era* (Urbana: University of Illinois Press, 1982), 223–46; David C. Rankin, "The Origins of Negro Leadership in New Orleans during Reconstruction," ibid., 155–89; Richard L. Hume, "Negro Delegates to the State Constitutional Conventions of 1867–1869," ibid., 129–53; August Meier, "Afterword: New Perspectives on the Nature of Black Political Leadership during Reconstruction," ibid., 393–406. For examples of ambitious blacks who immigrated

from the North during Reconstruction, see the essays on Aaron A. Bradley, Benjamin A. Boseman, and George T. Ruby, ibid., 281–308, 335–62, 363–92. See also Russell Duncan, *Freedom's Shore: Tunis Campbell and the Georgia Freedmen* (Athens: University of Georgia Press, 1986); Peggy Lamson, *The Glorious Failure: Black Congressman Robert Brown Elliott and the Reconstruction in South Carolina* (New York: W. W. Norton, 1973); Victor Ullman, *Martin R. Delaney: The Beginnings of Black Nationalism* (Boston: Beacon Press, 1971); Bettye J. Gardner, "William H. Foote and Yazoo County Politics, 1866–1883," *Southern Studies* 21 (Winter 1982): 398–407.

57. Occasionally, African-American politicians were frank about their reliance upon political offices for financial support. See, for example, Rapier to Henry K. Thomas, September 8, 1869, Rapier Mss., Howard University, Washington, D.C.; and Martin Delaney's request for a job from South Carolina Governor Robert K. Scott, quoted in Victor Ullman, *Martin Delaney: The Beginnings of Black Nationalism* (Boston: Beacon Press, 1971), 420. Blanche K. Bruce parlayed his earnings from political office into substantial wealth. See William C. Harris, "Blanche K. Bruce of Mississippi: Conservative Assimilationist," in Rabinowitz, *Southern Black Leaders*, 6–8. See also Lamson, *Glorious Failure*, 273–74; Euline W. Brock, "Thomas W. Cardozo: Fallible Black Reconstruction Leader," *Journal of Southern History* 47 (May 1981): 183–206; Duncan, *Freedom's Shore;* Thomas Holt, *Black over White*, 112; Eric Foner, *Reconstruction*, 361–62.

58. Michael Les Benedict, "Factionalism and Representation: Some Insight from the Nineteenth-Century United States," *Social Science History* 9 (Fall 1985): 361–98.

59. Michael Perman, *The Road to Redemption: Southern Politics, 1869–1879* (Chapel Hill: University of North Carolina Press, 1984), 22–56; Lawrence A. Powell, "The Politics of Livelihood: Carpetbaggers in the Deep South," in J. Morgan Kousser and James M. McPherson, eds., *Region, Race, and Reconstruction: Essays in Honor of C. Vann Woodward* (New York: Oxford University Press, 1982), 315–48; James L. Garner, *Reconstruction in Mississippi* (New York: Columbia University Press, 1901), 136; Thomas Holt, *Black over White*, 112; Ted Tunnell, *Crucible of Reconstruction: War, Radicalism, and Race in Louisiana, 1862–1877* (Baton Rouge, Louisiana State University Press, 1984), 148–49.

60. Unnamed black speaker in Mobile, Alabama, quoted in *Appleton's Annual Cyclopedia* (1867), 18; Edward Shaw, quoted in Armstead L. Robinson, "Beyond the Realm of Social Consensus: New Meanings of Reconstruction for American Historians," *Journal of American History* 68 (September 1981): 291.

61. Edward McPherson, *Political History during Reconstruction*, 374. These are the states in which voters were reported by race.

62. Charles H. Lewis to Senator Henry Wilson, November 19, 1867, Wilson Mss., L. C. In Louisiana, white Republican organizers reported that moderate Union men "are apprehensive that they will be thrown overboard by the negroes." "[T]hat will ruin us," one of them warned. Thomas B. Waters to Robert W. Taliaferro, May, 25, 1867, quoted in Tunnell, *Crucible of Reconstruction*, 128. Unionist leader Michael Hahn, who had served as governor of Abraham Lincoln's reconstructed

Louisiana government in 1865, echoed the complaint. "Instead of extending the Republican fold, old citizens of Union and Republican proclivities were ostracized and only new comers were placed in positions of power and emolument." Hahn, quoted in Richard N. Current, *Three Carpetbag Governors* (Baton Rouge: Louisiana State University Press, 1967), 49. U.S. Marshall J. P. M. Epping, who likewise warned against alienating southern whites, stormed out of the 1867 convention of the South Carolina Union League, blasting "[d]emagogues and renegades . . . having in view only their own selfish interests, [who] keep prating and howling about rebellion and slavery." In William C. Hine, "Frustration, Factionalism, and Failure: Black Political Leadership and the Republican Party in Reconstruction Charleston, 1865–1877" (Ph.D. diss., Kent State University, 1979), 67. North Carolina Unionist and U.S. Marshal Daniel R. Goodloe complained that the Reconstruction Act "was a signal for a scrub-race for office among demagogues. . . . Whoever made the loudest professions of devotion to black men's rights . . . was the soundest patriot. Life-long devotion to the Union . . . went for nothing." Goodloe, *The Marshalship in North Carolina* (n.p., 1869), 6. For the frustrated efforts of one influential South Carolinian to establish a Republican party that could appeal to whites, see Roger P. Leemhuis, *James L. Orr and the Sectional Conflict*, passim.

63. "Political Conditions in South Carolina," *Atlantic Monthly* 39 (February 1877): 177–94.

64. Judge Daniel L. Russell to Thomas Settle, September 16, 1874, quoted in Jeffrey J. Crow and Robert F. Durden, eds., *Maverick Republican in the Old North State: A Political Biography of Daniel L. Russell* (Baton Rouge: Louisiana State University Press, 1977), 29. See generally Current, *Those Terrible Carpetbaggers*. In Alabama, for example, more moderate Republicans allied with Governor William H. Smith and Senator Willard Warner struggled for influence with more radical Republicans allied with Senator George E. Spencer, who emerged triumphant when his faction secured control of federal patronage in 1870. Wiggins, *The Scalawag in Alabama Politics*, passim. In Mississippi, native southern Governor James Lusk Alcorn and his moderate allies battled Senator Adelbert Ames, who had come to the state as military commander in 1868. William C. Harris, *Day of the Carpetbagger: Republican Reconstruction in Mississippi* (Baton Rouge: Louisiana State University Press, 1979), 413–19, 459–80 and passim. In Louisiana, northern immigrant Governor Henry Clay Warmoth urged moderation in contrast to his rival, fellow immigrant William Pitt Kellogg and his allies among the federal officeholders. Joe Gray Taylor, *Louisiana Reconstructed, 1863–1877* (Baton Rouge: Louisiana State University, 1974), 209–52; Tunnell, *Crucible of Reconstruction*, 136–72 passim; Current, *Three Carpetbag Governors*, 49–56. In Florida, it was Governor Harrison Reed, another postwar arrival, against Senator Thomas W. Osborne and his allies among federal officeholders, who among other things rejected Reed's conciliatory program, which led him to oppose further civil-rights legislation. Canter Brown, Jr., "Carpetbagger Intrigues, Black Leadership, and a Southern Loyalist Triumph: Florida's Gubernatorial Election of 1872," *Florida Historical Quarterly* 72 (January 1994): 277–78 and passim; Jerrell H. Shofner, *Nor Is It Over Yet: Florida in the Era of Reconstruction, 1863–1877* (Gainesville: University of Florida Press, 1974),

198–224; Current, *Three Carpetbag Governors*, 20–26. South Carolina seems to have been an exception. There the Customs House faction of the party, centered in Charleston and environs and allied with conservative Republican Senator Frederick A. Sawyer, consistently bolted the party to form fusion movements with the Democrat / Conservatives. Thomas Holt, *Black over White*, 119; Hine, "Frustration, Factionalism, and Failure," passim.

65. Ames to Senator Justin S. Morrill, October 20, 1871, Morrill Mss., Manuscripts Division, L. C. Ames became governor of Mississippi in 1873, defeating Alcorn who ran as a reform Republican with Conservative backing. Harris, *Day of the Carpetbagger*, 459–80. In Louisiana, the conservative Warmoth lost control of the Republican party to Senator William Pitt Kellogg and his allies in the New Orleans customs house and other federal offices. In 1872, Kellogg was elected governor in Louisiana, defeating a coalition of Democrat / Conservatives backed by Warmoth. Taylor, *Louisiana Reconstructed*, 209–52; Tunnell, *Crucible of Reconstruction*, 170–71. In Florida, Senator Thomas W. Osborne's federal office-holder wing of the party almost succeeded in ousting conservative Republican Governor Harrison Reed through impeachment. But, in contrast to events elsewhere, Republicans then turned to a moderate native Unionist, Ossian B. Hart, as their gubernatorial candidate. Carter Brown, "Carpetbagger Intrigues," 275–301.

In South Carolina, the formerly conservative Governor Robert K. Scott responded to black criticism of his passivity in the face of the Ku Klux Klan. Moving towards the left, he retained control of the party and secured reelection in 1870. The Conservative Charleston *News and Courier* reported events as follows: "The governor, in order to make his election sure, has appealed to all the passions of the colored men—hugged them to his bosom, appointed them to office, . . . pandered to their prejudices, all for the simple purpose of driving out of the party every decent white man in it, and ruling alone." Charleston *News and Courier*, March 4, 1870. Having secured his reelection, Scott alienated many black leaders by moving back towards conservatism. Franklin J. Moses, Jr., a Scott ally who nonetheless criticized Scott's retreat, won the gubernatorial nomination and then defeated a bolting Republican ticket, organized by the conservative Republican Senator Frederick A. Sawyer and supported by Democrat / Conservatives. See Joel Williamson, *After Slavery: The Negro in South Carolina During Reconstruction, 1861–1877* (Chapel Hill: University of North Carolina Press, 1965), 190–98, 206–208, 259–66; Lamson, *Glorious Failure*, 80–173 passim.

In Texas, Governor E. J. Davis and Senator Morgan C. Hamilton seized control of the party from Hamilton's more conservative brother, Andrew J. Hamilton, by promising vigorous action to counteract anti-black and anti-Republican violence. See Charles William Ramsdell, *Reconstruction in Texas* (New York: Columbia University Press, 1910); Ernest Wallace, *The Howling of the Coyotes: Reconstruction Efforts to Divide Texas* (New York: American University Press Services, 1979); John L. Waller, *Colossal Hamilton of Texas: A Biography of Andrew Jackson Hamilton*, 122–40.

Perman describes developments generally in *The Road to Redemption*, 22–56. Events in Arkansas and North Carolina, where African Americans made up smaller proportions of the population, followed a different course. There, Republicans advocating liberality towards ex-Confederates remained powerful within the party. Persistent factionalism in both states enabled Conservative / Democrats to regain power. See Thomas S. Staples, *Reconstruction in Arkansas, 1862–1872* (New York: Columbia University Press, 1923); Justin M. Harrell, *The Brooks and Baxter War* (St. Louis: Slawson Printing Co., 1893); Carl H. Moneyhon, *The Impact of the Civil War and Reconstruction on Arkansas: Persistence in the Midst of Ruin* (Baton Rouge: Louisiana State University Press, 1994); Raper, *Holden*, passim.

66. Foner, *Reconstruction*, 350–56; Perman, *Road to Redemption*, 139–41. For these developments in Mississippi, see Harris, *Day of the Carpetbagger*, 437–52; for South Carolina, see Thomas Holt, *Black over White*, 105–10; Williamson, *After Slavery*, 258–62.

67. Goodloe, *Letter of Daniel R. Goodloe to Hon. Charles Sumner, on the Situation of Affairs in North Carolina* (n.p., 1868), 10; Goodloe, *The Marshalship in North Carolina*, 6. The quoted material is taken from both of these published letters.

68. Davis Tillson to Jacob D. Cox, November 23, 1867, Cox Mss., Oberlin College, Oberlin, Ohio. See also Judge Richard Busteed to Senator William Pitt Fessenden, March 11, 1868, Fessenden Mss., Western Reserve Historical Society, Cleveland, Ohio; Michael Hahn to Elihu B. Washburne, October 21, 1868, Washburne Mss., L.C.; J. P. M. Epping to James L. Orr, May, 1867, quoted in William C. Hine, "Frustration, Factionalism, and Failure: Black Political Leadership and the Republican Party in Reconstruction Charleston" (Ph.D. diss., Kent State University, 1979), 67.

69. For the effect of the economic collapse of 1873 on southern Republicans' economic program, see Summers, *Railroads, Reconstruction, and the Gospel of Prosperity*, 268–98. Michael Perman describes the new stress on retrenchment of expenditures in the South after 1873 without expressly linking the change to the economic downturn. See Perman, *The Road to Redemption*, 143–48.

70. For southern whites' perception that it was they who were fighting for liberty against tyranny and the public policies that led to that perception, see Michael Les Benedict, "The Problem of Constitutionalism and Constitutional Liberty in the Reconstruction South," in Kermit L. Hall and James W. Ely, eds., *An Uncertain Tradition: Constitutionalism and the History of the South* (Athens: University of Georgia Press, 1989), 225–49.

71. Historians have paid slight attention to the differences among Democrats in the Reconstruction South. The best source is Perman's *The Road to Redemption*, 149–77, which describes what Perman calls "the forked road to redemption." But Perman does not stress enough the importance of the federal threat of intervention to maintaining the moderate Democratic position.

72. The correlations between party support and the ethnocultural variables are not reciprocal for Democrats and Republicans, because the party variables are based on the proportion of the eligible electorate voting Republican or Democratic, rather than on the two-party vote. The ethnocultural variables are based on the 1870 census unless otherwise noted.

73. Dale Baum, *The Civil War Party System: Massachusetts as a Test Case, 1852–1876* (Chapel Hill: University of North Carolina Press, 1985), 125–35; Kleppner, *The Third Electoral System*, 131–39.

74. Michael Les Benedict, *A Compromise of Principle: Congressional Republicans and Reconstruction, 1863–1869* (New York: W. W. Norton, 1974), 188–209.

75. The median estimated voter turnout in the northern and border states was 61.2 percent in 1866, compared to 56.4, 57.9, and 57.3 percent for the congressional elections of 1862, 1870, and 1874.

76. In the 1864 elections the Republicans had gained 47 congressmen over their number of Republicans in the previous Congress. In the 1866 elections they lost only 6, which they gained back in the presidential election of 1868. In the succeeding off-year congressional elections of 1870, 1874, and 1878, the Republicans would lose 15, 95, and 10 seats respectively.

77. Akerman to Thomas L. Tullock, June 23, 1876, Ackerman Mss., Alderman Library, University of Virginia, Charlottesville, Virginia.

78. Richmond *Daily Dispatch*, August 30, 1876, p. 2.

79. Ibid., July 25, 1876, p. 2.

80. De Santis, *Republicans Face the Southern Question*, 66–103.

81. *New York Herald*, March 31, 1879, p. 3.

82. Joel Silbey, *A Respectable Minority*, 181–87, 200–202. There is no study of the struggle between Bourbon and liberal Democrats leading to the "New Departure" movement of 1871. It may be followed by reading such Democratic and independent Democratic organs as the *New York World*, *New York Herald*, *Chicago Times*, and the *Cincinnati Enquirer*. Jerome Mushkat discusses the New Departure movement in New York in *The Reconstruction of the New York Democracy, 1861–1874* (Rutherford, N.J.: Farleigh Dickinson University Press, 1981), 173–75, 191–92 and passim.

83. The Tenure of Office Act kept federal officers in place until their successors were confirmed, thus making every sitting officer beholden to his senator, no matter who had been most influential in securing his nomination originally. Senators established a custom of "senatorial courtesy" by which any senator could block the confirmation of a nominee offensive to him. Not only did this enable senators to protect sitting allies, it meant that any aspiring officeholder and his patron had to secure at least the acquiescence of his senator to an appointment.

Of course, this system operated only when the President and senator were of the same party. Thus it was Republican senators rather than Democrats who established predominance in their state parties during the late 1860s and the 1870s.

84. Benedict, "Factionalism and Representation," 373–74; Morton Keller, "The Triumph of Organizational Politics," chapter 7 of *Affairs of State: Public Life in the Late Nineteenth Century* (Cambridge, Mass.: Harvard University Press, 1977), 238–83.

85. Robert Michels, *Political Parties: A Sociological Study of the Oligarchical Tendencies of Modern Democracy*, trans. Eden and Cedar Paul (New York: Hearst's International Library, 1915). This rule is widely accepted in the political science lit-

erature. See E. Spencer Wellhoffer and Timothy M. Hennessey, "Political Party Development: Institutionalization, Leadership Recruitment, and Behavior," *American Journal of Political Science* 18 (February 1974): 135–65; Joseph R. Gusfield, "Social Movements: The Study of Social Movements," *International Encyclopedia of the Social Sciences*, 16 vols. (New York: Macmillan and the Free Press, 1968), 14: 445–52; Robert K. Merton, "Bureaucratic Structure and Personality," in Merton, *Social Theory and Social Structure*, rev. ed. (Glencoe, Ill.: Free Press, 1957), 195–206.

86. New York *Nation*, August 1, 1867, pp. 91–92. For a fuller discussion of the role dissident, reform-oriented Republicans played in undermining support for Reconstruction, see Michael Les Benedict, "Reform Republicans and the Retreat from Reconstruction," in Alfred Moss and Eric Anderson, eds., *The Facts of Reconstruction: Essays in Honor of John Hope Franklin* (Baton Rouge: Louisiana State University Press, 1991), 53–78. See also Foner, *Reconstruction*, 488–99.

87. For an insightful discussion of the politics of "corruption" in the Reconstruction era, see Mark Summers, *The Era of Good Stealings* (New York: Oxford University Press, 1993).

88. See Mark Summers, "The Press Gang: Corruption and the Independent Press in the Grant Era," *Congress & the Presidency* 17 (Spring 1990): 29–44.

89. Foner, *Reconstruction*, 518.

90. Silbey, *The American Political Nation*, 224–30.

91. Stanley Coben, "Northeastern Business and Radical Reconstruction: A Re-Examination," *Mississippi Valley Historical Review* 46 (June 1959): 67–90; Peter Kolchin, "The Business Press and Reconstruction, 1865–1868," *Journal of Southern History* 33 (May 1967): 183–96; Harold Francis Williamson, *Edward Atkinson: The Biography of an American Liberal, 1827–1905* (Boston: Old Corner Book Store, 1934). Currency issues were crucial in alienating much of the Republican financial community from radical Republicans. Leading radicals, such as Benjamin F. Butler, Thaddeus Stevens, and Benjamin F. Wade, opposed contracting the money supply and returning to a specie-based currency. Northeastern business and financial interests bitterly condemned their position. Benedict, *A Compromise of Principle*, 262–65. See also Robert P. Sharkey, *Money, Class, and Party: An Economic Study of Civil War and Reconstruction* (Baltimore: Johns Hopkins University Press, 1959).

92. For the relationship between the "equal-rights, no special privileges" element of free-labor ideology and laissez-faire moralism, see Michael Les Benedict, "Laissez-Faire and Liberty: A Re-Evaluation of the Meaning and Origins of Laissez-Faire Constitutionalism," *Law and History Review* 3 (Fall 1985): 361–98.

93. Albert G. Riddle, *The Life, Character, and Public Services of James A. Garfield* (Cleveland: W. W. Williams, 1881), 298.

94. Stanley P. Hirshson, *Farewell to the Bloody Shirt: Northern Republicans and the Southern Negro, 1877–1893* (Bloomington: Indiana University Press, 1962), 190–250.

4

The Politics of the Gilded Age

R. Hal Williams

A title like "The Politics of the Gilded Age" has been known to empty a room in a matter of seconds. Political history has not been in fashion until recently, and I am not sure the Gilded Age *ever* was— except, ironically, for many of those who lived in it. They liked it, thought it important, believed it a time of excitement, growth, and progress.[1]

They knew it, too, as a political time, intensely so—a period of parties and politics, dramatic campaigns, and contested elections. And it *was*: we know that from letters and newspapers, from diaries, from the willingness of people to travel miles to stand in the hot sun and listen to stump speeches that lasted three hours or more, and from the massive voter turnouts that put our own paltry participation (barely over 50 percent in the last presidential election; under 45 percent in the 1994 congressional elections) to shame.[2]

"We love our parties as we love our churches and our families," as Senator Henry Blair of New Hampshire said in 1886. "We are part of them."[3]

For a long time we historians made the mistake of forgetting that. We read our Henry Adams and James Bryce, our Matthew Josephson and Mark Twain, and we paid little attention to the actual story of politics in the Gilded Age.[4] There were exceptions, to be sure, Vincent De Santis and other talented scholars who were working in the field, but their findings somehow rarely reached the college textbooks and more general literature.[5]

As a result, the Gilded Age often wound up as either "postscript" or "background," as the era that gave away the gains of the Civil War or as stage-setting for the "real" drama, which in most studies took place just after the turn of the twentieth century.

It was "the great barbecue" the liberal reformers tried to end; "the age of negation" the progressives managed to stop; the "distended society" the bureaucratic state arose to order; "the steel chain of ideas" the reform Darwinists struggled to break; the stifling "corporate state" the Populists arrived to fight.[6]

And while the Gilded Age may have been, in one way or another, all of these things, it was rarely allowed to be just itself.[7]

That situation has now changed—and changed rather dramatically. In some of the most recent studies, in fact, the politics of the Gilded Age has become a sort of paradigm, a lesson for us now: a time of popular politics, important issues, and responsive leaders.

Not all of this is new. Revisions in our views of Gilded Age politics date at least from the 1950s and 1960s, from Professor De Santis's own work, and from the work of historians like C. Vann Woodward, H. Wayne Morgan, Geoffrey Blodgett, Lee Benson, and Samuel P. Hays.[8] Since then, the work of revision has continued at a remarkable pace, reflected in both narrative history and the quantification-minded "new" political history—"the now middle-aged, 'new' political history," as William G. Shade has recently called it.[9]

There is irony in this, of course: at the same time political history was losing its place of dominance in college classrooms and the study of the American past, political historians were producing some of their most important studies of the party system, voter behavior, party structure, and the political elite.[10]

In part, these historians reflect the interests of a new generation, discontented with modern politics, concerned about current directions, that has found things to admire in the politics of the nineteenth century, in some cases the very same things the older "progressive" historians were prone to attack.

But a great deal more has been going on than simply a generational change, the kind of periodic revival that occurs when a lake bed "churns" and renews. The newer interpretations draw on new techniques of inquiry, issues of community and gender that were hitherto unexplored, a fresh attention to words and style, and a fruitful union of political and social history that has led historians to ask new questions and to take fresh looks at old ones.

The result has been eye-opening, and it has almost completely revised our view of the politics of the Gilded Age.

The main findings of the last couple of decades are now widely accepted and can be stated fairly briefly:

After the 1830s, when state after state gave the vote to all white males regardless of birth or property, the United States had the most open electorate in the world, part of a larger sense of openness in economic and social life that restructured American society.

That electorate, to be sure, was limited to those who were male and those who were white, but it was a stunning development nonetheless, emphasized again in recent historiography, that made the United States for much of the nineteenth century the only democracy in the world. The adoption of the Fifteenth Amendment in 1870 broadened the franchise still more, to most adult males, black as well as white—at least for a time.[11]

What was more, in twenty-two states, aliens as well as citizens could vote, and in much of the country, restrictions against office-holding diminished. Alabama, Missouri, Virginia, and Arkansas no longer required that their governors be born in the United States. New Hampshire, which had mandated that only Protestants could serve in state offices, dropped that provision in 1877, as did Massachusetts for its governor in 1892, and Delaware for its United States Senators in 1897.[12]

Real issues divided the parties, and elections occurred at the pace of heartbeats; the more elections, it seemed, the better. Voters were always voting, politicians always running. The advantages of incumbency as we know them today scarcely existed. Most congressmen served only two terms, and not until 1894 did the number of so-called "safe seats" outnumber the contested ones.[13]

In an era when the state of Maine, to take just one example, elected some of its mayors in June, its governor and state legislators in September, and the president in November, the next election was always just around the corner. For politicians, that meant primary elections and caucuses; the pyramid of town, county, and state conventions; conference after conference; and weeks spent on the stump, a different town, a different audience every night: it seemed never to end. People complained of the "everlasting politics. We work through one campaign, take a bath and start in on the next," a tired politician in Iowa said.[14]

The complaint overlooked a deeper meaning. It was democracy in action, as Robert H. Wiebe has recently argued, and if, as Wiebe says, democracy is "America's most distinguishing characteristic and its most significant contribution to world history," it flowered in the Gilded Age.[15]

It flowered, in fact, between the 1830s and 1890s, and therein lies another important recent finding about the Gilded Age.

The "new" political historians—middle-aged or not—have demonstrated that in terms of politics the Gilded Age *was* part of a larger period, the third or Civil War party system: a time of intense electoral competition, new and larger polarities between the sections, greater attention to party management, evolving ideologies and style, and remarkably high voter turnout.[16]

Between the 1830s and the 1890s, Joel H. Silbey has noted, the United States was a "political nation," with a system of two-party politics "unique in its power and in its depth of social penetration."[17]

"What the theatre is to the French, or the bull-fight or fandango to the Spanish, the hustings and the ballot-box are to *our* people," as one observer said. "We are all politicians, men, women, and children."[18]

We were, indeed, or at least nearly so: during the Gilded Age, people identified with their party and clung to it with loyalty and devotion.

In part, of course, party loyalties reflected the impact of the crises of the 1850s, the Civil War, and Reconstruction, influences so deep they lasted as long as people lived. Both Republicans and Democrats tapped the Civil War as an issue, appealing to "the passions of the strife," as Thomas Ewing, Jr., a prominent Democrat, moaned about the Republicans in 1879. They "hug the war, and fondle the war, as a loving mother does her first-born babe," Ewing said; and indeed they did, but so did Ewing and the Democrats who had, we should remember, their own, more effective version of the famous "bloody shirt."[19]

If a Republican or Democrat waved the "bloody shirt," why wonder? Waving it might hide other questions, to be sure, but just as often the act brought to mind the deeper issues of the Civil War, issues that were certainly worth discussing. Five of the six presidents elected between 1865 and 1900 had served in the war, as had a great many social, economic, and religious leaders. As late as 1890 there were well over a million veterans of the Union Army still alive, and Confederate veterans numbered in the hundreds of thousands. Few of them had forgotten their experience at war, the preservation of the Union, the surrender of the South, the end of slavery. "[I]n our youth," as Oliver Wendell Holmes, Jr., once put it, "our hearts were touched with fire."[20]

The fire of party loyalty was handed down from fathers to sons, and to daughters as well. When a journalist for the Springfield (Massachusetts)

Republican got home after casting his vote in the 1864 presidential election, he called his children into the garden and, as they watched, hung a Democratic ballot on a hook and set fire to it, while the children gave three cheers for "old Abe." He wanted, the reporter said, to teach the children "their political duty in their youth."[21]

For large numbers of people the lessons stuck. Most voters, one observer said, stayed with their party from reasons of "habit, sentiment, and finally of inheritance; so that John Smith is a Republican or a Democrat because his father was one before him; and hardly asks himself seriously why he prefers his party any more than he asks why he prefers Mrs. John Smith to other women, or John Smith, Junior, to other boys. And he regards a man who 'belongs' to neither party, but alternates between them according to their varying merits, somewhat as he regards a man who has a variety of wives."[22]

But more was at work than sentiment and inheritance. Partisan loyalties, as the "new" political historians have shown, tended to reflect membership in particular ethnoreligious groups. Using computers and sophisticated statistics, several historians have demonstrated the important relationship between religion and politics, but Paul Kleppner has developed it to the fullest, arguing that the political parties "were not aggregations of individuals professing the same political doctrines but coalitions of social groups sharing similar ethnocultural values." They were "political churches," he says, and the way people voted tended to reflect their membership in a certain type of church.[23] Members of pietistic churches tended to be Republicans. Roman Catholics, German Lutherans, and other liturgical or non-moralistic groups, on the other hand, gravitated toward the Democrats.[24]

Shaped by family and religion, voting returns displayed the intensity of party loyalties. Voters tended to stay with the same party year after year, though it is now clear that third parties like the Greenback, Prohibition, and People's parties, provided a helpful way-station for those who were restive, a chance to form new voting habits and weaken the commitment to an older party.[25] But for most people, the original commitment remained strong. In presidential elections in Massachusetts between 1864 and 1896, fewer than one voter in ten crossed party lines in any set of successive elections. The choice usually was not for which party to vote; it was more often whether to vote at all.[26]

Given a choice about voting, people almost always chose to vote. Women could vote in national elections only in Wyoming and Utah, in Colorado (after 1893), and in Idaho (after 1896). In recognition of their separate "sphere," women could vote in school board elections in seventeen states, and in three states those with property could vote on measures involving taxes and bonds. African Americans, Asian Americans, and other minorities were also often kept from the polls.[27]

But among those who could vote, turnout was astonishingly high, averaging just under 80 percent of eligible voters in the presidential elections between 1868 and 1892, numbers unequaled before or since.[28] In only one presidential election—1872—did the turnout sink below 75 percent, and in 1896, almost eight voters in every ten turned out to vote for president.[29]

In parts of the North, the numbers could be dazzling. In Indiana, turnout averaged 93 percent in the presidential elections between 1868 and 1892; in New Jersey, 89 percent. In the 1896 presidential election, more than 95 percent of the eligible voters cast ballots in the Midwest. Turnouts were highest in presidential races, but participation was relatively high in congressional, gubernatorial, and local elections as well.[30]

For a time, the same held true in the "Solid South," making it a good deal less solid than it sometimes seemed. Through the 1880s, in fact, Southern politics were lively and competitive, and Southern voters turned out in numbers comparable to those outside the South. Sixty-four percent of Southern adult males, on average, voted in elections during that decade, and it is of interest, too, that turnout rates among white and black voters did not vary greatly. The turnout of African Americans in the 1880s averaged just under 61 percent, compared to 69.7 percent for white, adult males.[31]

And one last finding: Gilded Age elections were close, the closest the country has ever experienced.[32] In the five presidential races between 1876 and 1892, an average differential of only 1.4 percent separated the Republican and Democratic candidates. The Republicans managed to win three of the five races, but they captured a majority of the popular vote in none of them, and they had a plurality only once, in 1880.[33] Republicans Rutherford B. Hayes and Benjamin Harrison won the presidency in 1876 and 1888 even though they actually trailed in the popular vote. In 1880, James A. Garfield beat out Winfield Hancock by fewer than forty thousand votes, and Grover Cleveland's margin in 1884 over

James G. Blaine came to about twenty-nine thousand out of over 10 million votes cast. Narrow margins often separated candidates, and in a climate where divisive issues and splinter parties could easily tip elections one way or another, politicians understandably grew cautious.[34]

"Gridlock," a familiar word in politics today, lasted for twenty years, virtually spanning the Gilded Age. Between 1875 and 1897, Republicans or Democrats managed to control the presidency and both houses of Congress at the same time for only four years, and in neither case did it turn out much to their advantage. The Republicans and the famous "Billion Dollar Congress," in power from 1889 to 1891, lost badly in the 1890 elections, a fate the Democrats also suffered between 1893 and 1895. Running for Congress could be a tricky business: fewer than two percentage points separated the total Republican and Democratic vote for congressmen in five of the six elections between 1878 and 1888.[35]

Little wonder Mark Twain could remark that it was a good thing Congress had not been present when God said, "Let there be light," for the world would still be in darkness. Bogged down in party stalemate, subject to high member turnover, with rules that were designed to impede instead of speed, Congress rarely got near the switch.

Taken together, these findings provide a much clearer picture of politics in the Gilded Age, a measure of the striking historiographical advances of the last several decades.

In retrospect, it seems obvious the discoveries were coming. Historians who mined letters and diaries, newspapers and speeches, looking for party policy, motivation, leadership, and behavior, had questions in common with the analysts of voting behavior, who soon began turning their attention from people as voters to people as people, and to the decisions they made not only about politics, but about religion, ethnicity, the family, and community. Political history and social history became interestingly intertwined.[36]

Much of the recent research has reflected this combination of political and social history, the recognition of the value of both narrative and cliometric approaches, and an incorporation in new ways of older or ignored issues such as policy and gender.

Party ideology, one of the older issues, has attracted fresh attention. Drawing on the work of antebellum historians and political scientists, Gilded Age historians have tried to track the ideology of the political parties, the "symbols of identification or loyalty," as William Nesbit Chambers has called them.[37] The result has been a closer attention to language, to symbols, to ceremony and "style." Words and phrases, including many that were once simply dismissed as tattered threads of the "bloody shirt," have provided ways to understand party values and programs and the emotional and psychological linkages between party leaders and voters.[38]

In an era of enormous residential transiency, when less than half of a town's population might remain in the town over a ten-year period, politics and partisanship contributed an element of continuity and stability to people's lives. Newcomers to a community, accustomed to the arguments of Republicans (or Democrats) in Maine and Massachusetts, could feel more comfortable (and to some degree at home) in hearing similar words in Illinois or Wyoming. The "new Western history" has noted how much trash people dropped as they moved west, but when it came to politics and party commitments, those who moved usually took their affiliations along.[39]

Belonging to a political party, it is increasingly clear, gave people a sense of community, "an internalized sense of history, tradition, and common values."[40] When new voters arrived on the scene—from other parts of the United States, from abroad, or simply from reaching voting age—they soon joined a party community and gained an immediate role in American life. "When he first landed in New York with his wife," as Mark Twain and Charles Dudley Warner jested about the typical immigrant, "he had only halted at Castle Garden for a few minutes to receive and exhibit papers showing that he had resided in this country two years—and then he voted the democratic ticket and went up town to hunt a house."[41]

Once perceived as divisive, the parties in this sense became schools instead, teaching "seasonal courses in how to be Americans. Party activities were one of the best civics lessons the nineteenth century offered." The rituals were visible and everywhere, the language plain and understood, and it all affirmed democracy, mass participation, and the role of the "People" in the political process.[42]

Election campaigns contained ceremonies that chose, acknowledged, explained, and ratified—and that culminated in the casting of the vote on election day. The torchlight parades, mass rallies, stump speeches, and election-day barbecues involved and empowered voters, who felt

themselves part of the process. Emotion and display—the announce-
ment of a person's partisan loyalties and his vote—made that vote more
meaningful. And in all of this there was "the sense," in Michael
McGerr's words, "of politics as a cross-class mass endeavor dependent
on the visible assent of the people."[43]

And the people assented; there was plenty of evidence for that. When
James G. Blaine came to Indianapolis to stump for Benjamin Harrison
in 1888, there were 25,000 marchers, forty brass bands, and dozens of
flag-laden floats; it took an hour and a half for the marchers to pass the
reviewing stand, and something on the order of 100,000 people looked
on. During the campaign itself Harrison spoke almost daily to groups
visiting his home, in sixteen weeks welcoming 110 delegations of voters, a total of nearly 300,000 people. William McKinley went Harrison
one better. In the famous "Front Porch" campaign of 1896, as many as
750,000 persons actually visited McKinley's home, a figure that
amounted to about 5 percent of the total vote and 13 percent of the entire
Republican vote that fall.[44]

Gradually, however, the mass party style gave way to campaigns of
education and advertising, approaches that placed an emphasis on reading and reflection, on a politics of reason instead of emotion and demonstration—but a politics that was also "more elitist and less accessible to
voters." Politics stirred and involved fewer voters, emphasized the per-
sonalities of candidates, and in the absence of mass involvement, promoted the participation of pressure groups.[45]

The result, some historians have begun to think, was unfortunate.
Something important was lost, a sense of involvement, a point of vital
contact between voter and system, a feeling that democratic politics
could work. "The driving force behind 19th century democracy," Robert
H. Wiebe has said just recently, "was thousands of people spurring
thousands of other people to act. Many little favors, many personal connections, wound a host of little springs to make the mechanism work."[46]

With the turn of the twentieth century, the little springs began to wind
down. Before they did, though, they did their work, much of it, as historians have begun to rediscover, in individual communities, cities, and
states.

Gilded Age observers often took note of this fact, but we have tended
to overlook it in our own preoccupation with events in Washington. If
James Bryce missed many a point when it came to American politics, he

did not miss this one, the differing roles of the federal government and the states within the American system. The states, he noted, exerted broad powers, meddling more in society than the British Parliament did back home.[47]

In some ways, the states simply picked up new powers during the Civil War. Under the pressures of the war, governors and state legislators found themselves organizing a draft, appointing military officers, purchasing arms, and overseeing the welfare of their soldiers in the field. The Civil War, a victory for federalism over the Confederacy's version of states' rights, actually wound up empowering the states, and some of them made wide use of their new status once the war was over.[48]

Their activities expanded dramatically. Government bodies outside of Washington spent about 60 percent of all public dollars in 1880, a percentage that remained about the same twenty years later. Boston alone spent $50 a person in 1880, while the federal government spent just $5.34, and most of that went for defense and the foreign service. During the Gilded Age, about three out of every four public employees worked outside Washington.[49]

What they did deserves further study.[50] Governors, commissioners, and state legislators worked under difficult conditions. They were underpaid, they had no professional staff, and in the case of state legislators they might meet for only a month or two every other year. Yet on the whole, the states enacted a striking body of law during the last half of the nineteenth century.

Massachusetts, to take one example, passed laws that provided for compulsory education; regulated banks and railroads; created a Bureau of Labor Statistics and boards of Charities and Labor Arbitration; established a state university; offered help to disabled veterans; protected some property rights for women within their marriages; imposed a maximum ten-hour workday for women and children; required fire escapes, toilets, and proper ventilation in factories; regulated "sweat shops"; and licensed engineers, dentists, physicians, and lawyers.

And if that were not enough, it also created an Agricultural Experiment Station and a Dairy Bureau; put into effect a sanitary code for Boston; established a State Board of Health and a Metropolitan Sewer Commission; mandated regulations for water standards; outlawed the sale of adulterated food and drugs; provided state aid for highways and created a Highway Commission; instituted civil service reform in state government; adopted the Australian secret ballot; ordered the registration of lobbyists; and regulated campaign finances.[51]

Commissions and boards: historians once thought they were a sure sign of the Progressive era. Massachusetts had fifty-six of them by 1900. *"Our whole state government has gone into commission,"* Ben Butler, the Massachusetts governor and congressman, said as early as 1871.[52]

As a state, Massachusetts was more active than most, but it did not stand alone. In another tendency that foreshadowed the progressives, states copied other states in establishing government boards, and by 1900 thirty-nine of them had boards of public health, thirty-four had railroad commissions, twenty-nine had bureaus of labor or labor statistics, twenty-eight had school departments or boards, and fourteen had boards of charity. Thirteen states limited the hours that women could work each day; twenty-eight states set limits on child labor.[53]

Interesting new issues came to the forefront. In New York State, conservation became a concern, at first in efforts to preserve the country's most famous work of nature, Niagara Falls.[54] As early as 1831, Alexis de Tocqueville, America's celebrated French visitor, was urging a friend to get to the Falls soon if he wished "to see this place in its grandeur." "If you delay," Tocqueville warned, "your Niagara will have been spoiled for you. Already the forest round about is being cleared. . . . I don't give the Americans ten years to establish a saw or flour mill at the base of the Cataract."[55]

Tocqueville, as usual, was right, though it actually took only three years before the work began—on dams, mills, and assorted tourist attractions. As shops, billboards, and hotels sprang up around the Falls, Frederic Church, Frederick Law Olmsted, Henry James, Charles Eliot Norton, Henry Hobson Richardson, William Dean Howells, Ralph Waldo Emerson, Henry Wadsworth Longfellow, Francis Parkman, and John Greenleaf Whittier, among others, grew concerned.[56]

So did conservationists; *and* private interests that saw ways to profit from a rescued Falls; *and* urban reformers who thought nature alone could relieve the bleakness of urban-industrial life. The Falls, one of the leaders of the preservation campaign said, had a "peculiar power to inspire wholesome and elevated emotions, to calm the fevered unrest of our crowded, hurried modern life; to delight and reinvigorate all who feel that 'the world is too much with us, late and soon,' and to minister to the sanity and happiness of millions of toiling men and women through all coming time."[57]

Adopting the slogan: "Save Niagara Falls," the preservationists put together a lobbying effort so skillful it could provide lessons for modern-day Washington. They wrote letters, published editorials and articles, circulated pamphlets, and collected statements of support from the presidents of colleges and universities in all parts of the country. Roscoe Conkling and Governor Grover Cleveland lent a hand, and once the New York legislature passed the Niagara Reservation bill in early 1883, Cleveland immediately signed it into law. Lawsuits from owners of property near the Falls brought delays, but the Niagara Falls State Reservation opened to the public on July 15, 1885, one of the first state parks in the nation. Thirty thousand people were present for the event.[58]

Conscious that they had accomplished something important, the leaders of the Niagara campaign promptly put together a series of lessons for others, which they printed and circulated. "The effort to save Niagara," one of them said in the language of the time, "was a new experiment, and it developed some facts or laws relating to methods for the propagation of ideas which had not been so fully recognized before, and which apply equally to many things in the life and thought of our time."

There were four lessons in all, beginning with an instruction that to remove an "evil," start with "a clear and truthful description of existing conditions, with a plain, brief presentation of the remedy proposed." Second, couch what is written in terms that can be understood by "people without 'culture,' who work with their hands. What is plain to them will be understood by all others. All rhetorical indirection or display is a fatal disadvantage. Nobody now takes fine writing seriously, not even the authors of it."

Third, follow up the initial statements with "frequent, brief restatements, each complete in itself, . . . and these must be continuously varied and multiplied, without any long pause, till their cumulative effect produces a reverberation filling all the air of the time, and compelling general attention." And finally, "employ an agent," essentially a lobbyist, "who understands the evil, and believes in the remedy proposed, who shall devote his whole time and energies to the work, with a large measure of freedom of judgment and action as to methods. This agent should be able to employ the pen and the press, as well as the power of personal appeal."[59]

The lessons worked well. By the time the new Niagara park opened, preservationists in New York State had already moved on to a campaign to save the Adirondacks in the northeastern corner of the state. Along with painters and poets, this time they enlisted hunters and fishermen, the well-to-do who owned summer cottages in the area, and business-men and city officials who feared that deforestation would pollute the Hudson River and Erie Canal.[60] On May 15, 1885, Governor David B. Hill, an unlikely conservationist, signed an act establishing a state forest preserve of nearly six million acres in the Adirondacks, the largest such reserve in the United States.[61]

In recent years, as the account of the Niagara campaign suggests, his-torians have begun to examine in some detail what was going on in com-munities across the nation. We know more than we did before about events and outlooks in rural communities in upstate New York, about sanitation and water supply in New York City and Cleveland, and about the issues of language and liquor in state houses in the Midwest.[62] There and elsewhere, a great deal, it is clear, was going on. Not all the mea-sures adopted were successful, nor were all of them even wise. But in knowing something about them, the story of politics and policy in the Gilded Age has gained in richness, in complexity, and in linkages with the eras around it.

"[T]he publicists," a thoughtful commentator noted in 1883, referring to E. L. Godkin, George William Curtis, and the other sources James Bryce had consulted in forming his opinions about Gilded Age politics, "tell us we are governed too much; but the people are demanding more government, and, in obedience to this demand, law-making bodies are rapidly expanding the scope of law." Even if the publicists somehow overlooked it, the commentator said, almost every community felt it: "a body of good and earnest people [were] demanding reform, or devising methods for the improvement of mankind in diverse ways."[63]

*Man*kind, indeed.

"Polytics ain't bean bag," Mr. Dooley liked to say to his friend Hennessy over the Archey Road bar. "'Tis a man's game; an' women, childher an' pro-hybitionists do well to keep out iv it."[64]

For years, historians agreed with Mr. Dooley: to the part about women, at least, many making the simple assumption that politics *was* "a man's game," and since women could not vote, they could not act politically. In recent years political historians have changed that view and have given us the benefit of putting women back into politics, "of seeing the formerly unseen," as Nancy F. Cott has put it.[65]

The result has been not only to broaden our view of politics in general, but to sharpen our understanding of male politics as well.

Gilded Age politics, Paula Baker and others have pointed out, was filled with masculine imagery. Campaigning and voting were man's business, a chance for men to interact, a proving ground for male identity. In a thoughtful study of the idea of "manliness," Gail Bederman has recently argued that in some communities at least, it was both proving ground *and* battleground, a place of struggle between men of the middle class and men of the working class, each side competing for "control over the masculine arena of politics." In contests for the command of city governments, in uprisings during the widespread labor unrest of the period, immigrants and workers challenged the authority of middle class men: and in the cities at least, often won.[66]

Party politics, as such perspectives suggest, stressed personal character and "manly" qualities: courage, loyalty, earnestness, and self-assertion. Politicians prided themselves on their manhood; candidates campaigned on it. "I am of age," a New York politician wrote Senator David B. Hill to say that he could not be toyed with, "and must be allowed to assert my manhood, occasionally at least."[67] John R. Lynch, the last black congressman from Mississippi, told the House of Representatives in 1882 that blacks "have said to those upon whom they were dependent, you may . . . take the bread out of the mouths of my hungry and dependent families. You may close the schoolhouse door in the face of my children. Yes, more, you may take that which no man can give—my life. But my manhood, my principles, you cannot have."[68]

The ability to attend political conventions, speak on the stump, and vote became a defining characteristic of being male, a gender identification that spanned class, religious, and ethnic differences. Male rituals dominated party rallies and parades, particularly the army-style marching companies, and men staffed the conventions and party committees. On election day, the men lined up to vote in front of saloons and barber shops, masculine locations; men drank to their party's triumph, or for that matter, to its defeat; and men and boys fired the cannons that celebrated the final outcome, sometimes losing a finger or two in the process. Political parties served as a kind of male fraternal organization. "[D]evotion to party," as one historian has put it, "was a male virtue and part of a male culture."[69]

Issues like the tariff could reflect male values. Higher tariffs, Republicans argued, would not only strengthen the economy and raise wages, but enable men to keep "their wives . . . at home and their children at school." In free trade England, in contrast, women did "unwomanly work," were "begrimed from head to foot," and had to "unsex themselves in their struggle for bread." With lower tariffs and lower wages, men delayed marriage or, worse, sent pregnant wives into the factory. Reducing families to desperation, free trade would fill "the brothel as well as the jail."[70]

"Were I a woman . . . ," William K. "Pig Iron" Kelley, Philadelphia Republican congressman, high tariff advocate, and the father of Florence Kelley, said in 1864, "I would clamor for a prohibitory tariff as a means of diversifying the industry of the country. It is only in semi-barbarous regions that women . . . follow the plow."[71]

Stressing the value of "manliness," the partisan press praised "tough-minded" political leaders, whom it contrasted with effeminate Mugwumps or patrician bolters of the kind that backed Horace Greeley in 1872: "namby-pamby, goody-goody gentlemen" who "sip cold tea." They were "a third sex," a Kansas Senator said in angry scorn, with "two recognized functions. They sing falsetto, and they are usually selected as the guardians of the seraglios of Oriental despots."[72] When New York Senator Roscoe Conkling in 1877 branded George William Curtis, the editor of *Harper's Weekly* and a frequent bolter, as one of "the man milliners, the dilettanti and carpet knights of politics" who "forget that parties are not built up by deportment, or by ladies' magazines, or gush," those who heard him understood instantly the nature and gravity of the attack.[73]

But if the Conklings could make fun of men whom they identified with womanly interests, they could ill afford to overlook the growing power that women actually exerted in the political arena. Movements for temperance, for social "purity," and for a wide range of labor, educational, and local reforms all reflected women's expanded political role during the Gilded Age.[74]

In many communities, temperance sparked the first involvement. In December 1873, a lecturer from Boston spoke on temperance to an audience in Hillsboro, Ohio, a small town to the east of Cincinnati. "The Duty of Christian Women in the Cause of Temperance" was his subject, and he said that if women prayed in local saloons, they might be able to close them down. Starting early the next morning two hundred women did just that. In each saloon in town, they knelt, prayed together, and asked the owner to pour out his stock. And there the owner stood, as Mark Twain said, waiting meekly "behind his bar, under the eyes of a great concourse of ladies who are better than he is and are aware of it, and hear[ing] all the iniquities of his business divulged to the angels above, accompanied by the sharp sting of wishes for his regeneration, which imply an amount of need for it which is in the last degree uncomfortable to him. If he holds out bravely, the crusaders hold out more bravely still. . . ."[75]

Spreading from town to town—through Ohio, Michigan, Indiana, and New Jersey, twenty-three states in all—the movement became the Woman's Crusade, "the first women's mass movement in American history."[76]

It closed countless bars and breweries, though many of them briefly. Saloonkeepers fought back, as did many voters who liked their drink or valued personal liberties. By the fall of 1874 the Woman's Crusade was dead, but it had "taught women," as Frances Willard, the well-known temperance leader, said, "their power to transact business, to mold public opinion by public utterance. . . ."[77]

Willard herself went on to lead the Women's Christian Temperance Union, the single largest women's organization of the century. In the WCTU, many women found their voice, and they turned more and more to social and political reform. Of the organization's thirty-nine social action departments in 1896, twenty-five dealt with issues like prison reform, woman suffrage, child labor, and improved working conditions for women who worked.[78]

Recent studies have also brought to light the network of women's clubs that used politics and persuasion to get political results. One of them, the Philadelphia Working Women's Society, convinced the Pennsylvania legislature to pass a law in 1889 regulating the employment of women and children and providing for two women factory inspectors to enforce it—the first female factory inspectors in the country. The Chicago Woman's Club, founded in 1876, adopted the motto "Nothing Human can be Alien to Us" and worked for the eight-hour day, prison reform, and seats for women on Chicago's board of education.[79] Across the country women joined clubs by the hundreds of thousands. "In Puritan days," one woman said in 1898, "the test of right living was church membership, now the test seems to be club membership."[80]

With the role of gender added in, the world of Gilded Age politics has taken on sharper meaning and importance, not only the story of currency and tariffs but the unfolding of an often local and personal affair: subtle, complex, gradual, built in part of human interactions, and in the end promotive of change. The political worlds of men and women, far from being separate spheres, interacted to shape politics and gender roles. Earlier than men, women engaged in organized, interest-group politics of the modern kind, a policy that men, too, gradually adopted. Through politics, Gilded Age men pursued their vision of a properly ordered social world, while women exploited the idea of domesticity to increase their political influence. Politics, in short, became "a public space where the ideals of manhood and womanhood could be acted out."[81]

The recent scholarship, it should be noted, has not blinked at the darker side of Gilded Age politics. There was corruption, to be sure, and racism of the worst sort, and maltreatment of women and others; there were issues missed and opportunities overlooked. The newspaper editor who warned of the 1884 presidential campaign that "Whiskey will be drunk, crime will be committed, boys ruined, industrious men made politicians, bad blood engendered, bad passions excited, and when it is all over, there will come a wild scramble for the loaves and fishes"— knew something about American politics.[82]

But the pendulum of Gilded Age political historiography has clearly swung. The movement is welcome, signifying an intent to take these years, like any others, with the seriousness they deserve. And so far, the dividends have been handsome. In the last several decades, the political history of the Gilded Age has been rewritten, with the promise of further insights, new questions, and a great many areas yet to explore.[83]

While there are certain to be some surprises, the upcoming agenda is fairly clear:

There is room, for example, for further exploration of the ethnoreligious model, especially in light of recent work that suggests other patterns in some counties and communities.[84] What do we do with the many people—a quarter or more of the population in some areas—who had no church affiliation at all, the "nothingarians," as the nineteenth century liked to call them?[85] And what, too, can be made of J. Morgan Kousser's recent appeal to go beyond "the static cultural determinism of the ethnocultural school," to integrate more fully "economic and political history, electoral behavior and policy, and thought and action"?[86]

We can make, it is clear, a great deal of it all. We know a lot about some communities and states in the urban North, a lot less about communities in the South and West and rural areas of the North.[87] Work on gender and politics, so excitingly begun, should continue. It would be valuable to learn more about the role of class and, as Kousser suggests, the interplay of economic issues, both of which received relatively scant attention in the studies of the 1970s and 1980s.[88] Key relationships—those, for example, between voting and issues; between voting and policy; among communities; and between community and nation—need development, as does our knowledge of party symbols and ideology, party organization, and the nature of political decision making.[89] Richard L. McCormick's repeated pleas that we "put governance back into the study of party history" deserve some answers.[90]

When Horace Greeley, the savvy editor of the New York *Tribune*, remarked in the late 1860s that the Democratic party had emerged from the Civil War as nothing more than "a myth, a reminiscence, a voice from the tomb, an ancient and fishlike smell," he woefully underestimated that party's resilience, a fact that has become apparent in the work of the "new" political historians. As early as 1868 the Democrats came close—astonishingly close, in the opinion of Republican leaders like Blaine—to beating Ulysses S. Grant, the great hero of the Union Army, and by 1874 they had retaken control of the House of Representatives, a control they maintained for all but four of the succeeding twenty years. Throughout the Gilded Age, Democratic doctrines appealed to large numbers of Americans. Yet there are few studies of the party at various levels, its organization and principles, its leadership, and its ongoing attraction to voters.[91]

In another important development, political scientists working on realignment theory have begun to think that political leaders and government policy play a crucial role in *confirming* electoral realignments, a conclusion that places leaders and their policies, as well as voters, at the core of American politics.[92] Along similar lines, studies of antebellum politics have shown the dynamic way in which voters responded to the economic policies of the Whigs and Democrats, a line of inquiry that might also bear fruit in the Gilded Age.[93] The data on population turnover suggest that political leaders often faced a daunting task, sitting atop a shifting electorate whose very mobility lay at odds with their own goals of political stability, ongoing policy, and reelection. "What was the role," as one scholar has recently asked, "of political life—participation, leadership, party, and elections—in continually integrating successive waves of transients and newcomers into the American community?"[94]

Political leadership in general deserves fresh scrutiny in light of the recent scholarship, including up-to-date biographies of major figures like Blaine, John Sherman, and Benjamin Harrison. Katherine Kish Sklar's new *Florence Kelley* opens numerous pathways, and a recent account of the troubled, patient, and loving marriage of Lucretia and James Garfield suggests what can be learned, even politically, from affairs of the heart.[95]

Put together, studies like these will add to the understanding of the "host of little springs" behind Gilded Age politics. Perhaps, as some historians are beginning to point out, there is even a lesson or two to be learned from the nineteenth century as the country creeps nearer the twenty-first. As public interest in politics and political history has dwindled in recent decades, John Morton Blum, among others, has lamented the loss, noting that political history at its best served to instruct generations of Americans in matters of government, leadership, and the law, "the creative possibilities for the state," Blum says, "and, too, the corruptibility of power."[96]

Most indications, including recent survey data, suggest that a large percentage of the population has little confidence in parties and politics just now, but it may be that matters have simply come full circle.[97] *George*, the nation's new political magazine—John F. Kennedy, Jr., at the helm; its first issue bearing a cover photograph of model Cindy Crawford dressed in George Washington coattails and powdered wig, a ruffled sports bra, and exposed navel—has been greeted as "yet another step between the ever-merging world of politics and entertainment."[98] There are ways in which the people of the Gilded Age would have readily understood this phenomenon.

And for Vincent De Santis, author of the influential *Republicans Face the Southern Question*, his work, I fear, is cut out for him, despite the pleasures of retirement. As Southern politicians—one after the other—switch to the Republican party; as Southerners themselves—one after the other—vote increasingly Republican; as the South once again takes on the old one-party hue: he must now turn to writing that crucial book—*Democrats Face the Southern Question*.

Notes

1. So much so that E. L. Youmans, editor of *Popular Science Monthly*, said in 1878 that nineteenth-century science had made even the doctrine of hell obsolete: E. L. Youmans, "Concerning the Belief in Hell," *The Popular Science Monthly* 12 (March 1878): 627–30, quoted in James J. Farrell, *Inventing the American Way of Death, 1830–1920* (Philadelphia, 1980), p. 82. Paula Baker, on the other hand, has beautifully described the deep suspicion of change and progress in communities that felt left behind: Paula Baker, *The Moral Frameworks of Public Life: Gender, Politics, and the State in Rural New York, 1870–1930* (New York, 1991), pp. 3–23.

2. Paul Kleppner, *The Third Electoral System, 1853–1892: Parties, Voters, and Political Cultures* (Chapel Hill, N.C., 1979), p. xv; New York *Times*, June 11, 1995.

3. Henry Blair, *One Hundred Years of Temperance* (New York, 1886), p. 85, quoted in Richard J. Jensen, *The Winning of the Midwest: Social and Political Conflict, 1888–1896* (Chicago, 1971), p. 3n.

4. For a recent demonstration of how to use Henry Adams to misread Gilded Age politics, see the extraordinary implication that James G. Blaine conspired in the assassination of President James A. Garfield, in Edward Chalfant, *Better in Darkness, A Biography of Henry Adams: His Second Life, 1862–1891* (New York, 1994), pp. 815–16n. Better in darkness, indeed.

5. For a commentary on the failure of college-level textbooks to reflect recent work on the Gilded Age, see Ballard Campbell, Jr., "Gilded Age Politics, The Textbooks, and Noncentralized Governance," paper given to the Organization of American Historians at the Annual Meeting, Washington, D.C., March 30, 1995. For De Santis, see Vincent P. De Santis, *Republicans Face the Southern Question: The New Departure Years, 1877–1897* (Baltimore, Md., 1959), and a perceptive recognition of his findings in the review by W. R. Brock, in *The English Historical Review* 76 (July 1961): 541–42.

6. Respectively, of course, Vernon Louis Parrington, *Main Currents in American Thought*, vol. 3, *The Beginnings of Critical Realism in America, 1860–1920* (New York, 1930), p. 23; Charles A. and Mary R. Beard, *The Rise of American Civilization* (New York, 1927), 2:341; Robert H. Wiebe, *The Search for Order, 1877–1920* (New York, 1967); Eric F. Goldman, *Rendezvous with Destiny: A History of Modern American Reform* (New York, 1952); Lawrence Goodwyn, *Democratic Promise: The Populist Moment in America* (New York, 1976).

7. Howard Mumford Jones, *The Age of Energy: Varieties of American Experience, 1865–1915* (New York, 1970), p. 16, tellingly makes this point in connection with art history. Also, Geoffrey Blodgett, "A New Look at the American Gilded Age," *Historical Reflections* 1 (Winter 1974): 231–34.

8. C. Vann Woodward, *Reunion and Reaction: The Compromise of 1877 and the End of Reconstruction* (Boston, 1951), *Origins of the New South, 1877–1913* (Baton Rouge, La., 1951), and *The Strange Career of Jim Crow* (New York, 1955); H. Wayne Morgan, ed., *The Gilded Age* (Syracuse, N.Y., 1963 / 1970), and *From Hayes to McKinley: National Party Politics, 1877–1896* (Syracuse, N.Y., 1969); Geoffrey Blodgett, *The Gentle Reformers: Massachusetts Democrats in the*

Cleveland Era (Cambridge, Mass., 1966); Lee Benson, "Research Problems in American Political Historiography," in Mirra Komarovsky, ed., *Common Frontiers of the Social Sciences* (Glencoe, Ill., 1957), pp. 113–83, and *The Concept of Jacksonian Democracy: New York as a Test Case* (Princeton, N.J., 1961); Samuel P. Hays, "History as Human Behavior," *Iowa Journal of History* 58 (July 1960): 193–206; and "The Social Analysis of American Political History, 1880–1920," *Political Science Quarterly* 80 (September 1965): 373–94. Vincent P. De Santis reviews the literature in "American Politics in the Gilded Age," *Review of Politics* 25 (October 1963): 551–61; "The Political Life of the Gilded Age: A Review of the Recent Literature," *The History Teacher* 9 (November 1975): 73–106; and "The Gilded Age in American History," *Hayes Historical Journal* 7 (1988): 38–57. Also, Walter T. K. Nugent, "Politics from Reconstruction to 1900," in William H. Cartwright and Richard L. Watson, Jr., eds., *The Reinterpretation of American History and Culture* (Washington, D.C., 1973), pp. 377–99.

9. L. Sandy Maisel and William G. Shade, eds., *Parties and Politics in American History: A Reader* (New York, 1994), p. 11.

10. As Joel H. Silbey notes in *The American Political Nation, 1838–1893* (Stanford, Cal., 1991), p. vii.

11. For the most recent and one of the most forceful statements, see Robert H. Wiebe, *Self-Rule: A Cultural History of American Democracy* (Chicago, 1995), pp. 1–85. Robert J. Steinfeld, "Property and Suffrage in the Early American Republic," *Stanford Law Review* 41 (January 1989): 335–76; and Chilton Williamson, *American Suffrage: From Property to Democracy, 1760–1860* (Princeton, N.J., 1960), trace the changes in suffrage requirements.

12. Morton Keller, *Affairs of State: Public Life in Late Nineteenth Century America* (Cambridge, Mass., 1977), pp. 522–23.

13. Donald A. Gross and James C. Garand, "The Vanishing Marginals, 1824–1980," *The Journal of Politics* 46 (February 1984): 226–28; James C. Garand and Donald A. Gross, "Changes in the Vote Margins for Congressional Candidates: A Specification of Historical Trends," *The American Political Science Review* 78 (March 1984): 17–30; Silbey, *American Political Nation*, pp. 185–86, 247; Morris P. Fiorina, David W. Rohde, and Peter Wissel, "Historical Changes in House Turnover," in Norman J. Ornstein, ed., *Congress in Change: Evolution and Reform* (New York, 1975), pp. 24–38. State legislatures also experienced high member turnover: Ballard C. Campbell, *Representative Democracy: Public Policy and Midwestern Legislatures in the Late Nineteenth Century* (Cambridge, Mass., 1980), pp. 31–45. On the issues dividing the parties, see Lewis L. Gould, "The Republican Search for a National Majority," in H. Wayne Morgan, *The Gilded Age*, pp. 171–87; Gould, "New Perspectives on the Republican Party, 1877–1913," *The American Historical Review* 77 (October 1972): 1074–82; and Robert S. Salisbury, "The Republican Party and Positive Government: 1860–1890," *Mid-America* 68 (January 1986): 15–34.

14. George M. Titus, "The Battle for Biennial Elections," *Annals of Iowa* 29 (January 1948): 164–65. Also, Joel H. Silbey, "Party Organization in Nineteenth-Century America," in Maisel and Shade, *Parties and Politics in American History*, pp. 83–101.

15. Wiebe, *Self-Rule*, p. 1.

16. Kleppner, *Third Electoral System*, pp. xv, 19–47; William N. Chambers, "Party Development and the American Mainstream," and Walter Dean Burnham, "Party Systems and the Political Process," both in William N. Chambers and Walter Dean Burnham, eds., *The American Party System: Stages of Political Development* (New York, 1967), pp. 3, 289–304; V. O. Key, Jr., "A Theory of Critical Elections," *Journal of Politics* 17 (February 1955): 3–18. For some cautionary thoughts about the idea of party systems, see Lee Benson and Joel H. Silbey, "Toward a Theory of Stability and Change in American Voting Patterns: New York State, 1792–1970," in Joel H. Silbey et al., eds., *The History of American Electoral Behavior* (Princeton, N.J., 1978), pp. 78–105.

17. Silbey, *American Political Nation*, p. 1, and quoting Morton Keller, "Powers and Rights: Two Centuries of American Constitutionalism," *Journal of American History* 74 (December 1987): 679.

18. Joseph Baldwin, *Party Leaders* (New York, 1855), p. 278, quoted in Jensen, *Winning of the Midwest*, p. 3.

19. "First Roar of the Democratic Gun!" Ovation to Ohio's Next Governor, Hon. Thos. Ewing, Washington, D.C., June 6, 1879, quoted in Silbey, *American Political Nation*, p. 219.

20. [Oliver Wendell Holmes, Jr.], *Speeches by Oliver Wendell Holmes* (Boston, 1891), p. 11; Theda Skocpol, "America's First Social Security System: The Expansion of Benefits for Civil War Veterans," *Political Science Quarterly* 108 (Spring 1993): 85–116; Paul H. Buck, *The Road to Reunion, 1865–1900* (Boston, 1937), pp. 44–114; Robert B. Beath, *History of the Grand Army of the Republic* (New York, 1888), p. 695.

21. Dale Baum, *The Civil War Party System: The Case of Massachusetts, 1848–1876* (Chapel Hill, N.C., 1984), p. 8; Joel H. Silbey, *A Respectable Minority: The Democratic Party in the Civil War Era, 1860–1868* (New York, 1977), pp. 5–14; Richard Hofstadter, *The Idea of a Party System: The Rise of Legitimate Opposition in the United States, 1780–1840* (Berkeley, 1969); Ronald P. Formisano, "Political Character, Antipartyism and the Second Party System," *American Quarterly* 21 (Winter 1969): 683–709; Norman H. Nie, Sidney Verba, and John R. Petrocik, *The Changing American Voter* (Cambridge, Mass., 1976), pp. 44–45, 59; Angus Campbell, Philip E. Converse, Warren E. Miller, and Donald E. Stokes, *The American Voter* (New York, 1960), pp. 146–49.

22. George S. Merriam, *The Life and Times of Samuel Bowles* (New York, 1885), 2:222–23. As Brand Whitlock, the progressive reformer and mayor of Toledo, Ohio, recalled of his youth: "in the Ohio of those days it was natural to be a Republican; it was more than that, it was inevitable that one should be a Republican; it was not a matter of intellectual choice, it was a process of biological selection. The Republican party . . . was a fundamental and self-evident thing, like life, and liberty, and the pursuit of happiness, or like the flag, or the federal judiciary. It was elemental, like gravity, the sun, the stars, the ocean. It was merely a synonym for patriotism, another name for the nation." Brand Whitlock, *Forty Years of It* (New York, 1914), p. 27. A young man from South Carolina or Georgia could have made the same statement about the Democratic party.

23. Kleppner, *Third Electoral System*, pp. 144, 189. For amplification of the eth-
noreligious interpretation (other than in the key works of Jensen, Kleppner, and
McSeveney, cited elsewhere), see Frederick C. Luebke, *Immigrants and Politics:
The Germans of Nebraska, 1880–1900* (Lincoln, Neb., 1969); Ronald P. Formisano,
"The Invention of the Ethnocultural Interpretation," *The American Historical
Review* 99 (April 1994): 453–77; Formisano, "The New Political History,"
International Journal of Social Education 1 (Autumn 1986): 5–21; Peter H.
Argersinger and John W. Jeffries, "American Electoral History: Party Systems and
Voting Behavior," in Samuel Long, ed., *Research in Micropolitics: Voting Behavior*
(Greenwich, Conn., 1986), 1:1–33; Samuel T. McSeveney, "Ethnic Groups, Ethnic
Conflicts, and Recent Quantitative Research in American Political History,"
International Migration Review 7 (Spring 1973): 14–33; Joel H. Silbey, " 'Let the
People See': Reflections on Ethnoreligious Forces in American Politics," in Silbey,
The Partisan Imperative: The Dynamics of American Politics Before the Civil War
(New York, 1985), pp. 69–84; and Robert P. Swierenga, "Ethnoreligious Political
Behavior in the Mid-Nineteenth Century: Voting, Values, Cultures," in Mark A.
Noll, ed., *Religion and American Politics: From the Colonial Period to the 1980s*
(New York, 1990), pp. 146–71. Questions about the ethnoreligious interpretation
can be found in Richard L. McCormick, "Ethno-Cultural Interpretations of
Nineteenth-Century American Voting Behavior," *Political Science Quarterly* 89
(June 1974): 351–77; J. Morgan Kousser, "The 'New Political History': A
Methodological Critique," *Reviews in American History* 4 (March 1976): 1–14;
Paula Baker, "The Culture of Politics in the Late Nineteenth Century: Community
and Political Behavior in Rural New York," *Journal of Social History* 18 (Winter
1984): 173–74; Melvyn Hammarberg, *The Indiana Voter: The Historical Dynamics
of Party Allegiance During the 1870s* (Chicago, 1977); and James E. Wright, "The
Ethnocultural Model of Voting: A Behavioral and Historical Critique," in Allan G.
Bogue, ed., *Emerging Theoretical Models in Social and Political History* (Beverly
Hills, Cal., 1973), pp. 35–56. Allan G. Bogue, *Clio and the Bitch Goddess:
Quantification in American Political History* (Beverly Hills, Cal., 1983), and
Bogue, "The Quest for Numeracy: Data and Methods in American Political
History," *Journal of Interdisciplinary History* 21 (Summer 1990): 89–116, nicely
describe the changing methodologies.

24. Benson, *Concept of Jacksonian Democracy*, p. 165; Jensen, *Winning of the
Midwest*, pp. 58–88; Paul Kleppner, *The Cross of Culture: A Social Analysis of
Midwestern Politics, 1850–1900* (New York, 1970), pp. 35–91, and Kleppner, *Third
Electoral System*, pp. 143–97; Richard Jensen, "The Religious and Occupational
Roots of Party Identification: Illinois and Indiana in the 1870s," *Civil War History*
16 (December 1970): 325–43.

25. Paul Kleppner, "The Greenback and Prohibition Parties," in Arthur M.
Schlesinger, Jr., *History of U.S. Political Parties*, vol. 2, *1860–1910: The Gilded
Age of Politics* (New York, 1973), p. 1550.

26. Baum, *Civil War Party System*, p. 20; Walter Dean Burnham, "The 'System
of 1896' and the American Electorate," in Burnham, *Critical Elections and the
Mainsprings of American Politics* (New York, 1970), p. 73.

27. Keller, *Affairs of State*, p. 442; Paula Baker, "The Domestication of Politics: Women in American Political Society, 1780–1920," *American Historical Review* 89 (June 1984): 634n.

28. And the figure would have been even higher were it not for a substantial drop in the vote in several states in the South.

29. On voting turnout, see Walter Dean Burnham, "The Changing Shape of the American Political Universe," *American Political Science Review* 59 (March 1965): 7–28; Burnham, *Critical Elections and the Mainsprings of American Politics*, pp. 18–21, 71–91; Burnham, "Those High Nineteenth-Century American Voting Turnouts: Fact or Fiction?" *Journal of Interdisciplinary History* 16 (Spring 1986): 613–44; Samuel T. McSeveney, *The Politics of Depression: Political Behavior in the Northeast, 1893–1896* (New York, 1972), pp. 3–31; and Gary W. Cox and J. Morgan Kousser, "Turnout and Rural Corruption: New York as a Test Case," *American Journal of Political Science* 25 (November 1981): 646–63.

30. U.S. Bureau of the Census, "Voter Participation in Presidential Elections by State: 1824 to 1968," in *Historical Statistics of the United States from Colonial Times to 1970, Bicentennial Edition* (Washington, D.C., 1975), 2:1071–72; Jensen, *Winning of the Midwest*, p. 2; Silbey, *American Political Nation*, p. 219.

31. J. Morgan Kousser, *The Shaping of Southern Politics: Suffrage Restriction and the Establishment of the One-Party South, 1880–1910* (New Haven, Conn., 1974), pp. 2–3, 12–29, 224–29 (the figure of 64 percent is for selected elections: pp. 224–25); J. Morgan Kousser, "Post-Reconstruction Suffrage Restriction in Tennessee: A New Look at the V. O. Key Thesis," *Political Science Quarterly* 88 (December 1973): 655–83; Kleppner, *Third Electoral System*, pp. 99–100; Jerrold G. Rusk and John J. Stucker, "The Effect of the Southern System of Election Laws on Voting Participation: A Reply to V. O. Key, Jr.," in Silbey et al., *History of American Electoral Behavior*, pp. 198–250.

32. For an excellent brief summary of Gilded Age elections, see McSeveney, *Politics of Depression*, pp. 3–31.

33. And then it was about one-tenth of one percent, or 9,457 votes out of 9.2 million votes cast.

34. "Electoral and Popular Vote Cast for President, by Political Party: 1789 to 1968," *Historical Statistics of the United States*, 2:1073; Vincent P. De Santis, "National Politics in the Gilded Age," in Vincent P. De Santis, J. Joseph Huthmacher, and Benjamin W. Labaree, *America Past and Present: An Interpretation with Readings* (Boston, 1968), 2:150–51; Peter F. Nardulli, "A Normal Vote Approach to Electoral Change: Presidential Elections, 1828–1984," in *Political Behavior* 16 (December 1994): 483–84; and Charles W. Calhoun, "The Political Culture: Public Life and the Conduct of Politics," in Charles W. Calhoun, ed., *The Gilded Age: Essays on the Origins of Modern America* (Wilmington, Del., 1995), pp. 189–90.

New York State, one of the most important states in the era's electoral politics, reflected the close competition between parties from 1860 to 1892. The Democrats' mean share of the vote in those years was 49.1 percent, the Republicans' 48.9 percent. The average difference between the parties in an election was a mere 3.2 percent; eleven times it was less than two percent: Lee Benson, Joel H. Silbey, and Phyllis F. Field, "Toward a Theory of Stability and Change in American Voting Patterns: New York State, 1792–1970," in Silbey et al., *History of American Electoral Behavior*, pp. 92–94.

35. Jensen, *Winning of the Midwest*, p. 10; R. Hal Williams, *Years of Decision: American Politics in the 1890s* (New York, 1978), pp. 19–96; James A. Garfield, "A Century of Congress," *Atlantic Monthly* 40 (July 1877): 49–64. Margaret Susan Thompson, "Corruption—Or Confusion? Lobbying and Congressional Government in the Early Gilded Age," *Congress and the Presidency* 10 (Autumn 1983): 169–93, and Thompson, *The "Spider Web": Congress and Lobbying in the Age of Grant* (Ithaca, N.Y., 1985), detail the difficulties Congress faced.

36. Too much so for some political historians: see, e.g., J. Morgan Kousser, "Restoring Politics to Political History," *Journal of Interdisciplinary History* 12 (Spring 1982): 569–95. "Political history is in danger of becoming a mere branch of social history": p. 569. See, on the other hand, Samuel P. Hays, "Politics and Social History: Toward a New Synthesis," in James B. Gardner and George Rollie Adams, eds., *Ordinary People in Everyday Life: Perspectives on the New Social History* (Nashville, Tenn., 1983), pp. 161–79; and Hays, "Politics and Society: Beyond the Political Party," in Paul Kleppner et al., *The Evolution of American Electoral Systems* (Westport, Conn., 1981), p. 246. Richard L. McCormick, "The Social Analysis of American Political History—After Twenty Years," in Richard L. McCormick, *The Party Period and Public Policy: American Politics from the Age of Jackson to the Progressive Era* (New York, 1986), pp. 89–140, reviews the most important findings.

37. Chambers, "Party Development and the American Mainstream," in Chambers and Burnham, *American Party Systems*, p. 5; Lucien Pye and Sidney Verba, *Political Culture and Political Development* (Princeton, N.J., 1965), p. 513.

"Ideology," as Samuel P. Hays has noted, "constitutes a linkage between voters and party; it forms the context of explanation as to current affairs, past history, and future hopes, all of which establish the party as worthy of commitment." Samuel P. Hays, "Society and Politics: Politics and Society," *Journal of Interdisciplinary History* 15 (Winter 1985): 490.

For work on antebellum ideology, see Lance Banning, *The Jeffersonian Persuasion: Evolution of a Party Ideology* (Ithaca, N.Y., 1978), p. 15; Bruce Collins, "The Ideology of the Ante-bellum Northern Democrats," *Journal of American Studies* 11 (April 1977): 103–21; Jean H. Baker, *Affairs of Party: The Political Culture of Northern Democrats in the Mid-Nineteenth Century* (Ithaca, N.Y., 1983); and William E. Gienapp, *The Origins of the Republican Party, 1852–1856* (New York, 1987).

38. See, e.g., Kleppner, *Third Electoral System*, pp. 74–96, 103; Silbey, *American Political Nation*, pp. 196–97, 216–18; Samuel P. Hays, "Political Parties and the Community-Society Continuum," in Chambers and Burnham, *American Party System*, p. 161; Joel H. Silbey, Allan G. Bogue, and William H. Flanigan, "Introduction," in Silbey et al., *History of American Electoral Behavior*, p. 3; Robert K. Kelley, "Ideology and Political Culture from Jefferson to Nixon," *The American*

Historical Review 82 (June 1977): 531–62; and Jo Freeman, "The Political Culture of the Democratic and Republican Parties," *Political Science Quarterly* 101, no. 3 (1986): 327–56.

39. Although her data was limited to one county in New York State, Paula Baker has argued that this might not be the case, suggesting that despite their nationally oriented appeals and policies, "parties meant different things to voters in different places." Some newcomers even changed parties to fit in with their new community: Paula Baker, "The Culture of Politics in the Late Nineteenth Century: Community and Political Behavior in Rural New York," *Journal of Social History* 18 (Winter 1984): 167–93. On the other hand, see the arguments of Wiebe, *Self-Rule*, pp. 75–85; Lewis L. Gould, *Wyoming: A Political History, 1868–1896* (New Haven, Conn., 1968), pp. 1–22; and Howard Roberts Lamar, *Dakota Territory, 1861–1889: A Study of Frontier Politics* (New Haven, Conn., 1956), among many others. Paul F. Bourke and Donald A. DeBats, "Individuals and Aggregates: A Note on Historical Data and Assumptions," *Social Science History* 4 (May 1980): 238–47, consider the problems that transiency poses for voting studies. Richard Jensen questions whether so much transiency occurred at all: "History from a Deck of IBM Cards," *Reviews in American History* 6 (June 1978): 233. Using poll book data, Kenneth J. Winkle has found widespread migration in certain Ohio townships, in which transient voters entered a town's electorate soon after arrival and then withdrew, in a pattern that occurred over and over again: Winkle, "A Social Analysis of Voter Turnout in Ohio, 1850–1860," *Journal of Interdisciplinary History* 13 (Winter 1983): 411–35. Howard P. Chudacoff, *Mobile Americans: Residential and Social Mobility in Omaha, 1880–1920* (New York, 1972), pp. 130–47, finds some complex patterns, including a higher voting rate among people who moved than among those who did not.

40. Silbey, *American Political Nation*, p. 216.

41. Mark Twain and Charles Dudley Warner, *The Gilded Age: A Tale of To-Day* (Hartford, Conn., 1873), pp. 301–2.

42. Jean H. Baker, "The Ceremonies of Politics: Nineteenth-Century Rituals of National Affirmation," in William J. Cooper, Jr., Michael F. Holt, and John McCardell, eds., *A Master's Due: Essays in Honor of David Herbert Donald* (Baton Rouge, La., 1985), pp. 168–75 (quotation is from p. 168); Michael McGerr, "Political Style and Women's Power, 1830–1930," *The Journal of American History* 77 (December 1990): 865; Susan G. Davis, *Parades and Power: Street Theatre in Nineteenth-Century Philadelphia* (Philadelphia, 1986).

43. McGerr, "Political Style and Women's Power," pp. 865–70 (quotation is from p. 870). Also, William E. Gienapp, " 'Politics Seem To Enter into Everything': Political Culture in the North, 1840–1860," in William E. Gienapp, Thomas B. Alexander, Michael F. Holt, Steven E. Maizlish, and Joel H. Silbey, eds., *Essays on American Antebellum Politics, 1840–1860* (College Station, Tex., 1982), pp. 14–66; and Paul F. Bourke and Donald A. DeBats, "Identifiable Voting in Nineteenth-Century America: Toward a Comparison of Britain and the United States Before the Secret Ballot," in Donald Fleming, *Perspectives in American History* 11 (1977–1978): 259–88.

44. Jensen, *Winning of the Midwest*, pp. 13–14; Harrison to Levi P. Morton, Oct. 29, 1888, Levi P. Morton Papers, New York Public Library; Harry J. Sievers, *Benjamin Harrison*, vol. 2, *Hoosier Statesman: From the Civil War to the White House, 1865–1888* (New York, 1959), pp. 371, 423–25; Burnham, "The 'System of 1896' and the American Electorate," in Burnham, *Critical Elections and the Mainsprings of American Politics*, p. 73.

45. McGerr, "Political Style and Women's Power," p. 869; McGerr, *The Decline of Popular Politics: The American North, 1865–1928* (New York, 1986); Richard Jensen, "Armies, Admen and Crusaders: Types of Interparty Election Campaigns," *The History Teacher* 2 (January 1969): 33–50. Also, Jerrold G. Rusk, "The Effect of the Australian Ballot Reform on Split Ticket Voting: 1876–1908," *American Political Science Review* 64 (December 1970): 1226; and L. E. Fredman, *The Australian Ballot: The Story of an American Reform* (East Lansing, Mich., 1968).

46. Wiebe, *Self-Rule*, p. 71.

47. James Bryce, *The American Commonwealth* (London, 1888), 1:432–52, 2:145–71. A citizen paid his direct taxes to officials acting under state laws, Bryce noted. "The State . . . registers his birth, appoints his guardian, pays for his schooling, gives him a share in the estate of his father deceased, licenses him when he enters a trade . . . marries him, divorces him, entertains civil actions against him, declares him a bankrupt, hangs him for murder. The police that guard his house, the local boards which look after the poor, control highways, impose water rates, manage schools—all these derive their legal powers from his State alone." Quoted in Campbell, *Representative Democracy*, p. 2.

48. Bryce, *American Commonwealth*, 1:500–501. In the post-war years, the Supreme Court gave broad discretion to both state and federal legislatures: *Veazie Bank v Fenno*, 8 Wall. 533, 548 (1870); Keller, *Affairs of State*, pp. 18–20, 74.

49. Ballard C. Campbell, "Federalism, State Action, and 'Critical Episodes' in the Growth of American Government," *Social Science History* 16 (1992): 569; Campbell, "Gilded Age Politics, The Textbooks, and Noncentralized Governance," p. 9; Solomon Fabricant, *The Trend of Government Activity in the United States Since 1900* (New York, 1952), esp. pp. 28–33; Lance E. Davis and John Legler, "The Government in the American Economy, 1815–1902: A Quantitative Study," *The Journal of Economic History* 26 (December 1966): 514–52; R. A. Musgrave and J. M. Culbertson, "The Growth of Public Expenditures in the United States," *National Tax Journal* 6 (June 1953): 97–115.

50. A number of studies have shown how fruitful such inquiry can be: e.g., on politics in the cities, Jon C. Teaford, *The Unheralded Triumph: City Government in America, 1870–1900* (Baltimore, Md., 1984); Carl V. Harris, *Political Power in Birmingham, 1871–1921* (Knoxville, Tenn., 1977); and William Cronon, *Nature's Metropolis: Chicago and the Great West* (New York, 1991). On the states, William R. Brock, *Investigation and Responsibility: Public Responsibility in the United States, 1865–1900* (Cambridge, England, 1984); Richard L. McCormick, *From Realignment to Reform: Political Change in New York State, 1893–1910* (Ithaca, N.Y., 1981); David P. Thelen, *The New Citizenship: Origins of Progressivism in*

Wisconsin, 1885–1900 (Columbia, Mo., 1972); Gould, *Wyoming*; Campbell, *Representative Democracy*; and Blodgett, *Gentle Reformers*.

51. And these measures, as a historian who has studied them observes, "merely skim the surface of statutory development in the Bay State": Campbell, "Public Policy and State Government," in Calhoun, *The Gilded Age*, p. 314; Raymond L. Bridgman, *Ten Years of Massachusetts* (Boston, 1888), pp. 6–7; Barbara Gutmann Rosenkrantz, *Public Health and the State: Changing Views in Massachusetts, 1842–1936* (Cambridge, Mass., 1972), pp. 37–127.

52. Butler quoted in Keller, *Affairs of State*, p. 168. Also, Gerald D. Nash, *State Government and Economic Development: A History of Administrative Policies in California, 1849–1933* (Berkeley, 1964), pp. 139–224; and Nash, "Government and Business: A Case Study of State Regulation of Corporate Securities, 1850–1933," *Business History Review* 38 (Summer 1964): 144–62.

53. Campbell, "Gilded Age Politics, the Textbooks, and Noncentralized Governance," p. 12; Campbell, "The State Legislatures in American History: A Review Essay," *Historical Methods Newsletter* 9 (September 1976): 185–94; William G. Shade, "State Legislatures in the Nineteenth Century," in Joel H. Silbey, ed., *Encyclopedia of the American Legislative System* (New York, 1994), 1:208–11; Albert Bushnell Hart, *Actual Government* (New York, 1903), pp. 113–50; Keller, *Affairs of State*, pp. 464–66; Brock, *Investigation and Responsibility*, pp. 2–8; Arthur S. Link, "The Progressive Movement in the South, 1870–1914," *North Carolina Historical Review* 23 (April 1946): 183–88; James F. Doster, *Railroads in Alabama Politics, 1875–1914* (University, Ala., 1957), pp. 9–36.

54. Alfred Runte, "The Role of Niagara in America's Scenic Preservation," in Jeremy E. Adamson, ed., *Niagara: Two Centuries of Changing Attitudes, 1697–1901* (Washington, D.C., 1985), pp. 117–27; Henry Norman, *The Preservation of Niagara Falls* (New York, 1981).

55. Quoted in George Wilson Pierson, *Tocqueville in America* (Garden City, N.Y., 1959), p. 210.

56. Alfred Runte, "Beyond the Spectacular: The Niagara Falls Preservation Campaign," *The New York Historical Society Quarterly* 57 (January 1973): 39–40, 45; W. D. Howells et al., *The Niagara Book* (New York, 1893); Laura Wood Roper, *FLO: A Biography of Frederick Law Olmsted* (Baltimore, Md., 1973), pp. 378–82, 395–97; and J. B. Harrison, "Charles Eliot Norton and Niagara Falls," Charles Eliot Norton Papers, Manuscripts Division, Library of Congress, Washington, D.C. The Falls, Olmsted complained, were in danger of becoming just another sensational exhibition, with "rope-walking, diving, brass bands, fireworks, and various 'side-shows' ": Frederick Law Olmsted, "Notes by Mr. Olmsted," in *Special Report of the Commissioners of the New York State Survey of 1879* (Albany, N.Y., 1880), pp. 28–29.

57. J. B. Harrison, "The Movement for the Redemption of Niagara," *The New Princeton Review* 1 (March 1886): 244–45; Thomas R. Cox, Robert S. Maxwell, Phillip Drennon Thomas, and Joseph J. Malone, *This Well-Wooded Land: Americans and Their Forests from Colonial Times to the Present* (Lincoln, Neb., 1985), p. 137; Charles M. Dow, *The State Reservation at Niagara: A History*

(Albany, N.Y., 1914); Chester E. Pond, *The Falls of Niagara: Our School of Sublimity* (Topeka, Kan., 1888); and Elizabeth McKinsey, *Niagara Falls: Icon of the American Sublime* (Cambridge, Eng., 1985).

58. *New York Times*, July 15–16, 1885; Runte, "Beyond the Spectacular," pp. 43–48; Harrison, "Movement for the Redemption of Niagara," pp. 237–42; Hans Huth, *Nature and the American: Three Centuries of Changing Attitudes* (Berkeley, Cal., 1957), pp. 171–73; Allan Nevins, *Grover Cleveland: A Study in Courage* (New York, 1932), pp. 143–44.

David B. Hill, who had become governor when Cleveland moved on to the White House, said in accepting the gift of the park: "The preservation of the beauty of this, the greatest of wonders, is indeed a noble work. Its conception is worthy of the advanced thought, the grand liberality, and the true spirit of the nineteenth century": *New York Times*, July 16, 1885.

59. Harrison, "Movement for the Redemption of Niagara," p. 243. Also, J. B. Harrison, *The Condition of Niagara Falls and the Measures Needed to Preserve Them: Eight Letters Published in the New York Evening Post, the New York Tribune and the Boston Advertiser* (New York, 1882).

60. Frank Graham, *The Adirondack Park: A Political History* (New York, 1978), pp. 37–44, 79–120; Donald J. Pisani, "Forests and Conservation, 1865–1890," *The Journal of American History* 72 (September 1985): 354–57.

61. Graham, *Adirondack Park*, pp. 105–6; Jane Eblen Keller, *Adirondack Wilderness: A Story of Man and Nature* (Syracuse, N.Y., 1980), pp. 173–79; Samuel Trask Dana, *Forest and Range Policy: Its Development in the United States* (New York, 1956), pp. 43–44; Philip G. Terrie, *Forever Wild: Environmental Aesthetics and the Adirondack Forest Preserve* (Philadelphia, 1985), pp. 95–103; Gordon B. Dodds, "The Historiography of American Conservation: Past and Prospects," *Pacific Northwest Quarterly* 56 (April 1965): 77; H. Wayne Morgan, "America's First Environmental Challenge, 1865–1920," in Margaret Francine Morris, ed., *Essays on the Gilded Age: The Walter Prescott Webb Memorial Lectures* (Austin, Tex., 1973), p. 106; William G. Robbins, *American Forestry: A History of National, State, & Private Cooperation* (Lincoln, Neb., 1985), pp. 34–41.

62. Thanks to Baker, *Moral Frameworks of Public Life*; Teaford, *Unheralded Triumph*; Jensen, *Winning of the Midwest*; Kleppner, *Cross of Culture*. See also Jon C. Teaford, "New Life for an Old Subject: Investigating the Structure of Urban Rule," *American Quarterly* 37 (1985): 346–56.

63. *Science*, July 27, 1883, quoted in Brock, *Investigation and Responsibility*, p. 43; Ballard C. Campbell, *The Growth of American Government: Governance from the Cleveland Era to the Present* (Bloomington, Ind., 1995); for similar views, see Albert Shaw, "The American State and the American Man," *Contemporary Review* 51 (1887): 695–711.

64. Philip Dunne, ed., *Mr. Dooley Remembers: The Informal Memoirs of Finley Peter Dunne* (Boston, 1963), p. 106.

65. Nancy F. Cott, "On Men's History and Women's History," in Mark C. Carnes and Clyde Griffen, eds., *Meanings for Manhood: Constructions of Masculinity in Victorian America* (Chicago, 1990), p. 208.

66. Gail Bederman, *Manliness & Civilization: A Cultural History of Gender and Race in the United States, 1880–1917* (Chicago, 1995), pp. 13–15.

67. C. F. Peck to Hill, Aug. 23, 1891, quoted in Baker, *Moral Frameworks of Public Life*, p. 30.

68. Quoted in Kousser, *Shaping of Southern Politics*, p. 14n.

69. Paula Baker, "The Domestication of Politics," pp. 620–47, especially 628–30; and *Moral Frameworks of Public Life*, pp. 24–55; John Mack Faragher, *Women and Men on the Overland Trail* (New Haven, Conn., 1979), pp. 116–19.

70. Robert Ellis Thompson, *Protection to Home Industry* (New York, 1886), pp. 79–80; Giles B. Stebbins, *The American Protectionist's Manual* (Chicago, 1888), pp. 62, 145–46; Joanne Reitano, *The Tariff Question in the Gilded Age: The Great Debate of 1888* (University Park, Penn., 1994), pp. 52–53, 79–81. In a forthcoming book, Charles W. Calhoun will explore the tariff and Republican ideology, including gender: see his insightful "Political Economy in the Gilded Age: The Republican Party's Industrial Policy," paper given to the Organization of American Historians at the Annual Meeting, Washington, D.C., March 30, 1995.

71. Quoted in Kathryn Kish Sklar, *Florence Kelley and the Nation's Work: The Rise of Women's Political Culture, 1830–1900* (New Haven, Conn., 1995), p. 37.

72. *Congressional Record*, 49th Cong., 1st sess. (March 26, 1886), p. 2786; Richard Hofstadter, *Anti-Intellectualism in American Life* (New York, 1963), p. 188; *Harper's Weekly* 30 (April 10, 1886): 226–27, 240.

John J. Ingalls was the Senator, and he said (p. 2786): "But there is a third sex, if that can sex be called which sex has none, resulting sometimes from a cruel caprice of nature, at others from accident or malevolent design, possessing the vices of both and the virtues of neither; effeminate without being masculine or feminine; unable either to beget or to bear; possessing neither fecundity nor virility; endowed with the contempt of men and the derision of women, and doomed to sterility, isolation, and extinction. But they have two recognized functions. They sing falsetto, and they are usually selected as the guardians of the seraglios of Oriental despots." Ingalls's wife thought the speech damaged his political career: Burton J. Williams, *Senator John James Ingalls: Kansas' Iridescent Republican* (Lawrence, Kan., 1972), pp. 107–9.

73. Alfred R. Conkling, *The Life and Letters of Roscoe Conkling, Orator, Statesman, Advocate* (New York, 1889), pp. 540–41; Clyde Griffen, "Reconstructing Masculinity from the Evangelical Revival to the Waning of Progressivism: A Speculative Synthesis," in Carnes and Griffen, *Meanings for Manhood*, p. 192. For an argument that such attacks were actually directed against women, since males would "often displace their fears of being womanized or symbolically emasculated not by direct attacks against women but by describing male opponents in female terms," see David G. Pugh, *Sons of Liberty: The Masculine Mind in Nineteenth-Century America* (Westport, Conn., 1983), p. 103.

74. The literature on women's political activism has grown rapidly in the past several decades. See, e.g., Gerda Lerner, "New Approaches to the Study of Women in American History," *Journal of Social History* 3 (Fall 1969): 53–62; Ruth Bordin, *Woman and Temperance: The Quest for Power and Liberty, 1873–1900* (Philadelphia, 1981); Mary P. Ryan, *Women in Public: Between Banners and*

Ballots, 1825–1880 (Baltimore, Md., 1990); Ellen Carol DuBois, *Feminism and Suffrage: The Emergence of an Independent Women's Movement in America, 1848–1869* (Ithaca, N.Y., 1978); DuBois, "Outgrowing the Compact of the Fathers: Equal Rights, Woman Suffrage, and the United States Constitution, 1820–1878," *The Journal of American History* 74 (December 1987): 853–62; DuBois, "Taking the Law into Our Own Hands: *Bradwell, Minor,* and Suffrage Militance in the 1870s," in Nancy A. Hewitt and Suzanne Lebsock, eds., *Visible Women: New Essays on American Activism* (Urbana, Ill., 1993), pp. 19–40; DuBois, "The Radicalism of the Woman Suffrage Movement: Notes toward the Reconstruction of Nineteenth-Century Feminism," *Feminist Studies* 3 (Fall 1975): 63–71; Lori D. Ginzberg, *Women and the Work of Benevolence: Morality, Politics, and Class in the Nineteenth-Century United States* (New Haven, Conn., 1990); Mary H. Blewett, *Men, Women, and Work: Class, Gender, and Protest in the New England Shoe Industry, 1780–1910* (Urbana, Ill., 1988); Vincent P. De Santis, "Belva Ann Lockwood," *Timeline* 46 (December 1987–January 1988), pp. 45–47; Thelen, *New Citizenship*, esp. pp. 86–112; and David J. Pivar, *Purity Crusade: Sexual Morality and Social Control, 1868–1900* (Westport, Conn., 1973). Elizabeth R. Varon, "Tippecanoe and the Ladies, Too: White Women and Party Politics in Antebellum Virginia," *The Journal of American History* 82 (September 1995): 494–521, is the most recent statement. For an articulate and shrewd contemporary argument, see Florence Kelley, "Need Our Working-Women Despair?" *International Review* 13 (November 1882): 517–27.

75. Mark Twain, *Collected Tales, Sketches, Speeches, & Essays, 1852–1890* (New York, 1992), p. 564; Ruth Bordin, " 'A Baptism of Power and Liberty': The Women's Crusade of 1873–1874," *Ohio History* 87 (Autumn 1978): 395; Frances E. Willard, *Woman and Temperance or, The Work and Workers of the Woman's Christian Temperance Union* (Hartford, Conn., 1883), pp. 50–67; and Jack S. Blocker, *"Give to the Wind Thy Fears": The Women's Temperance Crusade, 1873–1874* (Westport, Conn., 1985).

For women and temperance, see Baker, *Moral Frameworks of Public Life*, pp. 108–13; Eliza Daniel Stewart, *Memories of the Crusade: A Thrilling Account of the Great Uprising of the Women of Ohio in 1873, Against the Liquor Crime* (Columbus, Ohio, 1889); Jed Dannenbaum, "The Origins of Temperance Activism and Militancy Among American Women," *Journal of Social History* 15 (Winter 1981): 235–52; Jack S. Blocker, Jr., "The Politics of Reform: Populists, Prohibition, and Woman Suffrage, 1891–1892," *Historian* 34 (August 1972): 614–32; Barbara Leslie Epstein, *The Politics of Domesticity: Women, Evangelism, and Temperance in Nineteenth-Century America* (Middletown, Conn., 1981), pp. 95–107; and Anne Firor Scott, *The Southern Lady: From Pedestal to Politics, 1830–1930* (Chicago, 1970), pp. 145–63.

For the WCTU, see Bordin, *Woman and Temperance*; Ruth Bordin, *Frances Willard: A Biography* (Chapel Hill, N.C., 1986); Ian R. Tyrell, *Woman's World / Woman's Empire: The Woman's Christian Temperance Union in International Perspective, 1880–1930* (Chapel Hill, N.C., 1990); Jed Dannenbaum, *Drink and Disorder: Temperance Reform in Cincinnati from the Washingtonian*

Revival to the WCTU (Urbana, Ill., 1984); and Joseph R. Gusfield, *Symbolic Crusade: Status Politics and the American Temperance Movement* (Urbana, Ill., 1963), pp. 88–96.

A young man who was in a Hillsboro saloon described the experience to a reporter: "He and half a dozen others, who had been out of town, and did not know what was going on, had ranged themselves in the familiar semicircle before the bar and had their drinks ready and cigars prepared for the match, when the rustle of women's wear attracted their attention, and looking up they saw what they thought a crowd of a thousand ladies entering. One youth saw among them his mother and sister, another had two cousins in the invading host, and a still more unfortunate recognized his intended mother-in-law!" Epstein, *Politics of Domesticity*, p. 96.

76. Bordin, " 'A Baptism of Power and Liberty,' " pp. 393–404 (quotation is from p. 396); Mrs. Annie Wittenmyer, *History of the Woman's Temperance Crusade* (Philadelphia, 1878), pp. 34–50; Jon C. Teaford, *Cities of the Heartland, The Rise and Fall of the Industrial Midwest* (Bloomington, Ind., 1993), p. 92. "Here, for the first time, groups of women pitted themselves against what they saw as institutions of male culture": Epstein, *The Politics of Domesticity*, p. 1.

77. Bordin, " 'A Baptism of Power and Liberty,' " p. 403. Entering saloons in 1874 as "a gentle, well-dressed, and altogether peaceable mob," Willard said, women "have become an army, drilled and disciplined": Frances E. Willard, *Glimpses of Fifty Years: The Autobiography of an American Woman* (Chicago, 1892), pp. 472–73. They were "[t]he first female sit-ins in American history," a historian of the movement has written, "perhaps the first sit-ins of any variety": Epstein, *Politics of Domesticity*, pp. 95–96.

78. Sklar, *Kelley*, p. 74; Gusfield, *Symbolic Crusade*, p. 86; Bordin, *Woman and Temperance*, pp. 52, 62, 89, 92–118. Also, Richard W. Leeman, *"Do Everything" Reform: The Oratory of Frances E. Willard* (New York, 1992); and Mary Martha Thomas, *The New Woman in Alabama: Social Reforms and Suffrage, 1890–1920* (Tuscaloosa, Ala., 1992), which also details the involvement of African-American women in the WCTU and women's clubs.

79. Sklar, *Kelley*, pp. 141–42, 177.

80. Margaret Gibbons Wilson, *The American Woman in Transition: The Urban Influence, 1870–1920* (Westport, Conn., 1979), pp. 91–105 (quotation is from p. 101). Besides Sklar, *Kelley*, see J. C. Croly, *The History of the Woman's Club Movement in America* (New York, 1898); Mary I. Wood, *The History of the General Federation of Women's Clubs* (New York, 1912); Theodora Penny Martin, *The Sound of Our Own Voices: Women's Study Clubs, 1860–1910* (Boston, 1987); Karen Blair, *The Clubwoman as Feminist: True Womanhood Redefined, 1868–1914* (New York, 1979); Howard Furer, "The City as a Catalyst for the Women's Rights Movement," *Wisconsin Magazine of History* 52 (Summer 1969): 285–305; Nancy F. Cott, *The Bonds of Womanhood: 'Woman's Sphere' in New England, 1780–1835* (New Haven, Conn., 1977); Estelle B. Freedman, *Their Sisters' Keepers: Women's Prison Reform in America, 1830–1930* (Ann Arbor, Mich., 1981), pp. 22–52.

81. Baker, *Moral Frameworks of Public Life*, pp. xv–xvii (quotation is from p. xvii); McGerr, "Political Style and Women's Power," pp. 867–68; Baker,

"Domestication of Politics," pp. 632–35; Mary P. Ryan, "The Power of Women's Networks: A Case Study of Female Moral Reform in Antebellum America," *Feminist Studies* 5 (Spring 1979): 66–85; Freedman, *Their Sisters' Keepers*, pp. 22–35.

82. Westfield *Republican*, March 19, 1884, quoted in Baker, *Moral Frameworks of Public Life*, p. xvi. There is continuing scrutiny, for example, of political corruption: see, e.g., Peter H. Argersinger, "New Perspectives on Election Fraud in the Gilded Age," *Political Science Quarterly* 100 (Winter 1985–86): 669–87.

83. Richard L. McCormick, "Political Parties in American History," in McCormick, *Party Period and Public Policy*, pp. 157–76, summarizes recent findings.

84. E.g., Baker, "Culture of Politics in the Late Nineteenth Century"; James Edward Wright, *The Politics of Populism: Dissent in Colorado* (New Haven, Conn., 1974); Lawrence M. Lipin, *Producers, Proletarians, and Politicians: Workers and Party Politics in Evansville and New Albany, Indiana, 1850–87* (Urbana, Ill., 1994); Dale Baum, "Know-Nothingism and the Republican Majority in Massachusetts: The Political Realignment of the 1850s," *The Journal of American History* 64 (March 1978): 959–86; and Stephen E. Maizlish, *The Triumph of Sectionalism: The Transformation of Ohio Politics, 1844–1856* (Kent, Ohio, 1983).

85. Shade, "State Legislatures in the Nineteenth Century," p. 210, outlines the problem and suggests that about two-thirds of the "nothingarians," in Midwestern legislatures, at least, were Democrats. See also, Jensen, *Winning of the Midwest*, pp. 310–14.

86. J. Morgan Kousser, "Toward 'Total Political History': A Rational-Choice Research Program," *Journal of Interdisciplinary History* 20 (Spring 1990): 548–49.

87. There are some outstanding exceptions, of course, including Harris, *Political Power in Birmingham*. James Tice Moore, "Redeemers Reconsidered: Change and Continuity in the Democratic South, 1870–1900," *The Journal of Southern History* 44 (August 1978): 360–61n, lists studies of post-Reconstruction politics in the South. John Mack Faragher, *Sugar Creek: Life on the Illinois Prairie* (New Haven, Conn., 1986), shows what can be learned from a study of a northern rural community. Also, Brian Greenberg, *Worker and Community: Response to Industrialization in a Nineteenth-Century American City, Albany, New York, 1850–1884* (Albany, N.Y., 1985); and Don Harrison Doyle, *The Social Order of a Frontier Community: Jacksonville, Illinois, 1825–70* (Urbana, Ill., 1978).

88. Formisano, "Invention of the Ethnocultural Interpretation," pp. 470–77, esp. 472–73n, lists studies dealing with socioeconomic and class divisions.

89. Richard L. McCormick, "The Party Period and Public Policy: An Exploratory Hypothesis," *The Journal of American History* 66 (September 1979): 279–98; Hays, "Society in Politics: Politics in Society," pp. 481–499. Larry M. Logue, "Union Veterans and Their Government: The Effects of Public Policies on Private Lives," *Journal of Interdisciplinary History* 22 (Winter 1992): 411–34, poses the interesting argument that while Union veterans voted for the Republican party, those who belonged to the Grand Army of the Republic did so in even greater proportions, motivated by group identity and government pension policies.

Gilded Age political historians have profited a great deal from the work of antebellum historians. In an important argument, Michael F. Holt showed a decade ago that in the Jacksonian period "economic issues and contrasting party records were the central determinants of voting behavior," as voters responded to the perceived successes and failures of Whig and Democratic economic policies: Holt, "The Election of 1840, Voter Mobilization, and the Emergence of the Second American Party System: A Reappraisal of Jacksonian Voting Behavior," in Cooper et al., *A Master's Due*, pp. 16–58 (quotation is from p. 58).

90. Richard L. McCormick, "Political Parties in the United States: Reinterpreting Their Natural History," *The History Teacher* 19 (November 1985): 16. Ballard C. Campbell, *The Growth of American Government: Governance From the Cleveland Era to the Present* (Bloomington, Ind., 1995), takes a broad look at the issue. Also, J. Morgan Kousser, "Are Political Acts Unnatural?" *Journal of Interdisciplinary History* 15 (Winter 1985): 468–69; Kousser, "Toward 'Total Political History,' " pp. 521–60; Peter H. Argersinger, "The Value of the Vote: Political Representation in the Gilded Age," *The Journal of American History* 76 (June, 1989): 59–90, which gives attention to the important issue of representation; and Jon C. Teaford, "Finis for Tweed and Steffens: Rewriting the History of Urban Rule," *Reviews in American History* 10 (December 1982): 133–149. Urban government, Teaford says (p. 147), "is not simply an ethnocultural feud between clashing social factions. It is a struggle to provide vital services for millions of Americans demanding unprecedented levels of comfort and convenience. It is a story of technological achievement and sophisticated financing, a story of greater breadth and complexity than has yet been recorded."

91. New York *Tribune*, April 3, 1868, quoted in Silbey, *Respectable Minority*, p. x; James G. Blaine, *Twenty Years of Congress: From Lincoln to Garfield* (Norwich, Conn., 1884), 2:407–409; De Santis, *Republicans Face the Southern Question*, pp. 20–21; Jean H. Baker, *The Politics of Continuity: Maryland Political Parties from 1858 to 1870* (Baltimore, Md., 1971); R. Hal Williams, " 'Dry Bones and Dead Language': The Democratic Party," in Morgan, *The Gilded Age*, revised ed., pp. 129–48. Robert D. Marcus, *Grand Old Party: Political Structure in the Gilded Age, 1880–1896* (New York, 1971), examines the inner workings of the Republican party, the kind of study needed for the Democrats.

92. See, e.g., Jerome M. Clubb, William H. Flanigan, and Nancy H. Zingale, *Partisan Realignment: Voters, Parties and Government in American History* (Beverly Hills, Cal., 1980), pp. 12, 155–88. Also, Paul Lenchner, "Partisan Conflict in the Senate and the Realignment Process," *The Journal of Politics* 41 (May 1979): 680–86; Lenchner, "Partisan Realignments and Congressional Behavior: Some Preliminary Snapshots," *American Politics Quarterly* 4 (April, 1976): 223–26; and Barbara Sinclair Deckard, "Party Realignment and the Transformation of the Political Agenda: The House of Representatives, 1925–1938," *American Political Science Review* 71 (September 1977): 940–54.

93. E.g., Holt, "Election of 1840, Voter Mobilization, and the Emergence of the Second American Party System," pp. 16–58.

94. Winkle, "Social Analysis of Voter Turnout in Ohio," p. 434.

95. Sklar, *Kelley*; John Shaw, ed., *Crete and James: Personal Letters of Lucretia and James Garfield* (East Lansing, Mich., 1994); Eileen L. McDonagh, "Gender

Politics and Political Change," in Lawrence C. Dodd and Calvin Jillson, eds., *New Perspectives on American Politics* (Washington, D.C., 1994), pp. 58–73.

96. John Morton Blum, "History As It Should Be Taught," *The Washington Monthly* 27 (May 1995): 43–46.

97. In 1980, 45 percent of those sampled agreed that "it would be better if, in all elections, we put no party labels on the ballot." Thirty percent said that "the truth is we probably don't need political parties any more." In a 1983 Gallup poll, a majority saw interest groups as more effective in representing them than either of the political parties: Martin P. Wattenberg, "Dealignment in the American Electorate," in Maisel and Shade, *Parties and Politics in American History*, pp. 228–29; Burnham, "The Onward March of Party Decomposition," in Burnham, *Critical Elections and the Mainsprings of American Politics*, pp. 130–34. Walter Dean Burnham has suggested that political parties in the current climate may be losing their significance altogether: "The End of American Party Politics," *Trans-Action* 7 (Dec. 1969): 12–22. For a more hopeful point of view, see Nie, Verba, and Petrocik, *The Changing American Voter*, p. 2.

98. Dallas *Morning News*, September 18, 1995.

5

American Political Biography

Robert V. Remini

For American political biography, it is, to borrow a phrase, the best of times, it is the worst of times. It is the best of times for a number of reasons. The first and perhaps the most important is that, according to a survey conducted some years ago by the Library of Congress, the American public reads biographies more than any other type of book.[1] Intrigued, I decided to do a little research in the matter myself and discussed it with my editor at HarperCollins. He informed me that approximately fifty thousand general works are published each year, of which about two thousand are biographies; but he could not give me figures of the other types and categories of books published each year.[2] Still two thousand titles are impressive. Although these figures do not document the statement put out by the Library of Congress, it is nonetheless very encouraging for a biographer to know that there is a large audience out there ready to buy, if not always read, works of nonfiction in biography. Of course, political biographies that are serious and scholarly do not compare with the exposés and celebrity nonbooks that regularly appear on the lists of publishing houses. What proportion of nonbooks disguised as biographies are published each year I cannot say. I do know that W. W. Norton's Spring 1996 publication list includes seven biographies and ten works of fiction, not including poetry. Books under the history category are approximately 8 per cent of the list.[3]

The question then entered my mind as to why the reading public prefers biographies. I have my own suspicions about the reason but then, last July, I read an essay in the *New York Times Book Review* section, entitled " 'None Ever Wished it Longer': How to Stamp out Book Inflation," which offered an explanation.[4] With a little investigation I discovered that its author, Terry Teachout, writes about music for *Commentary* and ballet and modern dance for *The New Dance Review*. He is also currently at work on a biography of H. L. Mencken.

According to Mr. Teachout, the reading public of the past enjoyed what he called "serious middlebrow novels," the kind of novels that Charles Dickens, Anthony Trollope, and, to a lesser extent, Joseph Conrad and Robert Louis Stevenson regularly turned out. However, today such novels seem to have gone out of fashion. Therefore, concludes Teachout, since there is a growing scarcity of these "traditional character-driven narratives" in the world of fiction, the reading public has turned to biographies, that is, big, massive biographies several inches thick, so large that they can easily serve as doorstops. Such works satisfy the natural appetite of literate Americans—and I emphasize *literate* Americans—for storytelling. And almost by definition biographers are storytellers, which is not to imply that they offer only a string of anecdotes to move their narrative along. They are responsible historians, and their research, organization, and writing is just as exacting, just as professional, just as rigorous in its scholarship as any historical monograph.[5]

My own thinking about why biographies are popular is that the general public believes, as I do, that individuals make a difference in history. Individuals are not merely captives of the flow of events which are beyond human control. Events are frequently made to happen by strong, determined, and even sometimes deranged individuals who fight, struggle, and connive their way into positions of influence where they can control the conduct of public affairs. A Roosevelt, a Lincoln, a Jackson, a Truman, a Wilson, as well as an Oswald, a John Wilkes Booth, a Hitler, and a Stalin can markedly change the course of history, for better or worse. The public is anxious to know about these individuals, their background, how they acquired power, and what influences shaped their lives. Biographies will always be written of the great men and women whose lives made a difference. But even a man like Oswald will draw the attention not only of historians but, as Norman Mailer has recently shown, literary artists as well.

Events like the American Revolution, the Civil War, the Great Depression, World War II, and the Cold War are shaped and determined by individuals, collectively and singly, sometimes within, sometimes without the country. But, I hasten to add, these events also shaped the individuals in how they responded and what they did. Put another way, we would not have had as great a president as Abraham Lincoln without the Civil War. That war provoked the greatness that lay deep within him, by which he was able to save this nation from permanent rupture. As he himself said: "I claim not to have controlled events, but confess plainly that events have controlled me."[6] The same is true of Franklin Delano Roosevelt and the Great Depression, and Churchill and World War II. The combination of events and individuals directs the course of history. That is why great biography will always provide readers with an in-depth view of the times in which the subject of the biography lived.

The major leaders of this country remain popular figures today. And the popular appeal of their biographies does not seem to diminish with the increased size of the volumes necessary to portray their lives and works. As a matter of fact, that is today's fashion. Many, if not most of the biographies published these days are behemoths, running close to a thousand printed pages or more. Take the biography of Harry Truman by David McCullough—it runs to 1,117 pages. Robert Ferrell had the distinction of bringing out a study of Truman's life just under 500 pages, but Alonzo Hamby's most recent work is 760 pages long. Robert Caro's biography of Lyndon Baines Johnson, in progress, is 1,388 pages and counting. Robert Dallek's is 721 pages and counting. I confess I added to this pile with my three-volume Jackson that runs—I'm ashamed to admit it—to 1609 pages. But, let me add, size is essential in order to provide the details by which the life of a major figure is revealed.

Not unexpectedly, the big books are coming out every day. In late 1995, David Donald published his long-awaited biography of Abraham Lincoln, and even before the official date of publication it had become a best-seller. Early that summer Emory Thomas published a splendid new life of Robert E. Lee. Edmund Morris will soon bring out his study of Ronald Reagan. As you know, Morris has already completed the first volume of a multi-volume biography of Theodore Roosevelt. I assume that after the Reagan book he will return to TR. And we will hear again from Robert Dallek and Robert Caro as they continue their respective studies of LBJ.

Another reason it is the best of times is that in the last decade, the interest in women's history has produced an extraordinary collection of excellent biographical studies of important women in American political history. One outstanding example is the study of Eleanor Roosevelt by Blanche Wiesen Cook. The first volume runs to nearly 600 pages. A colleague at Notre Dame, Professor Jeanne Kilde, at my request, sent out a query on the Internet asking about feminist *political* biography.

The reaction was instantaneous and most encouraging. I never realized how much has already been done and is being done by women on women in politics, for example, biographies of Helen Gahagan Douglas, Belle Moskowitz, Susan B. Anthony, Frances Willard, and Mercy Warren, written respectively by Ingrid Scobie, Elizabeth Perry, Kathleen Barry, Ruth Bordin, and Rosemarie Zagarri. And there are many more.[7]

African-American political feminist figures have not been overlooked. Work has been done or is being done on Sojourner Truth, Fannie Mae Hamer, Jane Edna Hunter, Mary Church Terrell, and Ida B. Wells. And not all these works on American women have been written by women. Charles Capper won the 1993 Bancroft Prize for the first volume of his life of Margaret Fuller.[8] It is, as I say, the best of times.

What is really significant in all these studies, feminist or not, is that new and important facts are brought to light and new interpretations are presented that advance our knowledge of the past. For example, the Thomas biography of Robert E. Lee provides a totally new portrait of the general. Douglas Southall Freeman, in his massive four-volume study of Lee, had presented a godlike figure, worshipped by all southerners and by many Civil War buffs. Freeman himself reportedly tipped his hat every time he passed the statue of Lee in Richmond. The Thomas portrait of Lee is quite different. Thomas presents a man who liked to flirt with young ladies of his acquaintance, supposedly with the full knowledge of his wife, a man who avoided confrontation at all costs and who may have sacrificed a victory at Gettysburg because of this failing. A brave and courageous man, Lee could face combat and crisis, but in his day-to-day encounters with others he went to great lengths to escape disagreements or unpleasant situations. Throughout his life he physically and regularly fled from friction. He fled from in-laws, wife, children, recalcitrant slaves, and quarrelsome army officers, politicians, and bureaucrats. Thomas suggests that "in a real sense" Lee even became a Confederate to avoid the certain conflict at home had he chosen to remain in the United States Army and fight for the Union!

David Donald, in his new biography of Abraham Lincoln, shows us a more human, a more pragmatic, and a more complex Lincoln than we had known before. What is particularly striking about this book is the evidence Donald advances to demonstrate the extent to which Lincoln was controlled by events rather than the other way around. And there are many other examples of new interpretations provided by recent biographies.

What I am trying to say here is that biographies, that is, character-driven narratives of the lives of important individuals in our history—what too many younger historians call "old-fashioned history"—not only enjoy a huge audience among literate Americans but regularly provide new information and understanding of our past. In the most recent issue of the *Journal of American History*, the reviewer of Doris Kearns Goodwin's biography of Franklin and Eleanor Roosevelt, *No Ordinary Time*, underscores some of the points I have been trying to make. The reviewer faults the author for overstating "the advances in racial justice, just as she is overly enthusiastic about (and uncritical of) New Deal liberalism generally and its postwar legacies." The reviewer concludes, "this is a wide-ranging account that too often slips into the realm of nostalgia," but also admits that "it reflects sentiments that resonate with a significant segment of the book-buying and reading public today. After months on the best-seller list, *No Ordinary Time* indicated that half a century after the death of FDR and the end of World War II, Americans of many stripes are dissatisfied with the present political and social scene; across the political and ideological spectrum, Americans vote in bookstores as well as in elections."[9]

Just so. Historians might well remember that.

Which brings me back to the beginning of this paper: I stated that for American political biography it was the best of times and the worst of times. And indeed, in some respects, it really is the worst of times. When we in the profession do not see, do not address, and will not or can not articulate past political events of present concern, when we chase after subjects of little public interest, it is no wonder that our words and works get short shrift.

Young historians, I fear, are in hot pursuit of other, more "exotic," and frequently esoteric subjects dealing with class, race, and gender, what someone has termed the "holy trinity" of modern historical research.[10] Now I am not denying anyone's right to choose any subject he or she wishes. Nor am I denying the importance of studies concerned with race, class, and gender. They are very important. But not at the sacrifice of traditional, old-fashioned history; and I firmly believe that traditional biography, that is, character-driven narrative about the past, has been abandoned to a large extent by the rising generation of scholars. I regularly examine the list of doctoral dissertations in political history published each quarter by the *Journal of American History* and I am astounded at what I find: titles involving "nonlinear developments" and "synecdochic and metonymic phenomena." I frankly do not know what these dissertations can be about, and I wonder who besides the writers and their committees will read them.

One of the main problems confronting any biographer at the outset of his or her work is the problem of balancing the presentation of the individual under study with the times in which the subject lived. The individual must not be lost in the thicket of context, nor must context be severely diminished, since it helps explain and illuminate the subject's life. Determinist interpretations or so-called "scientific" historical models proposed today, constructed under the influence of anthropological or sociological explanations, too often employ biography to develop particular conceptions of a predetermined past. Such biographies, and there are a number of them, tend to utilize a "life" to advance a given view of the period under study, one that must necessarily concern itself with race, gender, and class.[11]

Furthermore, biographies, and especially political biographies, are by their very nature narrative in form, and I find that this so-called old-fashioned methodology is being discriminated against in our journals and at our annual conventions. In my opinion, the *Journal of American History* is probably more notorious for its unsympathetic approach to traditional political history than any other scholarly historical publication. In checking articles that have appeared in the *Journal* within the past five years, I found that there is not one dealing with politics that is not related directly to the "holy trinity." I had always presumed that this journal published the most important articles available in American history whatever their subject. But I no longer think that is true if the subject is biographical and political but not in any way related to themes of class, gender, and race.

Lest I am misunderstood, I am quite prepared to concede that some very important insights have been uncovered by all the new techniques and approaches of the "new-fashioned" history. But I fear that few beyond the academy are listening to what the "new history" has to say. It is a great pity that too many historians today seem to be talking exclusively to one another. Maybe that is just as well. But there is a great danger here, the danger that historians are making themselves irrelevant. We seem hell-bent on killing our profession.

I noticed in the newspapers recently that a panel formed by a private group called the Council for Basic Education[12] concluded that the recommendations for national history standards drawn up by respected scholars in American history "deserved criticism," that the standards were "too gloomy and politically motivated," that the "biased language" should be eliminated, that "more attention should be given such presences as Washington and Jefferson and seminal documents such as the Bill of Rights and the Constitution," that the absence of names in general needed correction, that the standards "should be rewritten to emphasize the founding fathers, the Constitution and America's opportunities."[13] And, let it be noted, President Bill Clinton's Education Secretary, Richard W. Riley, has agreed with the findings of the Council of Basic Education. He declared that the recommendations "are an important step forward in the resolution of controversy regarding proposed voluntary national history standards . . . and should form the basis for further developing a new consensus regarding what our young people need to know regarding America's proud history."

Now I do not wish to engage in the national history standards controversy. That is hardly my purpose in presenting this paper. What I am concerned with is the relationship of historians to the general public, both in what we write and what we teach. It is a question that seriously troubles the American Historical Association. The AHA recently formed an Advisory Committee of citizens from the media, public life, and private industry to counsel it on how the work of historians can be made more accessible to the public. After the Enola Gay incident and the national standards brouhaha, we have come to realize that a gulf exists between the academy and the American public, and it is rapidly widening.

It seems to me that too many young historians disdain what the public wants and needs. We take the very pious position that it is the public that must be taught the value of this new research and new approach, whether they like it or want it or not. We argue from authority. We take an elitist position about what is valuable and what is not valuable in American history, even if that means downgrading (and sometimes discarding) important considerations of the Constitution, the Declaration of Independence, the Bill of Rights, and so on, to make room for social history, feminist history, ethnic history, and other minorities history. As a result, other areas of history that deserve attention are given short shrift. And it is now quite apparent that the public will not buy this "refocused" interpretation of our past, not in the bookstores and, when they have a say in the matter, not in their schools. One trouble with the new generation of historians—to my admittedly prejudiced view—is that they can not and will not take the taste and interest of the average reader as seriously as they should. But I would remind them what a distinguished English critic once said about the common reader. "I rejoice," declared Dr. Samuel Johnson, "to concur with the common reader; for by the common sense of readers uncorrupted with literary prejudices . . . must be finally decided all claim to poetical honours."[14]

Old-fashioned political biographies of "dead white males" that are "character-driven narratives" seem to have little appeal for graduate students. For example, there is a real need for "old-fashioned" biographies of such Tennesseans from the Jacksonian era as John H. Eaton, John Coffee, William Carroll, John Overton, William and Willie Blount, William B. Lewis, John McNairy, John Rhea, Archibald Roane, John Sevier, Hugh Lawson White, and Andrew Jackson Donelson, to name a few. These biographies could be written by doctoral candidates and would add significantly to our understanding of the Jacksonian era. However, the current generation of historians is largely uninterested in such topics.

Still, American political biographies are and will continue to be written, whether we in the academy do it or not. And more and more nonacademics, such as David McCullough, Robert Caro, Doris Kearns Goodwin, and the late Barbara Tuchman, have taken over the task of providing the American people what they most like to read about their history. But there are others, less talented and less careful in their research, who are also writing political biographies.

Worse, the art of biography writing, I find, is not taught in our graduate schools. Graduate programs should offer courses to instruct students about the value, the nature, the purpose, and the problems of writing biography. In the past we older historians read narratives almost exclusively, so perhaps we did not need as much instruction in this genre as I think is essential today, when the emphasis is away from narration and towards quantification and other subtler and more intricate forms of research and analysis. I was personally fortunate to do my doctoral work on Martin Van Buren under Dumas Malone, the renowned biographer of Thomas Jefferson. He was a close friend of Douglas Southall Freeman, and our seminar sessions frequently involved discussing Freeman's methods in writing the biographies of Robert E. Lee and George Washington. I therefore felt especially fortunate to have Malone guide me in the early stages of my academic career.

I suppose what I am saying is that I would like to see a better balance between the "old-fashioned" and the "new-fashioned" history. I would like to see a rapprochement between the two. I grow tired of reading reviews that start off by sneeringly referring to the book under review as "old-fashioned," with the presumption that it has nothing new, important, or interesting to say. And I would like to see better writing on the part of academics. As a group we are wretched writers, a fact long recognized and commented upon, both within and without the academy. Small wonder the public prefers the McCulloughs and Goodwins.

Now I do not wish to be misunderstood here. I am not advocating that historians should simply attend to popular taste. That would be a disaster. We cannot and should not be controlled in our research and in what we write and say by public opinion. We must be free to pursue what we believe will lead to a better understanding and appreciation of the past; and in that pursuit every historian must choose the methodology that is personally congenial and most appropriate to the subject. Moreover, we must be free to talk to one another on whatever subjects and using whatever technology we wish. But I do not think we can totally disregard the public and expect to gain their attention, interest, or support.

I began this paper by stating that in my view it is the best of times and the worst of times for American political biography. I think on balance, however, that it really is the best of times. I rejoice that we biographers have a large reading audience among literate Americans hungry for what we can provide.

A book reviewer in the most recent issue of the *American Historical Review* wrote: "Narrative history currently is out of fashion."[15] Well, it may be out of fashion in the academy, but it is certainly not out of fashion with the "common reader"—thank God. And mark my words, old-fashioned narrative history and biography will rise again. Just wait and see.

Notes

1. Stephen B. Oates, prologue to *Biography as High Adventure: Life-Writers Speak on their Art* (Amherst, Mass., 1986), p. ix.

2. Hugh Van Dusen to author, September 30, 1995.

3. Tabitha Griffith to author, October 15, 1995.

4. *New York Times*, July 30, 1995.

5. Dumas Malone, "Biography and History," cited in Oates, *Biography as High Adventure*, p. 32.

6. Lincoln to Albert G. Hodges, April 4, 1864, quoted in David Herbert Donald, *Lincoln* (New York, 1995), p. 9.

7. Blanche Wiesen Cook, *Eleanor Roosevelt* (New York, 1992), Ingrid Scobie, *Helen Gahagan Douglas: A Life* (New York, 1992), Elizabeth Perry, *Belle Moskowitz: Feminine Politics and the Exercise of Power in the Age of Alfred E. Smith* (New York, 1987), Kathleen Barry, *Susan B. Anthony: A Biography of a Singular Feminist* (New York, 1988), Ruth Bordin, *Francis Willard: A Biography* (Chapel Hill, N.C., 1986), and Rosemarie Zagarri, *A Woman's Dilemma: Mercy Otis Warren and the American Revolution* (Wheeling, Ill., 1995).

8. Charles Capper, *Margaret Fuller: An American Romantic Life* (New York, 1992).

9. *Journal of American History* 82 (September 1995): 814–15.

10. I am grateful to Ronald Formisano, who reminded me of the term, although he did not coin it himself.

11. The ideas expressed here come from John Niven, "The Great Western," in *Reviews in American History* 13 (June 1985): 193.

12. The Council describes itself as "national advocates of the liberal arts for all elementary and secondary schools." Nine members comprised the panel, of whom six were American historians. *OAH Newsletter*, November 1995.

13. *New York Times*, October 12, 1995; *OAH Newsletter*, November 1995. There were several more recommendations which are not relevant to this paper.

14. *The Oxford Dictionary of Quotations* (New York, 1979), p. 281.

15. *The American Historical Review* 100 (October 1995): 1338.

6

Vincent P. De Santis:
Political Historian

Wilson D. Miscamble, C.S.C.

It is likely that more boys grow up hoping to make history rather than to write it, but Vincent De Santis preferred the latter calling. Born and reared in Birdsboro, Pennsylvania, the young De Santis early developed what turned out to be his life-long interest in and passion for history. His interest was nurtured by an excellent high school history teacher and solid training as a history major at West Chester State College, from which he graduated in 1941.

Major historical events interrupted whatever possibilities De Santis had to continue further studies in history. The United States was on the eve of its entry into World War II and intent on building its armed forces. Soon after his graduation De Santis joined the United States Army and served until December 1945. He rose from private to captain and as a member of the Nineteenth Infantry Regiment of the Twenty-fourth Infantry Division saw action in the Southwest Pacific Theater, deploying through Australia on his way to fierce fighting in New Guinea. In the midst of the harsh battle conditions, De Santis found some outlet for his desire to record and interpret events by keeping a diary with meticulous care, much to the amusement of his comrades.

After his military discharge De Santis spent a year teaching history at the high school level while he applied to enter graduate programs at both Johns Hopkins University and the University of Pennsylvania, because of their strong reputations in history. He had no detailed information on the faculty in either place, but he chose to attend Johns Hopkins cognizant of its special tradition for graduate education and assisted by the provisions of the GI Bill and a graduate fellowship.

On his arrival at Johns Hopkins, De Santis faced a number of possibilities. His interests lay in American history, and he could have studied either intellectual history with Charles Barker, the distinguished biographer of Henry George, or diplomatic history with the able Charles C. Campbell. Instead, the beginning graduate student gravitated towards a younger historian of the post-Civil War South named C. Vann Woodward. He gained entry to the seminar Woodward ran on southern history, and this course selection was decisive for De Santis as a historian. It profoundly influenced the kind of historian he would become, the questions he would ask of the past, and the subjects he would explore.

When De Santis entered Woodward's seminar, he entered the orbit of one of the most talented of the brilliant postwar generation of historians—among them Oscar Handlin, Arthur Schlesinger, Jr., and Richard Hofstadter. Woodward, a southerner born in Arkansas in 1908, had studied at the University of North Carolina in the mid-1930s under the direction of Howard K. Beale and there wrote the dissertation published in 1938 as *Tom Watson: Agrarian Rebel*.[1] Woodward deeply opposed southern segregation and institutionalized racism and had begun his work, as he later put it, in order to furnish "evidence against the once prevalent . . . assumption that 'things have always been the same.' "[2] Woodward was intent on challenging the southern historiography then dominated by the interpretations of Ulrich B. Phillips and William A. Dunning, which were severely biased against blacks.

Interrupted in his great intellectual project by his own service in World War II, Woodward resumed his work at Johns Hopkins in 1946 and emerged in the 1950s as "the dominant figure in studies of the South in Reconstruction and thereafter."[3] It was De Santis's good fortune to study with Woodward during the very years when he was researching and writing the major works which would establish his leadership in this highly energized field. Woodward brought to his graduate seminar for discussion and critique his draft chapters from two major studies, both of which appeared in 1951—*Reunion and Reaction: The Compromise of 1877 and the End of Reconstruction* and his magisterial *Origins of the New South, 1877–1913*.[4] In his careful and quiet manner he also challenged his graduate students—De Santis among them—to ask new questions and to reconsider traditional explanations of important events.[5]

As he would demonstrate in *Reunion and Reaction*, Woodward believed that the traditional interpretation of the Compromise of 1877 needed reconsideration. The issue of Rutherford B. Hayes's presidential victory and the removal of federal troops from the South was the topic Woodward suggested to De Santis for his seminar paper. He emphasized the importance of archival research and directed his student to examine the Hayes Papers lodged in the Hayes Memorial Library in Fremont, Ohio, thus forcing the Pennsylvanian to venture into the Midwest for the first but not the last time. The paper De Santis wrote on the topic was eventually presented to a meeting of the seminar, to which Woodward invited Howard Beale and John Hope Franklin of Howard University as well as the regular graduate student participants, among them Suzanne Carson Lowitt and Louis Harlan. De Santis was thus appropriately baptized into the world of professional historians.

His explorations on Hayes and the removal of the troops led the young historian on to what became his dissertation and first book. Following Woodward's lead of clearing up misconceptions about the South, De Santis sought to tell the story of Republican policy and strategy in the South during the years that followed the Compromise of 1877. As he explained it later, "because the South has been overwhelmingly Democratic since the Compromise of 1877, it has been assumed in many quarters that the Republicans, apart from Reconstruction, have never really been seriously active or interested in building a strong party in this section of the country." He noted that "among students of American politics there has been a widespread and persistent belief that with the withdrawal of the troops, the Republicans gave up the fight in the South as hopeless and unprofitable and wrote off this part of the country as a possible area to contend for, maintaining there only a skeleton organization composed almost entirely of federal office holders."[6] De Santis set out to test this belief and he eventually challenged it head-on in his dissertation, in a string of articles published in the fifties, and finally and most importantly, in his first book, *Republicans Face the Southern Question: The New Departure Years, 1877–1897.*[7]

In his book De Santis described as "one of the great myths of American politics" the conclusion that the Republican lack of success in the South during the Gilded Age resulted from a lack of effort. Quite to the contrary, he demonstrated conclusively that in the twenty years after the end of Reconstruction, Republican leaders "constantly worked to break up the Democratic South and to rebuild their party in these states on a strong and permanent basis."[8] He examined in detail the shifting strategies of the various Republican leaders—Hayes, Garfield, Arthur, and Harrison—and appraised their effectiveness.

In *Reunion and Reaction* Woodward had argued that the "compromise" in 1877 resulted in large part from a desire on the part of the Republicans to reconstitute a North-South coalition like the old Whig party. De Santis's work added weight to this argument. It showed Hayes as intent on conciliating southern whites and aiming to rebuild the Republican Party by reducing the roles of the freedmen and carpetbaggers and relying instead on new support from conservative, southern (Whiggish) whites, who were to be attracted by a federal program of internal improvements. Such support, however, proved scarce and James Garfield tried a different approach during his brief presidency. When General William Mahone broke with the dominant Democrats in Virginia and led the Readjuster movement, Garfield offered limited Republican cooperation. After Garfield's assassination, President Chester Arthur sought to cooperate not only with the Virginia Readjusters but also with the various other Independent movements which had sprung up over the South. But the Garfield / Arthur strategy of cooperation with Independents failed as badly as had Hayes's approach.

Benjamin Harrison tried another tactic to win Republican support in the South, although it bore some resemblance to the approach of Ulysses S. Grant during Reconstruction. It centered on the Force Bill of 1890 designed to allow the enforcement of the Fourteenth and Fifteenth Amendments and to remedy the situation in which Republican voters, especially blacks, increasingly were suppressed in the South. The Force Bill never passed the Senate, however, because the majority Republicans "abandoned their party in the South in 1890 because they had a greater interest in a high tariff and a silver measure, and because they feared that a revival of Reconstruction tactics would disrupt the community of business interests that had developed between the North and the South . . ."[9]

The agrarian revolt of the 1890s provided another and final resurrection of Republican hopes of profiting from Democratic schisms in the South. So-called fusions of Populists and Republicans appeared across the South. Yet, despite some limited and temporary Republican victories, this strategy proved as barren as all its predecessors. In fact, De Santis concluded, the Republicans were weaker in the South in 1896 than they had been in 1876, despite the fight they had made for the region. In explanation, De Santis offered "factionalism among their southern brethren, . . . fear of another Reconstruction among southern whites [and] . . . bickering among top strategists over what to do about the south."[10]

The De Santis book attracted attention for the light it shed on the actions of the Republican Party towards African Americans. Here his judgments were harsh. De Santis argued that "the Republican party turned out to be among the poorest of friends that the southern negro (*sic*) had in the post-Reconstruction years." As De Santis portrayed it, "instead of protecting the Negro and looking after him as the ward of the nation, they deserted him and left him as the ward of the dominant race in the South."[11] The experiments to attract white support in the South had been done at the expense of blacks, although not necessarily deliberately.

Republicans Face the Southern Question rested upon extensive archival research in papers of the Republican presidents and those of other Republican worthies like John Sherman, William Chandler, and Carl Schurz. It was written in a careful manner and was grounded firmly in the evidence. It made use of election data and other voting and electoral details, although one would not present it as a progenitor of the now aging "new political history." The work was unapologetically that of a straightforward political historian, and the enduring reliability of its findings and the significance of its conclusions attest to its quality.

De Santis's book gained immediate and favorable attention.[12] During the fifties and early sixties the South was the subject of much scholarly attention. This was hardly surprising in the era of the Civil Rights movement and given "the importance and fascination of the reversal of Reconstruction, the fate of the freedman, the creation of the Democratic 'Solid South,' Southern Populism, and the pimply adolescence of Jim Crow."[13] De Santis's book became the standard work on its subject and established him as an important scholar of Gilded Age politics. Opportunities followed as a result. In some contrast to his mentor, who remained primarily committed to the study of the South and race relations, De Santis focused during the 1960s on the political life of the Gilded Age more generally.[14]

By the time he turned his attention to Gilded Age politics, De Santis was well-established in the history department at the University of Notre Dame. He was recruited in 1949, before he had completed his dissertation, by Rev. Thomas T. McAvoy, C.S.C., the longtime department chair. He spent his whole academic career there, aside from various visiting appointments and a year's recall to active military service during the Korean War.[15] He joined a department where research was valued and where able scholars—among them Marshall Smelser, Aaron Abell, Matthew Fitzsimons, and William Shanahan—were colleagues and friends. Eventually, De Santis assumed a leadership role in the department. He was promoted to full professor in 1962 and served as department chair from 1963 to 1971. He also taught literally thousands of undergraduate students, helped (so to speak) by a teaching load of four courses a semester during his first two decades at Notre Dame. He proved an effective graduate mentor, supervising numerous master's theses and directing fifteen doctoral dissertations on a range of topics in American political and diplomatic history.[16]

Despite his heavy teaching and administrative commitments, De Santis continued to write. At the invitation of the publishers, Scott, Foresman and Company, he joined forces with a number of important scholars—among them David M. Potter, Carl N. Degler, Arthur S. Link, and Thomas Cochran—to produce "a concise yet scholarly textbook of American history."[17] *The Democratic Experience* made its first appearance in 1963 and was revised regularly with its fifth and final edition appearing in 1981. The format of the book changed with each revision to reflect developments in scholarship and the profession's increasing emphasis on social history. In the first edition the self-declared focus was on "the evolution of our nation's institutions and ideas," and each of the eight chronological parts contained initial chapters covering the basic political and economic history of the period under consideration with a third devoted to intellectual and cultural history. By the time of the fifth edition, the text promised "a solid interpretation of traditional economic and political history" but also offered "new insights into social and cultural changes that have influenced and been influenced by economic and political events." Now the lead chapter in each part focused on "the social changes, the cultural trends and the ideas that dominated [the] time period."[18] De Santis accommodated the changes easily. He welcomed the insights of the new political historians and of the social historians for the additional light they shone on the American past. He incorporated them effectively without losing grasp of the essential narrative of the national story.

De Santis naturally bore responsibility for the section in *The Democratic Experience* covering the period from Reconstruction through the turn of the century. He emphasized the change wrought in America during this time and in particular the emergence of a new industrial and urban society. He discussed in insightful fashion the amazing array of developments of the period—the passing of the frontier and the Old West, the eclipsing of countryside and farm by city and factory, the dramatic improvement in communications, the flood of new immigrants, the growth of organized labor, and the emergence of the United States as a world power. In the later editions he added analyses of the lives of ordinary Americans and popular culture to his first edition's discussions of political ideas, philosophy, religion, and high culture.

In the first edition De Santis, reflecting the continuing influence of progressive historians like Charles Beard and Matthew Josephson, focused on the great inequities which resulted from the growth of industry and noted the triumph of a small capitalist class whose economic stakes were protected by the government. Politics during the Gilded Age was presented as largely remote from public opinion and in the service of big business. Writing a decade and a half later, he provided a more nuanced view of industrial development which reflected the work of business historians like Thomas Cochran and Edward Kirkland. He also presented a view of Gilded Age politics notably different from that outlined by Beard and Josephson. Gone was the remoteness of the public from politics. Without ignoring the corruption and blandness of some areas of politics, he now noted the importance of politics to Americans of the Gilded Age and the vitality of the democratic spirit.[19]

In what was a distinct service to the profession, De Santis evaluated at roughly decade-length intervals the historical literature on Gilded Age politics. His first evaluation in 1963 noted the enduring influence of Beard and especially of Matthew Josephson's *The Politicos*. The Gilded Age had fared badly at the hands of historians, who largely had adopted the negative interpretations of the social reformers and intellectual critics who lived during the period, foremost among them Henry Adams and the English observer James Bryce. De Santis issued a call for historians to present the politics of the period through the perspective of its politicians and especially of those who elected them.[20] By the mid-seventies much new specialized work had been undertaken by scholars like

Geoffrey Blodgett, John G. Sproat, H. Wayne Morgan, and the group of new political historians—among whom Paul Kleppner, Richard Jensen, and Samuel McSeveney led the way. De Santis recorded this literature carefully in a detailed bibliography he published and enthusiastically reported on the new work and its implications in an essay published in 1975.[21] He commented favorably on historians' "extensive and significant re-examination of the political life of the Gilded Age."[22] Yet, with a seeming air of resignation, he also noted that some of the recent general surveys of the period—those by Ray Ginger, Robert Wiebe, John Garraty, and John M. Dobson were named—still reflected the older interpretation and continued to brand the party system of the late nineteenth century as corrupt, meaningless, inefficient, and unresponsive to public problems. When he reported on the historiography of the Gilded Age in the 1980s, De Santis noted further progress in rescuing the era's politics from the disparaging condemnation of the dominant interpretation at the time he began his career.[23] His own historiographical essays, of course, had played a role in encouraging this reconsideration.

In addition to evaluating the historical literature on the Gilded Age, De Santis contributed to it with a number of insightful interpretative essays and a survey of the period from the end of Reconstruction to American entry into World War I. In 1963 he provided an overview of the Republican Party for an important volume edited by H. Wayne Morgan aimed at reappraising the Gilded Age.[24] Here he qualified the conventional view that the Republican Party was merely conservative, evaded issues, and served only greedy interests. He called that view "overdone" and asked that late nineteenth-century Republicans be assessed in the context of the times in which they operated. He reflected a disposition to understand the past on its own terms and not to distort the past with the arrogant stance of a hanging judge.

Proving quite bipartisan in his interests, De Santis also devoted attention to the dominant Democrat of the era, Grover Cleveland. He accepted the invitation of Morton Borden to explain why historians considered Cleveland among the greatest of presidents—the Buffalo Democrat having been rated as number eight among presidents in a 1948 poll of historians conducted by Arthur Schlesinger, Sr., and number ten in his 1962 survey. De Santis's essay on Cleveland in Borden's *America's Ten Greatest Presidents* drew on Allan Nevins's exhaustive and favorable biography but accepted many of the qualifications of the

Nevins portrayal of Cleveland offered by Richard Hofstadter and Samuel Merrill. He admitted Cleveland was an honest man of character but, refusing the opportunity to exaggerate the "greatness" of his "greatest president," he presented Cleveland's achievements as essentially negative. Cleveland was "a symbol of civic staunchness" but hardly a "constructive force in public affairs."[25] Nonetheless, De Santis conceded in a later essay that Cleveland played some role in revitalizing the presidency during a period of congressional dominance and, in fact, in the Pullman strike and the Venezuelan boundary dispute, he actually expanded the powers of the presidency.[26]

De Santis incorporated his views of Cleveland and the Republican Party into interpretative introductions he wrote for a two-volume collection of contemporary historical documents, which he edited with J. Joseph Huthmacher and Benjamin W. Labaree, and more especially in the general survey of the era which he published in 1973.[27] *The Shaping of Modern America: 1877–1916* proved a most useful and popular introduction to and overview of the Gilded Age and the Progressive Era.[28] Clearly written and drawing on the research of scores of historians, the work was notable for its avoidance of caricatures and stereotypes and the absence of exaggerated theoretical pyrotechnics. It told the nation's story with care and treated the Gilded Age with due regard and not simply as a preface to Progressivism. The transformation wrought within America by the processes of industrialization and modernization during the combined Gilded Age-Progressive era was emphasized. Needless to say, however, the book also gave considerable attention to the exertions of Theodore Roosevelt and Woodrow Wilson. De Santis presented the Republican Roosevelt as devoted to stability and measured his contribution to the Progressive movement as "educative rather than legislative."[29] Influenced heavily by Arthur Link's interpretation, De Santis presented Wilson's presidency as involving a remarkable transformation in which the scholar-president "completely abandoned his original New Freedom program and accepted the concepts of the advanced progressives and Theodore Roosevelt's New Nationalism."[30]

De Santis included two chapters on American foreign policy in his book—the first examining the "New Manifest Destiny" and the second recording America's actions as a world power from its War with Spain to the eve of its entry into World War I. His interest in diplomatic history was manifested further in several essays written on U.S.-Italian relations in the postwar era, the seeds of which were planted during his Fulbright professorship in Italy in 1967–68.[31] But his most significant foray into the field of diplomatic history came with his collaboration with Joseph M. Siracusa in the revision of Julius W. Pratt's classic *A History of United States Foreign Policy*.[32] De Santis enjoyed a close friendship with Pratt, whom he recruited to teach at Notre Dame upon the venerable scholar's retirement from The State University of New York at Buffalo. His effort to keep Pratt's book in circulation resulted largely from their friendship. In the revision De Santis and Siracusa added sections to trace the course of U.S. foreign policy during the 1970s and maintained the high scholarly tone which had so marked the earlier editions of Pratt's book.

Despite these and other later flirtations with American diplomatic history, De Santis always remained without apology a political histo-rian.[33] His interest in the political dimension of the American experi-ence led him to explore a range of political episodes, particularly the intersection of Catholicism and politics in America. Prompted no doubt by the attention given to John F. Kennedy's campaign for the presi-dency, De Santis examined early in 1960 the role which Catholicism played in presidential elections from 1865 to 1900. He acknowledged the anti-Catholic propaganda exploited during the various campaigns but concluded that "Catholicism had no real significance in any one of the presidential elections of the post-Civil War generation."[34]

An issue that drew De Santis's passionate concern as well as his scholarly attention was the relationship between American Catholics and McCarthyism. As a young faculty member at Notre Dame he had written a long letter to *The New Republic* in 1954 suggesting that Catholics "should condemn McCarthy because he believes that the end justifies the means."[35] In his presidential address to the American Catholic Historical Association in 1964, the now established scholar returned to the topic. He traced the attitudes and associations of American Catholics with McCarthyism and concluded that "while Catholics were definitely split on the McCarthy issue, there was . . . a preponderance of pro-McCarthy sentiment among Catholics." At least pro-McCarthy sentiment predominated among vocal Catholics. Yet De Santis noted that much of McCarthy's Catholic support "came from the essentially isolationist element of American Catholicism" whose frus-trations were voiced by the Wisconsin senator.[36] De Santis's essay became the basic work on this topic replaced only by the publication of Donald Crosby's *God, Church, and Flag* well over a decade later.[37]

In addition to his essays on Catholics and American politics, De Santis contributed occasional essays on other political themes to *The Review of Politics*, the scholarly journal edited at Notre Dame. In 1953 he evaluated the election of 1952 in its pages.[38] Over two decades later he reviewed the literature on the presidency of the candidate who had come to power in that election. He presciently identified the first major wave of Eisenhower revisionism which eventually developed into a flood. Noting the work of historians like Herbert Parmet, Peter Lyons, and Charles Alexander, he noted how "the early harsh judgments of Eisenhower have been revised by the recent literature on him." He explained that Ike now "appears to be a more astute and more sophisticated politician, a stronger and more concerned chief executive, a more successful president both in domestic and foreign affairs."[39] This widely read and cited essay helped alert scholars to the major reconsideration of Eisenhower then just beginning.

De Santis's gifts for mastering a body of literature and discerning trends within it were put to good use in the years after he earned emeritus status in 1982. He was not the kind of historian who could simply lay down his pen (or, in his particular case, his retractable pencil!). Instead he began to draw upon his decades of reading and teaching to write articles for *The Notre Dame Magazine*, the publication of the Notre Dame Alumni Association. Such essays allowed him to connect with the University's graduates, many of whom had been his students. In these thoughtful pieces he addressed a wide array of topics, some among them quite controversial, such as the Kennedy assassination, Truman's decision to drop the atomic bomb, and the debate over Columbus's discovery of the New World.[40] All of his essays were clearly and engagingly written and reflected both careful reading of the specialized literature and a wise historian's thoughtful analysis. They attracted favorable response from readers and, on occasion, considerable criticism. His endorsement of the Warren Commission's final conclusion predictably drew the most fervent ire.

Vincent De Santis has enjoyed his career as a historian and teacher—indeed he has reveled in it. He developed close relationships with students and especially appreciated his colleagueship and association with other historians, many of whom—such as Robert Gunderson of Indiana University—he still meets regularly at the annual meetings of the Southern Historical Association. He contributed well to the profession he loved, writing innumerable book reviews and serving on conference program committees and as a referee for countless journals and publishers.

Throughout his long and distinguished career Vincent De Santis maintained a clear vision of his work as a political historian and, perhaps as a result, he employed a rather straightforward methodology. He did not seek to use history to establish the intellectual or moral superiority of the present over the past. He approached the past with compassion, simply seeking to understand, with genuine empathy, what had happened and why. In the eyes of relativists his epistemology might appear somewhat old-fashioned. De Santis believed and still believes that a good scholar, through the collection and ordering of evidence, can come close to knowing the truth about the past "as it really was," even if the full and complete truth is not attainable. Such an approach might be deemed by some to rest on shaky philosophical foundations, but De Santis applied it with integrity and this honest approach allowed him to speak with authenticity of the past. In so doing, he contributed to a deepened understanding of the political history of the United States. His readers and students have truly been beneficiaries of his notable contribution and the historical profession has been enriched by his presence.

Notes

1. C. Vann Woodward, *Tom Watson: Agrarian Rebel* (New York: Macmillan, 1938).

2. Woodward quoted in Peter Novick, *That Noble Dream: The "Objectivity Question" and the American Historical Profession* (Cambridge: Cambridge University Press, 1988), p. 228.

3. Novick, *That Noble Dream*, p. 353. On Woodward's career, see John Herbert Roper, *C. Vann Woodward: Southerner* (Athens, Ga.: University of Georgia Press, 1987); and Woodward's own reflections in *Thinking Back: The Perils of Writing History* (Baton Rouge: Louisiana State University Press, 1986).

4. C. Vann Woodward, *Reunion and Reaction: The Compromise of 1877 and the End of Reconstruction* (Boston: Little, Brown, 1951); and *Origins of the New South, 1877–1913* (Baton Rouge: Louisiana State University Press, 1951).

5. Woodward had notable success in his graduate teaching and trained many fine historians, of whom De Santis was one of the first. For a tribute to Woodward by some of his students, including De Santis, see James M. McPherson and J.

Morgan Kousser, eds., *Region, Race, and Reconstruction: Essays in Honor of C. Vann Woodward* (New York: Oxford University Press, 1982).

6. Vincent P. De Santis, *Republicans Face the Southern Question: The New Departure Years, 1877–1897*, Johns Hopkins University Studies in Historical and Political Science, ser. 77, no. 1 (Baltimore: Johns Hopkins Press, 1959), p. 11.

7. For the De Santis articles, see: "Negro Dissatisfaction with Republican Policy in the South, 1882–1884," *Journal of Negro History* 36 (April 1951), pp. 148–59; "Republican Efforts to 'Crack' the Democratic South," *Review of Politics* 14 (April 1952), pp. 244–64; "President Arthur and the Independent Movements in the South in 1882," *Journal of Southern History* 19 (August 1953), pp. 346–63; "President Hayes' Southern Policy," *Journal of Southern History* 21 (November 1955), pp. 476–94; "Benjamin Harrison and the Republican Party in the South, 1889–1893," *Indiana Magazine of History* 60 (December 1955), pp. 279–302; "President Garfield and the Solid South," *North Carolina Historical Review* 36 (April 1960), pp. 442–65; "The Republican Party and the Southern Negro," *The Journal of Negro History* 45 (April 1960), pp. 71–87.

8. De Santis, *Republicans Face the Southern Question*, p. 12.

9. Ibid., p. 213.

10. Ibid., p. 261.

11. Ibid., p. 215. (One should note here that until the mid-sixties the term "Negro" was considered more technically correct and more polite. The term "Colored" was seen as condescending and "black" had negative connotations. This changed after 1964–65 with the emergence of the black pride movement.)

12. See for example the attention given the book by Robert F. Durden in his review essay, "Politics in the Gilded Age, 1877–1896," in William H. Cartwright and Richard L. Watson, Jr., eds., *Interpreting and Teaching American History* (Washington, D.C.: National Council for the Social Studies, 1961), p. 182.

13. Walter T. K. Nugent, "Politics from Reconstruction to 1900," in William H. Cartwright and Richard L. Watson, Jr., eds., *The Reinterpretation of American History and Culture* (Washington, D.C.: National Council for the Social Studies, 1973), p. 388.

14. Woodward wanted to contribute to fundamental change in the South and his work reflected that commitment. See his *The Strange Career of Jim Crow* (New York: Oxford University Press, 1955); and *The Burden of Southern History* (Baton Rouge: Louisiana State University Press, 1960).

15. De Santis held a Guggenheim Fellowship in 1960–61 and held Fulbright Professorships in Italy in 1967–68, in Australia in 1979, and in India in 1991–92. During the Korean War he held a safe desk job at the Pentagon.

16. A list of the dissertations directed by Vincent De Santis is included as an appendix.

17. Preface to Carl N. Degler et al., *The Democratic Experience* (Chicago: Scott, Foresman and Co., 1963), p. v.

18. Preface to Carl N. Degler et al., *The Democratic Experience*, 5th ed. (Chicago: Scott, Foresman and Co., 1981), p. v.

19. This analysis relies on a comparison between the first edition (1963) and fourth edition (1979).

20. Vincent P. De Santis, "American Politics in the Gilded Age," *The Review of Politics* 25 (October 1963), pp. 551–61.

21. Vincent P. De Santis, *The Gilded Age—A Bibliography* (Northbrook, Ill: AHM Publishing Co., 1973).

22. Vincent P. De Santis, "The Political Life of the Gilded Age: A Review of the Recent Literature," *The History Teacher* 9 (November 1975), pp. 73–106. For a detailed examination of the new political history, see Allan G. Bogue, "The New Political History in the 1970s" in Michael Kammen, ed., *The Past Before Us: Contemporary Historical Writing in the United States* (Ithaca, N.Y.: Cornell University Press, 1980), pp. 231–51.

23. Vincent P. De Santis, "The Gilded Age in American History," *Hayes Historical Journal* 7 (Winter 1988), pp. 38–57.

24. Vincent P. De Santis, "The Republican Party Revisited, 1877–1897," in H. Wayne Morgan, ed., *The Gilded Age: A Reappraisal* (Syracuse, N.Y.: Syracuse University Press, 1963), pp. 91–110.

25. Vincent P. De Santis, "Grover Cleveland," in Morton Borden, ed., *America's Ten Greatest Presidents* (Chicago: Rand McNally and Co., 1961), pp. 161–84; direct quotations from p. 183.

26. Vincent P. De Santis, "Grover Cleveland: Revitalization of the Presidency," in Harry J. Sievers, S.J., ed., *Six Presidents from the Empire State* (Tarrytown, N.Y.: Sleepy Hollow Restorations, 1974), pp. 84–100. De Santis is still regularly called upon to write on Cleveland. See his "Grover Cleveland," in William C. Spragens, ed., *Popular Images of American Presidents* (Westport, CT.: Greenwood Press, 1988), pp. 131–46; and "Grover Cleveland, President, 1885–1889 and 1893–97," *Encyclopedia of the American Presidency*, 4 vols. (1993).

27. For the documentary collection, see Vincent P. De Santis, J. Joseph Huthmacher, and Benjamin W. Labaree, *America Past and Present: An Interpretation with Readings*, 2 vols. (Boston: Allyn and Bacon, 1968).

28. Vincent P. De Santis, *The Shaping of Modern America, 1877–1916* (Boston: Allyn and Bacon, 1973). This book was published in a second and expanded edition in 1989. See *The Shaping of Modern America, 1877–1920* (Arlington Heights, Ill.: Forum Press, 1989).

29. Ibid., p. 186.

30. Ibid., p. 225.

31. See Vincent P. De Santis, "The United States and Italy," in Omer De Raemaeker and Albert Bowman, eds., *American Foreign Policy in Europe* (Louvain, Belgium: Nauwelaerts, 1969), pp. 45–56; and "Italy and the Cold War," in Joseph M Siracusa and Glen Barclay, eds., *The Impact of the Cold War: Reconsiderations* (Port Washington, N.Y.: Kenikat Press, 1977), pp. 26–39.

32. Julius W. Pratt, Vincent P. De Santis, and Joseph M. Siracusa, *A History of United States Foreign Policy*, 4th ed. (Englewood Cliffs, N.J.: Prentice Hall, 1980).

33. On his later excursions into the field of diplomatic history, see Vincent P. De Santis, "Carter's Policy of the Two Chinas," *Asia and the World Forum* 2, no. 19 (June 1980) pp. 49–58; and his "Jimmy Carter and Human Rights," *Human Rights: Problems and Perspectives* (London and Taipei, 1982), pp. 167–79.

34. Vincent P. De Santis, "Catholicism and Presidential Elections, 1865–1900," *Mid-America: An Historical Review* 42, no. 2 (April 1960), pp. 67–79; direct quotation from p. 79.

35. Letter ("A Catholic View of McCarthy"), *The New Republic* 130 (June 7, 1954), p. 22.

36. De Santis's address was published as "American Catholics and McCarthyism," *The Catholic Historical Review* 51 (April 1965), pp. 1–30.

37. Donald F. Crosby, S.J., *God, Church, and Flag: Senator Joseph R. McCarthy and the Catholic Church, 1950–1957* (Chapel Hill, N.C.: The University of North Carolina Press, 1978).

38. Vincent P. De Santis, "The Presidential Election of 1952," *The Review of Politics* 15, no. 2 (April, 1953), pp. 131–50.

39. Vincent P. De Santis, "Eisenhower Revisionism," *The Review of Politics* 38, no. 2 (April 1976), pp. 190–207; quotations from pp. 206–7.

40. De Santis's essays in the following issues of the *Notre Dame Magazine* include: "A Man of Promise [John F. Kennedy]," 12 (October 1983), pp. 24–28; "Hell, Give 'Em Harry [Harry S. Truman]," 13 (Summer 1984), pp. 25–27; "From the Sublime to the Ridiculous [American Presidential Campaigns]," 13 (Winter 1984 / 85), pp. 28–32; "A Momentous Rush to Judgment [Truman's Atomic Bomb Decision]," 14 (Summer 1985), pp. 23–27; "Pearl Harbor Bombed," 15 (Autumn 1986), pp. 38–42; "The Great and Devastating Depression," 16 (Winter 1987 / 88), pp. 25–28; "Who Killed JFK?" 17 (Autumn 1988), pp. 51–56; "Whatever Happened to Horatio Alger?" 19 (Winter 1990 / 91), pp. 30–32; "An Inevitable War [World War II]," 20 (Autumn 1991), pp. 21–26; "Columbus Sailed the Ocean Blue," 21 (Summer 1992), pp. 46–49; "Until the Bombs Came [Japan's Decision to Surrender in 1945]," 24 (Spring 1995), pp. 16–20.

Appendix

Dissertations directed by Vincent P. De Santis Department of History, University of Notre Dame

Charles Joseph Tull, "Father Coughlin, The New Deal, and the Election of 1936" (1962)

Bro. Bernard F. Donahoe, C.S.C., "New Dealers, Conservatives, and the Democratic Nominees of 1940" (1965)

John F. Marszalek, "W. T. Sherman and the Press, 1861–1865" (1968)

Paul A. O'Rourke, "Liberal Journals and the New Deal" (1969)

Joseph A. Grande, "The Political Career of General Peter Buel Porter, 1799–1829" (1971)

Robert B. Clements, "*The Commonweal*, 1924–1938: The Williams-Shuster Years" (1972)

Richard John Del Vecchio, "Indiana Politics During the Progressive Era, 1912–1916" (1973)

James Michael Quill, "Northern Public Opinion and Reconstruction, April to December 1865" (1973)

James Robert Sweeney, "Byrd and Anti-Byrd: The Struggle for Political Supremacy in Virginia, 1945–1954" (1973)

Michael Paul Poder, "The Senatorial Career of William E. Jenner" (1976)

Peter Joseph Lombardo, Jr., "Connecticut in the Great Depression, 1929–1933" (1979)

John M. Pyne, "Woodrow Wilson's Abdication of Domestic and Party Leadership, November 1918–November 1920" (1979)

Wilson Douglas Miscamble, "George F. Kennan, The Policy Planning Staff and American Foreign Policy, 1947–1950" (1980)

James Gilbert Ryan, "Earl Browder and American Communism at High Tide, 1934–1945" (1980)

Thomas G. Bohlin, "United States–Latin American Relations and the Cold War: 1949–1953" (1986)

Contributors

Michael Les Benedict (Ohio State University) is in the first rank of scholars of the Reconstruction era. Among other works, he has authored *The Impeachment and Trial of Andrew Johnson: A Compromise of Principle*; *Congressional Republicans and Reconstruction, 1863–1869*; and *Fruits of Victory: Alternatives to Restoring the Union, 1863–1877*.

Carl N. Degler (Stanford University) is a past president of both the American Historical Association and the Organization of American Historians and one of the leading historians in the United States. He is the author of numerous works, including *Affluence and Anxiety in America since 1945* and *Out of Our Past: The Forces That Shaped Modern America*.

Jane Sherron De Hart (University of California, Santa Barbara) is a noted historian of twentieth-century American women's history, especially women and politics. She is author (with Donald G. Mathews) of *Sex, Gender, and the Politics of ERA: A State and the Nation* and (with Linda K. Kerber) *Women's America: Refocusing the Past*.

John F. Marszalek (Mississippi State University) is the author of books in the area of the Civil War and African American history, including *Sherman, A Soldier's Passion for Order*; *Assault at West Point*; and coeditor (with Charles D. Lowery) of *Encyclopedia of African American Civil Rights: From Emancipation to the Present*.

Wilson D. Miscamble, C.S.C. (University of Notre Dame) is the author of *George F. Kennan and the Making of American Foreign Policy, 1947–1950* and articles on a variety of topics in American diplomatic and political history.

Robert V. Remini (University of Notre Dame) is the prize-winning biographer of Andrew Jackson. He is also noted for his biographies of other nineteenth-century political figures, among them: *Henry Clay:*

Statesman for the Union; and *Martin Van Buren and the Making of the Democratic Party*.

R. Hal Williams (Southern Methodist University) is an important scholar of Gilded Age politics and the author of *The Democratic Party and California Politics, 1880–1896* and *Years of Decision: American Politics in the 1890s*.

Index